# BACKPACKER'S DIGEST

## 3rd Edition

## By Cheri Elliott

DBI BOOKS INC. NORTHFIELD, ILLINOIS

Editorial Director
JACK LEWIS

Production Director
SONYA KAISER

Art Director
DANA SILZLE

Production Coordinator
BETTY BURRIS

Copy Editor
DORINE IMBACH

Photo Services
BRANDON LEWIS

Contributing Editors
ROGER COMBS
DEAN A. GRENNELL

Publisher
SHELDON FACTOR

Produced by
Charger
Productions

ISBN 0-910676-21-6                                    Library of Congress Catalog Card Number 72-97509

# CONTENTS

# ACKNOWLEDGEMENT

Few books are the product of one individual, and BACKPACKER'S DIGEST is a primary example. Without the aid of the many manufacturers who provided up-to-date photographs and information on their products, as well as a wealth of information on backpacking this book could not have been produced.

Special gratitude is extended to the public relations departments of North Face, Early Winters, Stephenson's and Mountain Aire Foods, and the United States Marine Corps for their valuable knowledge and assistance.

To the staff and editors of Charger Productions and to my family, I offer my sincere appreciation and gratitude, and my deep respect for the countless hours, vast patience and unending support they have offered.

It is my sincere hope that the chapters included in this book will prove of value not only to novice backpackers, but also to experienced packers.

*Cheri Elliott*

Cheri Elliott
Burton, South Carolina

# CHAPTER 1

# WHERE IT'S AT

## Backpacking Has Gone From The Lonely Life Of The Mountain Man To A Family Sport

*The sport of backpacking truly needs no particular season. Late spring and early summer in California's Sierras will still present the family backpacking group with patches of cooling snow to refresh the long climb up.*

**T**HERE ARE countless ways of providing man with recreation, as vital a part of his life as sleep, work and food, if he hopes to maintain his sanity amid today's pressures. As those pressures increase so does his desire for recreation with new twists being added to old games to expand the challenge. Eighty-year-old women roller skate with 8-year-old boys. Families ride caravan-style on bicycles. The skateboard was once the hottest item in town. (Perhaps its decline was due to the impracticality of it as a source of recreation for *all* ages.

Not too many 8-year-olds could handle it well, and far fewer 80-year-olds ever tried.) But among the most popular of recreational sports today is *backpacking*, a sport that knows no age barrier, no seasons.

You can ski the mountains of Michigan in January, hunt the deer herds of Pennsylvania in December, or swim the waters of Arkansas in July — and fun will be yours. But there's little snow during a Michigan July, no deer season in March in Pennsylvania, and you'd need special wetsuits to brave a frigid Arkansas January. It's just not the season.

However, you *can* backpack all of these areas, during any of these times. There are no actual seasons. You simply dress to match the weather.

While today's backpacker looks upon backpacking as a method of enjoying life, it was not always so. The gold miners of the 1800s were also backpackers, as were the trappers and traders of that time.

Lacking the abundant cities and towns with groceries and shopping marts within minutes of each other, the only market available to the trapper was the market he carried on his back or, as often as was feasible, strapped to his pack mules. These trappers did not carry a few days' worth of supplies, but, rather, enough to last them for months at a time. They either carried everything they would need with them, or they did without.

For the trapper, backpacking was not a method of adding enjoyment to his life, as it is today. It was a method of living. It did not add to his existence, it *was* his existence. And he used all the ingenuity and natural supplies available to him to make that packing easier, his load a little lighter. Trees provided not only the fire he would use to warm himself and to cook with, but shelter against the cruelty of nature. A tree offered, as well, the material for his pack frame, patiently whittled into shape to fit his needs of the time, to be disposed of when he no longer needed it.

*Backpacking today is a far cry from the necessity of the frontier era. As a family sport, children can participate.*

*By today's standards, the backpacking equipment of the last century was crude, but nonetheless functional in design. The chief requirement was to be able to carry as much of the hiker's needs as possible with a minimum of bulk, effort.*

We are told that life was extremely difficult during those settlement/gold rush days, and we have no reason to doubt that; yet we also know that the miner, trapper and trader of that era took time out to admire nature, just as we strive to do today.

Although the advances of modern technology seem to make it all but impossible for anyone other than the most dedicated of backpackers to attempt to live as did our forefathers, even the least experienced packer can share in the wonders of nature just as did the California gold seekers. In so doing, we can ignite the pioneer spirit in all of us, and discover a little more about ourselves.

Those who enjoy fishing and/or hunting will find backpacking especially beneficial, for how else can they reach those virgin hunting grounds or untried rivers and streams too far from "civilization" to be congested? There are streams where the water is so pure you can drink it untreated, cold and bubbling with trout that have never been exposed to a hook or fly, and thus are not fisherman-wise. Forests that teem with deer and other game that have never heard the swish of an arrow or blast from a rifle. Such do exist we are told, but only in the hard-to-reach, far-from-the-city forests and mountains — areas that can only be reached by "packing in."

*Modern lightweight backpacking equipment not only provides rest and relaxation for the whole hiking family but allows the camper access to areas otherwise closed to travel. Alpine lakes by the thousands, such as this one in California's Sierras, also offer fishing opportunities not available to the motor traveler.*

A sport to be enjoyed year-round, backpacking is open to all age groups, young or old. In fact, there is hardly a human being who has not tried backpacking at some time or another in his or her lifetime. Perhaps it may not have been the sophisticated recreational sport we will discuss throughout this book, but anyone who has toted an object on his back has been involved in "backpacking." The local mailman on his appointed rounds may tote his letters in a pack on his back. Newspaper boys often carry their papers in a pack strapped to their back. And backpacks are as common among schoolchildren today as lunch pails were in the early 1900s. Yet it is doubtful that any of these people would refer to themselves as backpackers, because backpacking has come to mean something special and unique: a journey into nature, where civilization is nearly

forgotten for a period of time, and the only music to be heard may well be that of the wildlife or rumbling waterfalls.

To many, the real benefits of backpacking lie in the physical fitness it offers, strengthening legs, back and circulatory system while slimming waistlines. But a far greater benefit derived from backpacking may be of a mental nature. A day's journey into the San Gabriel Wilderness of California will put you among some of the most breathtaking of terrain. Surrounded by alder and willows, and miniature waterfalls, it is difficult to recall the agony of a lost contract, the anger of an unfair boss or the anguish of a defeat. Somehow, the irritations and mountains prominent in day-to-day living take on their proper perspective, becoming the challenges and mole hills

*Wildlife is often encountered on the typical backpack trip, such as these little beggers. Frame packs are fine for long dayhikes or fishing.*

that they should be. More often than not, the solution to a plaguing problem is seen amid the tumbling rocks of a chilly stream. While the body may find the going occasionally taxing, to the mind, backpacking is a highly restive, restorative time, a time to get your head together.

Whether you are experienced or a novice, the magnetism of backpacking should not be resisted. It takes but one journey to become "experienced." Naturally you will want to limit your initial hike to the well-known, well-patrolled trails that span the nation, where help can be expected to be within reasonable reach. It's a good idea to take that initial journey with an experienced backpacker, someone who will realize your limitations, and guide you through them. And why not make one of these early hikes a family hike? What better time to have that long put off discussion about life with an adolescent than amid nature's animate background, free from the constant interruptions of television, stereo and neighborhood friends. And what

*Gold panning has again become popular in many parts of the country. A lightweight plastic gold pan will keep children occupied for hours in camp.*

better way to tote that fifty pounds of supplies than to share the weight, divided among the family packers. True, the adults will have to carry more than the youngsters, but a thirty-pound pack can be carried for a much longer time, and with greater enthusiasm, while the other family members tote the additional supplies.

The opportunities to actually "spend some time with the kids" are becoming increasingly rare as the interest barriers between young and old increase. More than likely the hike intended to "teach the kids a thing or two about nature" will wind up teaching the parents as well. The movements of a grasshopper are never so animated as they become when described by a 9-year-old. The smell of a wildflower never quite as fragrant until held out for examination by a 7-year-old. And you may well be amazed at just how grown-up your teenager has become as you share thoughts on life as each of you see it.

However, just as you have sought out an experienced

*Modern fishing gear is light and easily carried by any packer. No backpack should start without a pole, line, reel and other equipment to let the kids "wet a line."*

backpacker for your initial hike who realizes your limitations, you, too, must realize the limitations inherent in hiking with youngsters. The thirty-inch stride of an adult means two or more strides by a youngster. And unless the pace is matched to the age and physical abilities of the child, a three-day hike that begins as an adventure may well dissolve into a nightmare before the first campfire.

Obviously a three-day hike with youngsters will involve a great deal less covered mileage, with frequent stops necessary. And you may find yourself spending more time admiring lizards and butterflies than the birds or rocks on which you had intended devoting your attention. If miles covered is your main goal, then perhaps the inclusion of children would be better left to another time. If not, definitely include them, but be prepared to stop and sample each berry patch you encounter, swim or at least wade in each stream and pond, and expand your view of the world as only can be done through a child. And don't be surprised to find yourself having trouble keeping up with your children occasionally. The stamina of a youngster has given many a researcher cause for admiration and exhaustion. While tiring easily, the younger generations also recover more quickly. It's a good idea to keep the children between the two parents during most of the hike, however, lest their enthusiasm exceed their capabilities. Try allowing them to take the lead only when you are certain of the terrain.

Senior citizens can enjoy the lure of backpacking just as do their offspring, particularly if daily walks are already a part of their routine. Again, the key is to know their limitations and adhere to those limitations at all times. This can prove more difficult, particularly if a stubborn streak prevents a senior backpacker from calling for a rest he feels only he requires. No one should ever hesitate to call for a rest period if he feels he needs it. Far worse is to continue on, finding yourself unable to maintain the pace, allowing fatigue to falter both your step and your senses, opening the door to tragedy. It's best to remember that during a group hike, all hikers are dependent on each other. An injury to one member of the party can easily lead to added stress and possible injury to one or more others, especially if concern gives way to panic. Remember that the primary purpose of the hike is fun, not fear.

Are you hesitant to enter into backpacking lest you find yourself in over your head, both financially and physically? Don't be. Just plan your trips before you take them, seek out methods of controlling or sharing the costs by controlling the expected needs. A three-week hike means three weeks-plus of foodstuffs to carry, placing a much heavier financial and physical demand on the hiker than does the three-day hike.

Although you'll probably want to take that three-week hike eventually, it need not and, in most cases, should not be during the early experiences of backpacking. Much better to wait until you've given your body an opportunity to tune-up to packing with the shorter hikes, while you give yourself time to gather the necessary equipment and supplies for the weeks-long safari. You'll find it easy to stockpile food items, since most backpacking items are intended to be stored for long periods of time when they are manufactured.

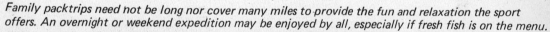

*Family packtrips need not be long nor cover many miles to provide the fun and relaxation the sport offers. An overnight or weekend expedition may be enjoyed by all, especially if fresh fish is on the menu.*

Many backpackers prefer the spring
and fall months for their treks,
although a cool glen among tall
trees in midsummer is refreshing.

One of the special memories for
most backpackers are the delicious
meals and snacks eaten on the trail.

**16**

Federal, state and local government agencies provide and maintain literally thousands of miles of hiking trails in all types of terrain throughout North America.

For the dayhike you'll need even less in terms of special gear. In fact, you might not need to purchase much or anything specifically for the hike. A good pair of shoes can be the work shoes you wear daily, provided they have a good, traction-grabbing sole and provide ample support for climbing the type of terrain you are entering. Your day-pack can be a converted school backpack, provided you travel well patrolled trails, where you can readily get help if needed. Regardless of where you go you'll want to carry water, and a basic first-aid and survival kit, but these needs do not require the use of one of the more sophisticated packs on your first hike.

The majority of backpackers, especially those new to the sport seem to prefer the spring and autumn months, when extremes of heat and cold are seldom a constant problem. However, winter and summer days can also prove both exciting and enjoyable provided your clothing can meet the climate. Just ask the college student who spends his summer vacation backpacking across the United States, and he'll fill your hours with tales of adventure and humor attendant with each sweating mile he has paced. There are countless manufacturers of backpacking and outdoor clothing who can guarantee you year-round comfort, with varying degrees of expense involved. In addition, if you've some degree of control over the basic sewing machine, you can even make many of your clothing and some of your backpacking items yourself, beginning from scratch or perhaps with a do-it-yourself kit. Sewing the items yourself can save you dollars while adding to your backpacking pleasures, and it need not be all that difficult.

In the chapters to follow we will take a hard look at these backpacking items, from packs to boots, tents to cooking utensils, seeking out the advantages and disadvantages of each, in the hope of aiding you in selection of the best gear for you — gear that will insure an enjoyable, rewarding experience as you discover a little more about yourself, and become — however briefly — a trader of the 1800s.

*"Today I have grown taller from walking with the trees."* — Karle Wilson Baker, 1878

# A PACK FOR YOUR BACK

## CHAPTER 2

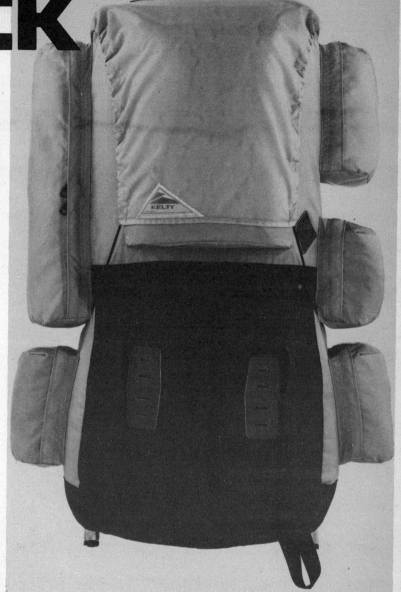

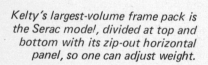

*Kelty's largest-volume frame pack is the Serac model, divided at top and bottom with its zip-out horizontal panel, so one can adjust weight.*

**B**ACKPACKING, as the word implies, means toting your gear on your back and, while not necessarily the most important item of gear you may purchase, the need of a well-fitting, comfortable backpack is essential to an enjoyable trip.

There are numerous styles and sizes of packs available from which to choose. To determine which pack best suits your needs, you must first define those needs: How long will you be gone? What type of terrain will you encounter? What weather conditions can you expect? Is the purpose of the trip to log backpacking miles or are you seeking something else?

Obviously, a three-day hike will require more gear than a day hike. Consequently, the space needs of your pack will differ. A winter hike in snow-covered mountains requires space for those extra sweaters and thermal underwear. A journey that includes photographing the covered terrain, or a trip to supply additional rock samples for a home collection will require added storage capabilities for that camera gear or rock samples. Whatever the purpose of your hike, your objective should be to include all of the necessary items, but to do so with as little weight as is prudently possible.

Toting a fifty-pound pack, even on a dayhike, can

## Selecting The Right Equipment For The Circumstances Pays Dividends In Comfort And Energy

become extremely difficult quickly. It is better to hold the weight to around twenty or thirty pounds if possible. With the myriad lightweight packs and equipment currently available, that weight restriction should be within your reach. Keep in mind when traveling with your family or companions that no two people can carry the same weight pack with the same degree of energy expenditure. What feels comfortable to you may soon prove taxing to your spouse or friend. Each hiker will need to make his own determination of his needs and capabilities.

Regardless of the overall size requirements of your pack, there are several guidelines that will aid in your selection. A good pack should hold the required weight snugly as well as comfortably. It should stand up to punishment while resisting the assaults of terrain and weather. With the pack on your back, you should be able to move with relative freedom, to stand reasonably straight. And finally, you should be able to carry that loaded pack whatever distance is required, without nearing exhaustion.

There are four basic categories of packs from which you can choose, each offering its own benefits and drawbacks. In choosing the pack for you, select one which will meet as many of your needs as possible. The four basic pack styles are external frame, internal frame, rucksack and fanny pack. Each was designed to meet specific backpacking needs.

The external-frame pack is generally considered to be the pack of choice for toting heavy loads over long distances, allowing you to carry the load in a more natural walking position. The lightweight aluminum frame, designed to match the curves of your back, holds the pack vertical. The center of gravity is high, allowing the hips to carry most of the weight. The shoulders are relieved of much of the pack weight. An important part of the external-frame pack is the well-padded shoulder harness and hip belt, which not only hold the pack securely in place, but provide added comfort to shoulders and hips. In purchasing an external-frame pack check the frame itself carefully. Special attention should be paid to the joints, which may be held together with screws, by machined joints or by welding. Screws can work loose during a lengthy or difficult hike, as can machined joints, although it is far less likely. The strongest joint is welded, using a heli-arc or tig weld. Generally, this welding is done by hand, which will

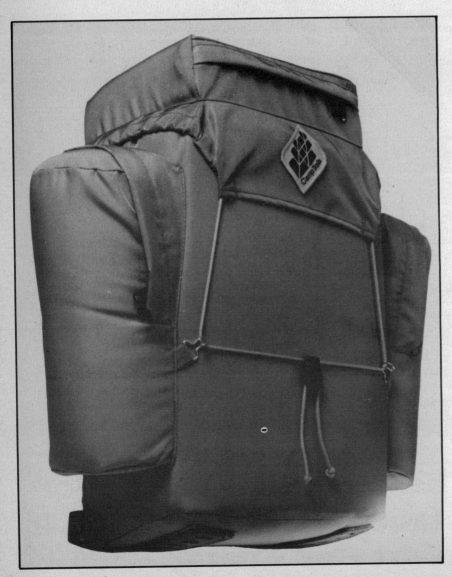

*Left: Camp Trails Trekker model has leather patches on the bottom, an expandable top, waiststrap with its touch-release buckle and is made of weatherproofed oxford weave nylon.*

Rock climbers tend to be selective
in their choice of packs, favoring
a soft pack that hugs the body such
as this Peak I style from Coleman.

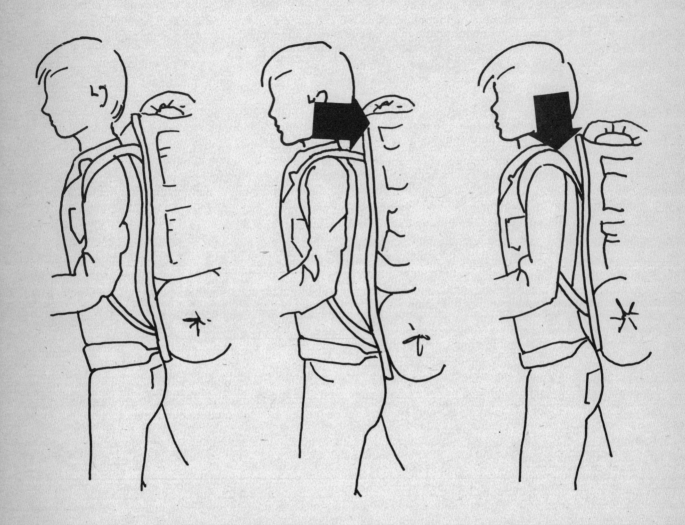

*The artist's rendition at left illustrates a pack that has the shoulder straps properly adjusted. The straps on the center figure are too short, dragging the pack too tightly against the shoulders, binding. Straps on the figure at right are too loose, causing the pack to sag.*

mean greater cost. It is also light in weight.

Your pack should be held securely to the frame, either by straps or tie-downs. Because the frame rests against the back, you'll want to be certain that the frame includes a webbed back band, usually made of nylon mesh. The band not only helps hold the frame in place, but allows for moisture escape.

Be certain that your pack frame fits you properly. Of particular benefit here are frames which can be moulded or shaped to your particular body. Proper fit includes the length of the frame. If it is too short it will pull down on your shoulders. If too long, it will pull back on them. Some manufacturers offer telescoping frames which can be adjusted to varying lengths allowing use of the same frame by several people of different sizes. For the youngster the telescoping frames allow the pack to grow as he grows.

Among recent innovations in pack frames is the flexible joint. Designed to allow for up-and-down, side-to-side movement as the hips carry you forward, the flexible joint prevents shoulder chafing while maintaining weight distribution. Among manufacturers of the flexible joint are JanSport and North Face. JanSport's Alpine Phantom uses four flex joints, two added to each side of the frame just below the shoulder bar. Made of stainless steel sandwiched between layers of nylon, the joints allow the frame and bag to move in unison with the upper body.

The Back Magic by North Face features a unique hour-glass-shaped frame contoured to the back as well as an adjustable suspension system. The heart of this system is a flexible nylon joint that attaches to the waist belt, allowing for side-to-side movement. With either frame, the intent is to provide a flexible, more fitted frame.

An excellent choice when hiking in open, trail-developed terrain, the external frame finds its greatest drawback amid

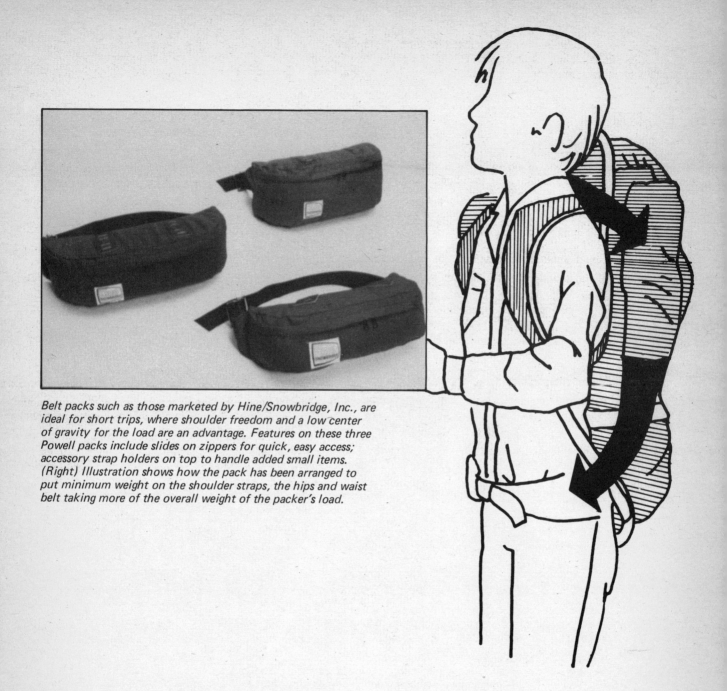

Belt packs such as those marketed by Hine/Snowbridge, Inc., are ideal for short trips, where shoulder freedom and a low center of gravity for the load are an advantage. Features on these three Powell packs include slides on zippers for quick, easy access; accessory strap holders on top to handle added small items. (Right) Illustration shows how the pack has been arranged to put minimum weight on the shoulder straps, the hips and waist belt taking more of the overall weight of the packer's load.

the less developed, closed terrain; here, the frame exhibits a tendency to hang up on the brush, seemingly reaching out to grab every limb within passing distance. It is in this type of terrain that the internal frame begins to shine. The frame is safely tucked *inside* the pack, away from interference. The internal frame pack should ride close to your back, increasing control of your center of gravity while flexing with your body movements. Many packs currently on the market actually wrap around your body, allowing the pack to become a part of you. Because they are far more compact than the external-frame packs, internal-frame packs offer increased arm movement, greater control in tough, rugged terrain where balance is of particular concern.

Internal-frame packs have plastic or metal stays sewn into the back section, often crossed in the form of an X. Combined with adjusting straps at shoulders, hips and

chest, the X-frame serves to stabilize the pack. It is in the use of the shoulder, hip and chest straps that the packer achieves his greatest flexibility. By tightening different straps, he can raise or lower the center of gravity, shifting the burden of weight from shoulders to chest muscles or hips. Shoulder straps, crossed at the front, distribute the weight of the pack more evenly across the shoulders, allowing the pack to move with the packer. The sternum strap reduces lateral sway while easing pressure on the shoulders.

The hip belt rides on the neutral part of your pelvic girdle, allowing your hip bones to carry the pack weight. Your center of gravity is low so it's easy to keep your balance.

Ample padding is important to relieve pressure points. In packing your internal frame pack, you also must take care to avoid pressure points; caused by pack contents poking

24

into your back. Remember that there is no external frame to run interference between you and the pack. Remember, too, that the internal frame pack is for moderate loads. Heavy loads are best left to the external frame and pack.

The third style of pack is the rucksack, a frameless pack that is shoulder suspended, fitting snug against the back. Also listed under the general heading of softpack, the rucksack is intended to carry lighter loads and for shorter periods of time. Some models, such as the Cannondale Softpack, feature a patented polyfoam liner to protect your back from pointed pack contents. Often it is the rucksack which becomes the novice backpacker's first pack, easily meeting the needs of those initial dayhikes or overnighters with friends. Some models have outside pockets for increased capacity, although it is not recommended that the packer tote more than the maximum twenty-pound capacity.

The fourth classification of pack is the fanny or hip pack. Actually a specialized pack, the fanny pack serves best as an emergency or dayhike carrier. Small enough to be carried inside an internal or external frame pack during the journey to camp, it is pulled out easily and strapped on for use during the day.

*Left: The buddy system can be of great advantage in backpacking, as it helps one to get the necessary adjustments of the pack to make hiking easier. This particular Coleman Peak I pack features a frame that has controlled flexibility. This type of frame has been designed to move, bend and flex with the body.*

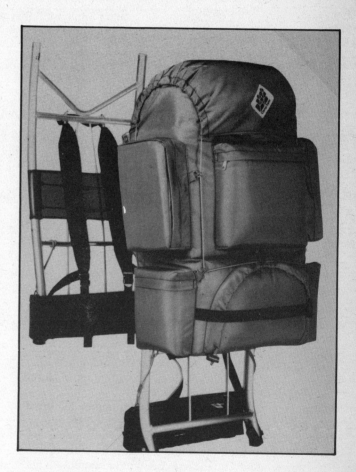

*Above: Designed to carry heavy loads, external frames like this Astral by Camp Trails feature an aluminum frame that is curved to match the curvature of the back. Note padded shoulder harness, waist belt, webbed back band of the unit. (Left) A premium internal pack, the Alpha Special offered by Hine/Snowbridge features a wrap-around hip belt for better fit. Snap clip tie-downs allow instant access to the top compartment, making life easier on the trail and in camp.*

The Loco internal-frame pack from Lowe Alpine Systems includes a chest or sternum strap for added stability over rough ground. Detachable side pockets also double as belt pouches.

As you can see, determination of the style of backpack is dependent on the purpose of your hike. You must select the pack that best suits your needs the majority of the time. Once you have made that determination, you will want to look more closely at the construction of your particular pack.

Among primary concern in pack construction should be dependability. Nothing is more frustrating than having your pack fall apart miles from civilization, and unless you've carried along a pack repair kit or a large tarp and some cord, you've got deep troubles. The type of materials used, the sewing techniques, attention to detail — all will play an important part in dependability.

For external and internal-frame packs as well as some softpacks, the material of choice is currently Cordura nylon, said to be the heaviest, most abrasion-resistant cloth available. For daypacks, most manufacturers lean toward Oxford nylon, a strong, abrasion-resistant, waterproof material. Although Oxford nylon may not be as strong as Cordura, it is considerably less expensive, which, combined with its waterproof characteristics, makes it the better choice for daypacks. Many manufacturers will go one step further by coating their packs, all styles, with a material known as Super K-Kote, a urethane film providing additional water resistance.

Because the bottom of the pack is the area that receives the most abuse and carries the greatest percentage of the load, you may want a second layer of material, either eleven-ounce Cordura or leather, wrapped around the bottom bathtub style.

Look for a pack that has as little piecing and sewn through stitching as possible. Each sewn-through seam offers moisture a prime point of entry into the interior.

Zippers play an important role in pack construction, and must be both light and tough. The preferred style of zipper today is the self-healing nylon coil zipper, chosen for its dependability and durability, even in extreme cold. Be wary of metal zippers. They are more likely to jam and will freeze in cold weather, if allowed to become wet. If the pack is fitted with an oversized rain flap to protect the zippers, all the better. The rain flap serves to channel rain away from the zipper seams, assuring a drier interior.

Consider the possibility of purchasing a bag with compressor straps if you intend on doing some hiking along rough, unstable terrain where a shift in your load is apt to cause a loss of balance. Compressor straps are intended to hold the load tight, and may be used to hold accessory gear to the outside of the pack when otherwise not needed. Many manufacturers sell the straps separately as an accessory item.

How do you tell if your bag is well made? Mostly it is a matter of look and see. Check seams and stress points. All load-bearing seams should have at least a double thread line. If the thread used is cotton, keep in mind that cotton thread is susceptible to breakage and rotting. Heavy-gauge nylon or dacron is preferred. A combination dacron with cotton is said to work well also, and prevents moisture

as seven thread lines to reinforce stress areas.

Many packs feature diamond-shaped pieces of leather sewn to the outside of the bag at various positions, frequently along the sides, bottom and outer side. These are called accessory patches, and allow for the addition of accessory pockets or simply a method of tying down additional items to the bag. Although not a necessary part of the pack, they are a nice-to-have feature on occasion.

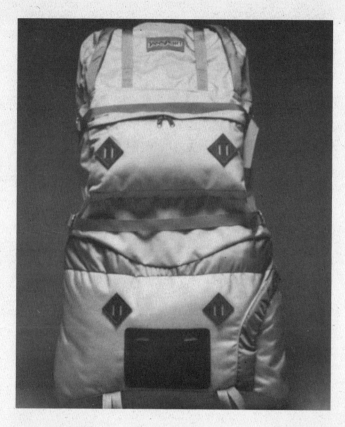

*JanSport's Alpine Phantom is built with numerous accessory patches for attaching poles and pockets. It also has oversize rain flaps and the model features several compressor straps.*

*Actually a specialized pack, this fanny type makes an ideal emergency pack. Zippered closures protected by rain flaps keep moisture from zipper.*

from wicking through the seams. The life of your pack will depend heavily on the type of thread used and the method in which it is used.

Heavy stress areas of the pack should be further reinforced using either bartacks, leather reinforcements or additional thread lines, termed X-tacks. Some manufacturers will use all three methods, some combinations of the three. One manufacturer uses as many

Straps on your pack should be well padded to protect your shoulders and hips. A popular padding material currently on the market is Ensolite, noted for its characteristic of conforming to your body. Stay stitching down the middle of the strap will prevent the Ensolite from slipping. Nearly all pack manufacturers offer a quick-release buckle on their straps — not only for convenience but for safety as well.

Once you've examined the outside of your pack carefully, it's time to check out the interior. Your prime concern here is whether or not you have ample storage space, and the degree of difficulty experienced in reaching that stored item. Basically, you will find two distinct styles of openings on backpacks: those that open from the top and those that open from the back. Each may offer separate compartments within or one large compartment. All have their advantages.

The top opening bag means less chance of water seepage as the cover pulls down well over the opening, secured by cords or straps. The lack of separate compartments means you can stuff a lot more into the bag. However, reaching a needed item at the bottom of the pack can prove a monumental task in poor weather, an irritation at best. Careful packing is of utmost importance to the backpacker with a top-loading pack. A hold-open bar that keeps the bag opening apart makes packing a lot easier. Stuff sacks are ideal here, allowing you to organize your gear into color-coded sacks readily located.

The back, panel-loading pack offers you ready access to your gear without the need to unpack. However, the three-quarter-length zipper can be a source of internal moisture, even though most manufacturers provide a weather flap over the entryway.

For the organized packer who likes to keep everything in its place, the inclusion of separate compartments within his pack is an answer to prayer. He knows just where to look for any item he might need. The single compartment backpacker has his advantages too, having the flexibility to pack a wide variety of items, including large sleeping bags or lengthy tent poles, inside with relative ease.

Because determining whether to go for the compartmentalized pack or not has proven difficult for many packers, manufacturers have tried to come up with a compromise, one which offers both choices in one bag. The divider simply drops down out of the way by use of a zipper when one compartment is needed. Coleman's 780

*Above: Tough Traveler's top-loading Mohawk features a unique hood assembly, with waterproof wings on each side to draw tightly around the bag. Straps fore and aft keep the bag anchored comfortably against the hiker's neck/shoulder area. (Left) Often a novice's first pack, an adult-size daypack doubles as a child's backpack. The outside pocket on this particular model can offer additional storage capacity.*

A-16's Hip Hugger packs come with hold-open bars to make top loading easier. Pull-over cover offers added protection against weather as well as compacting contents of the bag. Pack has 3422-cubic-inch capacity.

and Camp Trails' Timber are two examples of this versatile arrangement.

Versatility is an important part of backpack selection. If you can find a pack that will meet all of your needs, whether for daylong hikes or weeklong treks, you deserve to be proud of yourself. Unfortunately most packs that fit your dayhike needs are far too small in capacity for the seven-day journey, unless you can modify their carrying capacity. A prime way to do this is to add outer pockets. Pockets can add as much as eight hundred or more cubic inches of space to your pack, allowing you to carry that extra pair of socks, dehydrated food, sweater, camera gear, etc. Most packs come with at least one outside pocket. Some may have as many as four, nearly doubling your carrying capacity. Some manufacturers offer pockets as accessory items, to be attached to your pack with straps and the accessory patches, or perhaps with Velcro tabs. In examining these pockets look for good, stable attaching capabilities, or you're liable to lose your best camera in a clump of brush miles behind you. Be sure that the pockets will slide through the brush without pulling off. Zippers on the pockets should be large enough to allow for easy entry, covered with a protective weather flap that not only keeps

the rain out but the brush from grabbing.

Once you have selected a pack style that appeals to you, it is time to see if it will fit. If the pack is good, and it fits properly, the majority of the weight should fall to your legs. The only way to determine whether the pack fits is to try it on. If this is your first pack, you'll want the aid of an experienced salesman — preferably a backpacker himself — to help. If for any reason he will not let you try on the pack, then go somewhere else to purchase your backpack.

The length of your trunk is the determining factor in proper pack size, not your overall height. If you are ordering a pack through a mail-order company, you will need to provide them with that measurement.

Before hoisting the pack to your back load it with sufficient weight to approximate the weight you will be carrying in the field. This will allow you to "feel" the pack, the pressure you can expect. If the pack is uncomfortable now, it will be uncomfortable in the field as well.

Fasten and center the hip belt just below the waist. Remember it is a hip belt, not a waist belt. It should not hang off the waist. If it does, the pack is probably too small for you.

This front-loading double-compartment frame pack from Coleman offers easy access. The upper compartment has a full-drop-down opening feature.

Below: Primarily an expedition pack, the Serex offers 4500 cubic inches of usable volume. Pockets parallel each side of the pack as an option by Hine/Snowbridge. Snap clip tiedowns allow access to the top flap.

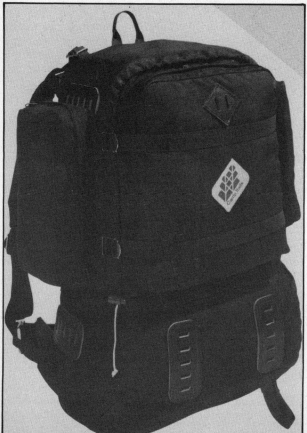

Left: Camp Trails' internal-frame half-dome provides a separate compartment below for your sleeping bag. The upper main compartment affords front-loading convenience with compressor straps that can be used to stabilize the load, a blessing on long treks.

These packs offered by Outdoor Products are listed in the current catalog as the 404 Traveler (left) and the 403 Sierra models. (Below) The same distributor has come up with this line of camouflaged packs. The fanny pack, the daypack and duffle bag all have been manufactured of waterproofed urethane-coated Oxford-weave materials.

Tighten the shoulder straps until the load feels balanced, the weight divided between the straps and hip belt. If the fit is too tight, the bulk of the weight will fall on the shoulders. If too slack, the hips must carry the weight. Shoulder straps should be about level with your shoulders. If they fall below your shoulders, try a larger size pack. If the straps rise several inches above your shoulders, you probably need a smaller pack. You want your legs to carry the weight, not your back. By balancing the pack's weight between your shoulders and hips, you direct that weight to your legs where it belongs. Every effort should be made to keep that weight within a reasonable limit, dependent on your physical capabilities.

If you allow yourself the opportunity, your body will tell you when you have exceeded your personal limits. Most adults will realize those limits and stay within them. Children, too, have limits. Unfortunately, they do not often understand them, and may exceed them if not guided by a wary parent. Fitting a child's pack to his capabilities can be as difficult as fitting him to a new pair of shoes. He doesn't know whether the pack fits or how it is supposed to feel, and you may not be sure either. A few tips from the folks at Camp Trails Company of Phoenix, Arizona, may well be worth considering:

*Comfortable fit is the overriding concern when purchasing a child's pack. Therefore, adjustability in a pack is the key feature to look for. Just as with an adult's pack, the child's pack should be fitted with weight in it. Keep in mind, however, that a child will carry considerably less weight than an adult. A good guideline is allowing the child's load, including the pack, to average twenty percent of their body weight but no more than twenty-five percent of their body weight. Keeping within the twenty to twenty-five percent ceiling insures that the weight won't make backpacking a painful experience. And it's a safe guideline for prevention of injury to developing bones and muscles caused by carrying too much weight.*

*Three important adjustments to check on children include: making sure that the hip belt fits snugly; checking that the shoulder straps have a buckle adjustment for loosening or tightening them and seeing that the straps won't slip out from these buckles when the pack has weight in it; seeing that the shoulder straps can be adjusted both for torso length and width.*

Camp Trails has a complete line of backpacks for youngsters, as do most of the major manufacturers. Some even offer adjustability that allows the pack to grow with the child for a period of time. That's efficiency, and efficiency is the name of the game in backpacking.

How you load your pack also plays a vital role in backpacking efficiency, and can mean the difference between devotion to the sport and disgust with it. To understand why a loading sequence works, you must first understand how your body works. When standing normally, without a pack, your body exhibits a center of gravity directly over your ankles. Weight is evenly distributed fore and aft, and you stand reasonably straight. Placing a loaded pack on your back alters that weight ratio, and your body naturally leans forward to accommodate the new weight, placing the pack's center of gravity over the ankles. Keeping that center of gravity as close to your back as possible

Above: This photo tends to depict what the well outfitted backpacker will wear. The unit is neat, arranged so the load is well proportioned for balance, carrying comfort. (Left) Backpacking has progressed from a frontier way of life to a family sport with packs for all family members.

limits the forward lean necessary to carry the load. Consequently you will want to load your heavier items close to your back.

Your sleeping bag is normally placed at the bottom of the bag, or tied beneath it, to give support to the load. Bulky items, such as extra clothing, are placed above that. Food items, preferably in plastic or foil bags come next, along with cooking wares. If your tent will fit inside your pack, it comes next. Tent poles can be carried either inside the pack or tied to the accessory patches alongside the pack.

Items you will need on the trail should be placed at the top of the bag. Include here your water supply, extra sweaters, noon meal and first-aid kit, if not placed in one of the outer pockets. Concentrate on placing heavier items closest to the back, keeping in mind that if yours is a frameless or soft pack you will not want hard objects poking you in the back as you hike. Nothing hard or pointed should rub against your body. Your intent is to enjoy yourself not injure yourself.

You've probably invested a good deal of money in your pack. Quality packs are expensive, though reasonably so. Consequently you'll want to protect it as well. Packing items that may leak in watertight bags is a good habit to develop. Never use detergents or washing machines for cleaning packs, as they can damage the coating or seams. Gentle hand washing, or possibly just wiping off with a damp cloth, should be all that is needed. Avoid heat in excess of 140 degrees Fahrenheit.

Between hiking trips store your pack in a cool, dry place, never against a cement floor or wall. Chemicals in the cement could damage the pack material. Empty the bag of all items that can leak or break open. Check for loose or split seams and repair them while you've plenty of time to do the job correctly. Lubricate zippers if they have jammed. If your pack has leather accessories, treat them with leather cleaner and conditioner. And if unsure of how to treat a particular cleaning or maintenance problem, telephone the manufacturer. He'd rather answer your questions now than listen to your complaints later. He knows that his best advertising comes from you, wearing his pack in the field for other backpackers to see. That's where all the fun takes place.

# CHAPTER 3

# YOU GOTTA HAVE SOLE

*Cooling one's feet in a clear creek can be invigorating, but when one is painfully crippled because of a poor fit in boots or shoes, this type of treatment is a temporary measure only.*

## ...Or If The Shoe Fits, Wear It!

TO A BACKPACKER, there is no single item of equipment more important to success than a good pair of boots.

Most other equipment items allow for improvising: If a pack ruptures, you can either repair it with your carried-along sewing kit, or, if necessary, you can enlist the aid of other equipment items to replace it. You might hold the seams together with compression straps or surround the pack with your ground cloth or tarp. Even a sleeping bag can be diverted to use as a temporary pack, at least long enough to get you back to civilization.

Admittedly each of these steps will result in some inconvenience for you, but a pair of boots that have lost a sole or ruptured a seam can mean a good deal more than

inconvenience. It could result in tragedy, depending on how badly the boots are damaged and how far from civilization you might be. Improvisation with boots is limited, with an extremely short success span.

If you are a space/weight-conscious backpacker — and most backpackers are — it is highly unlikely that you will carry backup boots with you. Consequently you must rely on the dependability of the pair you are wearing. You can economize on nearly all of your remaining equipment, but when your concern is boots, it is wise to purchase the best pair possible.

Selecting boots need not be a major decision, provided you go about it with some knowledge of what you are seeking and how the boots should fit. Be sure to give

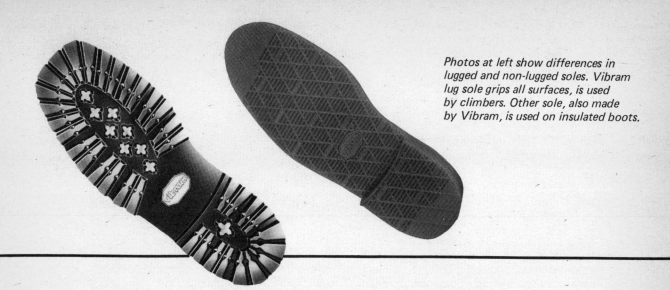

Photos at left show differences in lugged and non-lugged soles. Vibram lug sole grips all surfaces, is used by climbers. Other sole, also made by Vibram, is used on insulated boots.

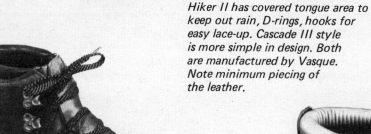

Hiker II has covered tongue area to keep out rain, D-rings, hooks for easy lace-up. Cascade III style is more simple in design. Both are manufactured by Vasque. Note minimum piecing of the leather.

Dunnam's Duraflex boots, in both low and high cut, offer plenty of padding for comfort, with uncluttered design.

yourself plenty of time to locate *the* pair of boots for you. It is unwise to wait until the last moment to purchase your boots, settling for a pair that doesn't quite fit, or not having time to break them in properly.

There are numerous types of boots available for the hiker, in various styles and heights. Which pair you will choose is dependent on the type of terrain you will hike the majority of the time. For most backpackers, the style needed is called a trail boot, similar in design to a work boot. The uppers will range from six to eight inches in height, laced from just behind the toes to the top of the boot. The boot should have a thick, lugged sole, not only to prevent slipping, but to insulate your foot from sharp stones. A scree guard will protect your ankles from injury as well as offer much needed support. A trail boot should be lined, not only for warmth but to provide a means of perspiration absorption. It should be comfortable, fully supportive, durable and water-resistant.

Similar in appearance to the trail boot is the mountain boot, but a backpacker need only to pick up the boot to notice a distinct difference. The mountain boot is heavy, weighing around six pounds as opposed to the average four or five-pound trail boot. There is little give in the mountain boot, which has a thick, inflexible sole. You'll want a trail boot with a well-insulated sole to protect your feet, but you need some degree of give in the sole as well.

You also want your hiking boot to be as light in weight as possible, while still offering support to arches and ankles. The mountain boot provides excellent support, but the difference in weight can prove dramatic when you multiply that extra pound or so by the thousands of steps you will take during your trip. Your feet take the load of both body and gear for many hours at a time during your backpacking trip. It can be foolish to enlarge that load unnecessarily, so choose your boot to match the majority of your terrain.

If your interest progresses beyond traditional

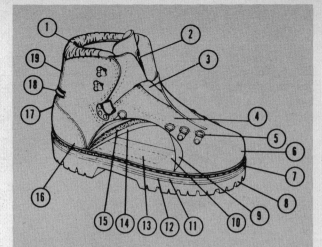

1. Foam rubber padding, covered with goat skin. Provides snug, comfortable fit, reduces pressure on Achilles tendon.

2. Velcro strip, locks tongue in position to inside quarter quickly and easily.

3. Bellows gusset provides barrier against dust, dirt, and water.

4. One piece upper leather eliminates unnecessary seam stitching.

5. Extra heavy duty nickel plated hooks.

6. Heavy duty box provides protection and helps retain shape of boot.

7. Norwegian welt, heavy duty construction for strength and water repellency.

8. Lug sole and heel, rugged and long-wearing. Screw at heels. Excellent sole for edging or snow and ice work.

9. Fully leather lined.

10. Heavy leather insole.

11. Heavy leather midsoles for extra firm support.

12. Full rubber and leather midsoles for additional support.

13. Extra reinforced spring steel shank.

14. Leather quarter lining for inside foot comfort and additional support.

15. Scree guard to protect and cushion the ankle (both sides).

16. Heavy reinforced outer leather heel pocket for added strength.

17. Thread, 100% nylon used at all strenuous points of boots to resist wear and decomposition due to water and perspiration.

18. Patented mantice double-action hinge.

19. Reinforced back stay for added strength.

*This lightweight backpacking boot by Vasque combines suede split leather and nylon. Both materials have been coated with a water-repellent finish. The outsole used on this particular model is a Vibram Kletter lift type.*

backpacking and mountaineering to the more advanced rock-climbing, you will need a specialty boot. The lug-soled tread that provides excellent traction on trails proves just the opposite on rocks. Rock-climbing boots feature smooth, rubber-soled bottoms for grasping and holding on to even the smallest of rock ledges. Extremely light in weight, the rock-climbing boot nudges the scales at less than three pounds, featuring a combination canvas and leather upper shoe. Excellent for smooth-surface climbing, rock-climbing boots are a poor choice for traditional backpacking. For most backpackers, the preferred boot will be the trail boot.

Selection of the best boot for you then becomes a question of construction and fit. All boots *look* good in the shoe store or shop window. They even *smell* good. It takes careful examination to determine whether they actually are well constructed; and you must get specific.

## CONSTRUCTION TIPS

Your first consideration in the overall worth of your trail boot might be of the material used. Leather is the primary component of most hiking boots, constructed with either the smooth or rough surface out. Both serve a purpose: Smooth-out boots provide the greatest water repellency and rough-out boots offer greater resistance to abrasions. Regardless of whether the leather is smooth or rough, it should be clean and firm.

Look for boots with as little piecing of the upper shoe as

Danner's insulated Fossil is made in both lowcut and 8-inch height, with Vibram soles.

Rock-climbing boot by Richmoor features smooth sole for better hold on rocks; poor choice for backpacking.

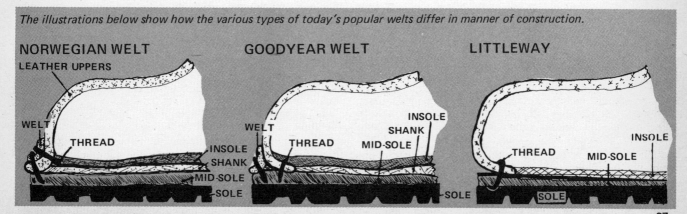

The illustrations below show how the various types of today's popular welts differ in manner of construction.

**NORWEGIAN WELT**
LEATHER UPPERS
WELT
THREAD
INSOLE
SHANK
MID-SOLE
SOLE

**GOODYEAR WELT**
WELT
THREAD
INSOLE
SHANK
MID-SOLE
SOLE

**LITTLEWAY**
INSOLE
THREAD
MID-SOLE
SOLE

Boot at left has been treated with good waterproofing compound — Mink Oil — and sheds water as a freshly waxed automobile. Boot on right is untreated, soaks up extra moisture almost like a sponge.

Three basic methods of attaching uppers to soles are illustrated at right. From left: Goodyear welt, Norwegian welt, and Littleway. Norwegian is generally considered best for backpacking boots, but is also the most expensive.

possible. Each additional seam provides a means for moisture to enter the boot. Your feet will sweat inside your boots anyway. The extra moisture is neither needed nor wanted.

A good deal of consideration should be given to the method in which these leather uppers are attached to the inner and midsole of the boot. Some boot manufacturers glue the boot together. Others sew it together, and some use a combination of both. There are three basic methods for sewing the upper to the sole: Norwegian welt, Goodyear welt and Littleway. Each has its advantages and disadvantages.

Perhaps the most popular of construction styles for heavy-duty hiking is the Norwegian welt. A narrow strip of leather, termed a welt, actually is sewn to the outside of the boot to protect the boot seams. Folding the end of the upper shoe toward the outside, the welt is laid on top of it. Stitches then are applied through both the welt and the upper shoe horizontally, into the insole. Then both are sewn again, this time directly through the midsole

vertically. This provides two separate thread lines to the upper and welt. In the event one seam fails, the shoe will be held together by the second thread line.

Similar to the Norwegian welt, the primary difference in the Goodyear welt is in the turn of the upper shoe. Rather than being turned out, the upper is turned inward, in a cupping formation. A seam then is sewn horizontally through both the upper shoe and welt into the insole. A second seam is sewn vertically through the welt into the midsole. The drawback to this style of construction may be in the single seam holding the uppers to the sole. It is, however, also much more inexpensive to manufacture than is the Norwegian welt.

The third style of construction is called the Littleway, popular in the manufacture of rock-climbing boots. The Littleway uses no welt. Instead, the upper is simply turned in, then stitched from the inside directly through the upper sole into the insole and midsole. While Littleway construction offers only a single seam, it has the advantage of having that seam inside the shoe, protected from the

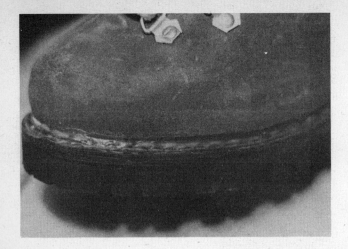

the Vibram sole, manufactured by Quabaug Rubber Company of Brookfield, Massachusetts. Developed in 1937 as the first all-purpose climbing sole, the sole has been highly imitated in recent years. The rubber sole is both abrasion-resistant and slip-resistant, yet offers ample flexibility. Chances are you'll need that flexibility. You'll also need ample support, not only of your foot but of your ankle as well.

In support of your foot, most good boots will have a metal shank, usually steel, offering reinforcement to the soles. Some will run the entire length of the boot, others spanning the ball of the foot. Protecting and supporting the ankles is the task of the scree (ankle) guard. Look for this extra padding to prevent twisted, sprained ankles. Check also for insoles that insulate, take the edge off rough seams and ease foot strain. If your boots do not have insulated insoles, you may wish to add them.

As you examine the construction of a considered boot, also think in terms of waterproofing capabilities. Regardless of where you backpack, the odds are that you will find

elements. There is no overhang of sole beyond the upper shoe, which allows your foot to hug rock ledges, a bonus when the going gets tight.

Good boots are made to outlast their outer sole, and its a lot cheaper to have your favorite boots resoled than to purchase a new pair. Whether new or resoled, the type of outer sole you choose can make a big difference in your ability to grasp the terrain without sliding or slipping.

For backpacking or mountaineering, one will need a thick, lug-soled boot. The most widely known of lug soles is

*Various patterns of lug soles used on backpackers' boots include American military boots used in Vietnam at left. More familiar patterns also shown include the popular Vibram, at right, with stitching sewn through toe area.*

*If good leather is to last, it must be properly cared for. Effects of neglect are evident on boot at left.*

yourself caught in a rainstorm at one time or another. Sloshing around in rain-soaked boots and socks not only is uncomfortable, but can be harmful, leading to fungus infections and possible crippling if allowed to go long enough. As previously mentioned, restricting the amount of piecing in a boot is a prime step toward waterproofing. Yet, even one-piece constructed boots have some seams: where the upper shoe joins the soles, along the heel guard and back stay. These seams should be sealable.

Look carefully at the tongue construction. You will want a boot that offers a tight seal between tongue and boot uppers. Some tongues are billowed, with folded flexible leather connecting the tongue to the upper shoe. Other manufacturers offer a cover for the tongue area that laps the outside of the boot, channeling water away from the tongue and down the side of the boot. Both styles offer excellent water resistance. Velcro tabs will help keep the tongue in place.

In an effort to provide a totally waterproof boot, the Danner Shoe Manufacturing Company has produced the lightweight Gore-tex boot. Gore-tex, a porous film with pores large enough to allow water vapor to pass, but too small to allow water drops to pass, is used as a sock lining for the new boots. More will be said about Gore-tex in following chapters.

*Despite the slogan on the backstay of the boot at right, no boot is 100% waterproof at all times. Some moisture will enter any boot, given the circumstances.*

## GETTING A GOOD FIT

Having settled on a style of hiking boot that meets your construction ideals, it is time to determine if the boot fits. Unfortunately there are many backpackers in the field today who, having purchased a quality boot, find themselves in as much discomfort as the individual with the poorly made boots. The problem is that their boots do not fit properly. If purchasing boots through the mail, the manufacturer will ask you to send a tracing of your foot, drawn while wearing the hiking socks you expect to wear with their boots. The purpose of the drawing is to obtain a more accurate fit to your particular foot. It would be better to purchase that first pair of boots from a local, reputable backpacking shop where you actually can try on the boot.

Give yourself plenty of time to size your new boots. You'll be much better off for it. Do not enter the shoe shop with a predetermined size in mind. You may be surprised, for not all boots of the same indicated size will fit you. The salesman should measure your foot with a Brannock or

Construction features shown above include reinforced heel, backstay and scree guard at boot top. Inclusion of pull loop makes pulling on damp boot easier.

Cutaway boot shows Goodyear welt construction and application of insulation inside leather upper.

similar device. This gives you a starting point from which to begin. Remember, it is only an approximate measurement. Allow the salesman to measure your foot even though you've worn a size 9D for ten years and know darn well what size you need.

If you have come to the shop prepared, you will find that you'll need a half size or more larger boot, and for good reason. You will be wearing, when the measurement is taken, the socks you intend to wear on the trail. Generally, you will have two pairs of socks, an inner and outer pair, both adding to the measurement. The best combination of sock is a thin inner sock under a heavier wool sock. The thin sock next to your foot acts as a sponge to wick away foot moisture. The heavier outer sock is intended to provide warmth and protection as well as some degree of padding for the foot.

Favored inner socks are made of nylon, orlon, cotton or a combination of two or more. For the outer sock the unanimous choice is wool, still believed to provide the

maximum of comfort and sweat absorption as well as insulation. Take care that the wool socks you purchase are of good quality, as cheap wool can contain impurities that will cause skin irritations. They may also insulate poorly and wear badly.

To begin fitting your boot, slip it on, leaving the tongue unlaced. Slide your foot back so that the heel is in proper position, then take a step or two. If the boot drops off or feels as if it would like to, the boot is probably too big for your foot. There should be no more than about ¼-inch of lift.

Next slide the foot all the way forward to the front or toe box of the boot. Try to slide your index finger between your heel and the boot. Use your own finger as it is of proportionate size to the remainder of your body; the salesman's finger may not be. If your finger will not slide between your heel and the boot, the boot is too short and can result in some extremely painful blisters.

Another test for length involves standing on an incline with the boot laced. Try to slide your foot forward in the boot. If your toes hit the toe box, the boot is too short. Some folks will even suggest that you kick the front of the boot against a wall or other hard object. If too short you will know it immediately, but you are also apt to know of the salesman's displeasure with similar speed. A scuffed pair of boots can be difficult to sell.

Returning your heel back into proper position, attempt

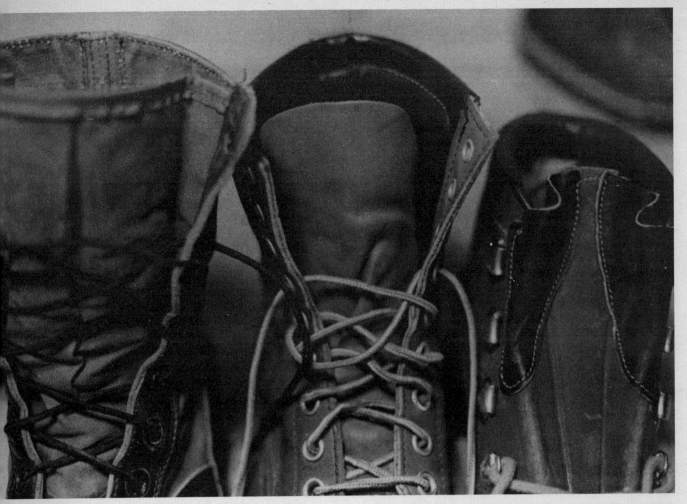

*Above: Boots at left and right have tongues attached with billowed material which channels excess water down and away from foot. Center boot has straight tongue attachment, preferred by some. Note wrinkles which may cause blisters.*

## GALIBIER MOUNTAIN BOOT CONSTRUCTION

1. Alpine rock climbing and technical ice boot
2. Top grain padded quarter lining
3. Separate padded cowhide tongue
4. Velcro tongue retainer
5. Double riveted lace hooks
6. Integral folding gusset closure
7. Double riveted lace grippers
8. Steel speed lace D-rings
9. Hard rubber toe notch in midsole (for increased sole life)
10. One piece reversed full grain double tanned cowhide
11. Patented Galibier Makalu sole
12. Norwegian veldshoen construction
13. Full grain double tanned one piece backstay

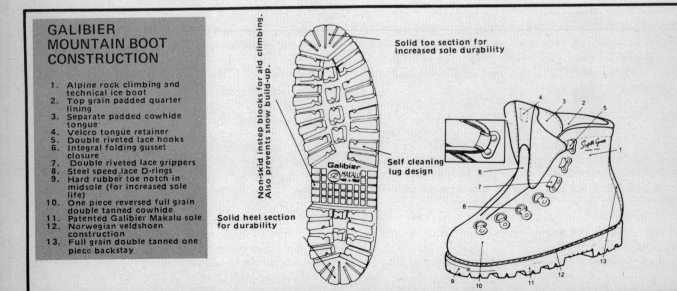

Solid toe section for increased sole durability

Non-skid instep blocks for aid climbing. Also prevents snow build-up.

Self cleaning lug design

Solid heel section for durability

to determine if the boot fits the ball of your foot. You must "feel" this measurement, and a qualified salesman will be of greatest advantage to you here. If all feels well it is time to lace up.

You will probably want a flat nylon lace for your boots, even though the round weave or leather strips may be more eye appealing. The flat laces will stay tied longer, and are not affected by weather as leather strips sometimes are. Your boots may come with eyelets, D-rings, hooks or a combination of the three. The shiny D-rings, also known as speed laces, and hooks look nice, and can make lacing your boots in limited light situations a good deal easier, but they also add weight to the boot. Neither of the three holds any better, so choose the one you prefer, but be certain it is strong. Lacing the boot to the bottom of the ankle area, then tying an overhand knot before continuing up the boot will keep the bottom secure while you finish the lacing.

After lacing, walk around in the boots for several minutes, allowing the boots to warm to your feet. At this point listen to what your feet have to tell you. Toes should wiggle, uncramped. You may feel some degree of pressure along the sides of the foot, but there should be no actual pinching. This pressure should ease as the boot warms and becomes more flexible. If the message you are receiving from your feet is one of honest discomfort, don't buy that boot. Keep in mind that, as the day wears on, a boot that began the hike with comfort may seem to tighten up. Under constant weight of body and pack, feet are prone to swell slightly. Be sure to try on both boots, as more than likely one foot will be larger than the other. Most people's are.

If after twenty or thirty minutes of test walking in the store the boots still feel comfortable or there is only a slight tightness along the sides of your foot, buy them. Take them home and begin the process of breaking them in.

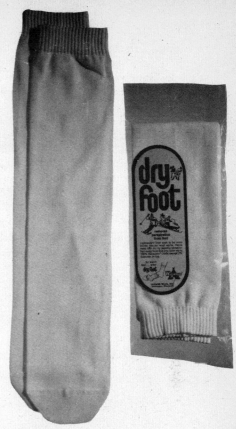

Wigwam Dry Foot keeps feet dry by wicking moisture away from foot and into outer sock. It's a lightweight liner to be worn under wool socks.

1. Top grain leather lining.
2. Heel and side counter.
3. Double-tanned, reversed, waxed full-grain cowhide.
4. Heel counter.
5. Toe counter.
6. Norwegian veldtshoen construction.
7. Full grain cowhide insole.
8. Rivets secure steel shank to midsole.
9. Contoured, double thickness wood provides stiffness and thermal insulation.
10. Full length, spoon-shaped steel shank.
11. Leather midsole with rubber inset at toe to resist damage by step kicking and rock climbing.
12. Leather midsole for lateral rigidity and better foot protection.
13. Galibier Makalu sole, especially developed for mountain use.

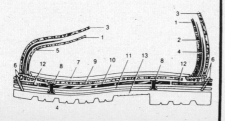

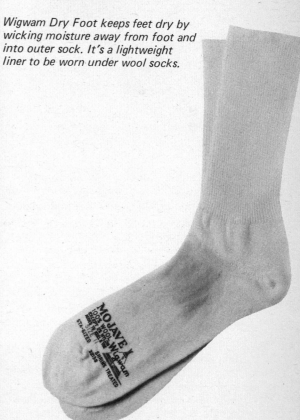

For those who want all wool worsted on their feet, the Wigwam Mojave is a lightweight undersock that features heels and toes that are well reinforced with nylon.

## BREAKING IN

As with fitting, breaking in boots need not be a difficult or uncomfortable task, but it should be time consuming. There was a time when the prescribed method for breaking in boots involved stepping into a tub of water, with the boots fully laced, and standing there for four or five seconds. The backpacker was then told to wear the boots until they dried thoroughly, the theory being that the soaked boots would stretch to his foot, and then mould to that shape as they dried. In reality, such "drownings" would only serve to tear down the boots unless the leather and seams were protected by a good water repellent. That being the case the water could have little effect on the boots in such a short time period. What did work, however, was the "wearing them until they dried" period.

That's what you will want to do with your new boots — wear them. Begin with short periods, around the house at first. Journey into the backyard or for walks around the

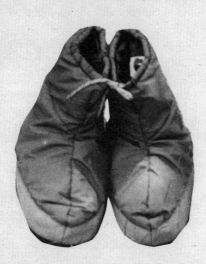

*The day's hike over, your feet can be pampered with a comfortable pair of booties. These are made of Polarguard, produced by Cedar River Mountaineering.*

neighborhood only when you are sure the boots fit. You can probably talk the shoe salesman into exchanging the boots for another size if you've only worn them indoors, on covered floors. But get the boots scuffed and grass-stained and you've slim chance of an exchange.

If you are fortunate enough to have a job which would allow for wearing hiking boots to work, then do so, but be sure to take along your normal work boots in the event you begin to feel pressure. Boot leather is rigid, and slow to mould to your foot, so give yourself time.

Give yourself time, as well, to waterproof your boots. It's wise to do this even though you do not expect to run into wet weather. Even the best of weather reports may meet with disagreement from Mother Nature, and if that happens it will probably come when you are farthest from civilization or a dry shelter. Be sure to read the directions that come with your boots to determine the recommended method of cleaning and waterproofing. That method is generally dependent on the method of tanning used on the leather.

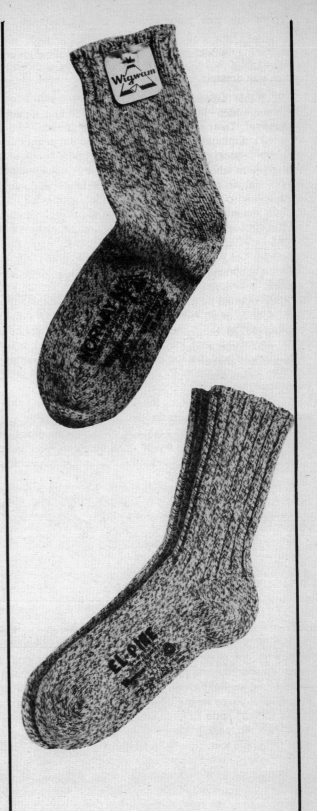

*The sock at top is called the Norway and is four-ply, combining 85% wool with 15% nylon; it's called Nywool. Lower photo is a Super-Stretch Ragg sock combining 85% wool, 2% Spandex, balance made up of nylon material.*

There are two basic tanning processes for leather, chrome or vegetable tanning. In chrome tanning the hide is soaked in a chromium salt solution which increases the leather's heat and abrasion resistance. Treat these boots with a wax dressing.

Vegetable tanning involves soaking the hide in plant extracts which make the leather more resilient and waterproof. Treat them with oil or grease, allowing it to set overnight, wiping the excess off in the morning.

If your boots do not come with an instruction tag, ask the salesman what to use for waterproofing and care. There are a number of quality leather products on the market from which to choose, If the boot has a smooth-out surface you will want to use a conditioner, such as Sno Seal. If the surface is rough-out you will use a silicone dressing.

Work the conditioner into all seams and joints, using a clean cloth or your fingers. After the initial treatment you will need to reapply the conditioner whenever the leather appears to be drying out.

Keep in mind that waterproofing compounds do not seal the boots from *all* moisture. If they did your feet would still get soaked, but from sweat rather than rain. Either way there will come a time when you must dry out those wet boots. When that time comes, use care. Leather is a lot like skin in that it cannot take exposure to intense heat. It may crack or shrink. Do not put wet boots over a stove or by a campfire. Dry them slowly, stuffing them with newspaper or cloth if it is available. If the interior has been soaked, hang the boots upside down to allow the moisture to drain out. Let the boots dry naturally.

## FOOT CARE

Regardless of how well your boots fit, the end of a day's hike will find tired feet in need of a rest. A change of shoes can be a delightful experience, and down booties are both warm and lightweight, taking up little space in your pack.

Proper foot care is essential to a successful hike, and it doesn't hurt to pamper those feet when you get the chance. A cool dip in a mountain spring or just simply sitting with your boots off, allowing your feet to air — both give tired feet a chance to relax.

Be alert to blisters. The smallest of rocks or a crease in a sock will cause a blister if given half a chance. At the first sign of a problem remove the boot. Apply a piece of moleskin to the area if you have it. If not, a Band-Aid or piece of adhesive may do. If a blister does develop, give it your attention right away. If large, you may need to drain it before covering with a dressing. Wash the area first, then apply an antiseptic to the skin. (You should carry this in your first aid pack.) Puncture the blister at its edge, and ease the liquid out, then cover with a sterile dressing. If the blister is small the liquid should be gradually absorbed by the body, and you need not puncture it at all. Check the healing process periodically to be certain that the remainder of your hike is the enjoyable experience you intended it to be.

Once you are home you will want to give your boots a final cleaning and conditioning. Pack the boots with newspapers or shoe trees and then store on an open shelf at room temperature. When the time comes to saddle up once again you will be ready, and your boots will be ready as well.

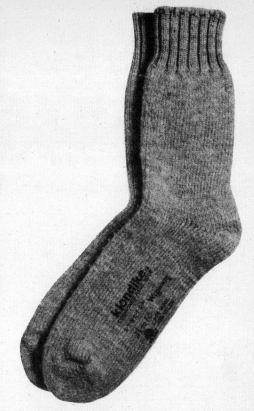

*Author's favored choice for an outer sock is wool. This style is Wigwam's Klondike in 90% wool. Nylon content is 10%, which adds comfort and helps retain sock's shape. The Klondike is fully cushioned from toe to top of rib.*

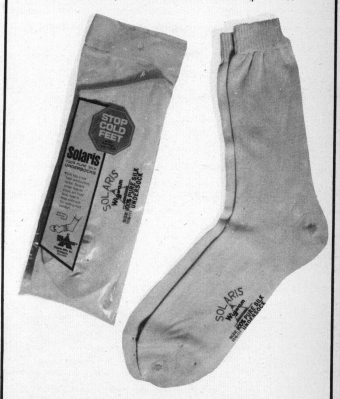

*One secret to heat retention in the feet is Wigwam's Solaris, which is 100% silk. This material has a low heat conductivity factor to keep out the winter cold.*

# THAT LAYERED EFFECT
## THAT LAYERED EFFECT
## THAT LAYERED EFFECT

## "A Hat Keeps Your Hands And Feet Warm."
## Is This A Time-Tested Truth Or Foolish Fable?

"WEARING A HAT can keep your hands and feet warm." That this adage of mountain men and experienced outdoorsmen can be true might surprise many readers. But, the hat you wear while backpacking *does* play a vital role in your comfort when exposed to cold weather conditions. It's just one part of what sage packers call "the layered effect."

To understand what layering is all about and why it works you must first know something of the system your body utilizes in regulating your internal environment.

Medical experts call that system "homeostasis" — the tendency of the body to maintain a uniform and beneficial physiological stability within and between its parts. In much simplified terms, it works something like this:

As adaptable as the human body may be, there is at least one area in which it shows remarkably little tolerance for change — internal temperature. We accept an internal temperature of 98.6 degrees Fahrenheit as being the "normal" temperature of man, although temperatures of as much as a half a degree above or below that level are still

*Lower left: The Gore-Tex all-weather parka from Marmot Mountain Works features a minimum of seams for greater waterproofing, more durability. Velcro-sealed cuffs, zipper shield keep out drafts. (Lower right) Gerry's Great Vest features a snap-front, down-filled collar. Pro Parka has elastic snap wrist closures, a drawstring bottom, two-way pockets that are protected by Velcro closures.*

## CHAPTER 4

considered within the acceptable range. Let that temperature alter by a mere full degree, however, and we begin to feel it. A rise in temperature and we start to sweat, perhaps flush. Let that temperature drop and we begin to shiver, or experience what we call "goose bumps" along our extremities. These are direct results of our body's attempts at regulating our temperature back to its normal range, attempts over which we have no control or direction.

We can, however, control the necessity for such actions by controlling our external environment, our *immediate* environment as it exists along our skin. That's what layering is all about — controlling that immediate environment by increasing or decreasing the depth and insulation capabilities of the clothing that surrounds the skin. Failing to do so, the body will take its own actions.

Admittedly the body has limited resources available to it, and can produce only so much heat or heat-carrying blood supplies. Consequently the body must set priorities. Its primary interest is in maintaining an optimum temperature around its vital organs, and it will concentrate on regulating the torso which houses those organs. If faced with a lowered body temperature, for instance, the body will draw the heat that it requires from the less vital areas of the body, the extremities. It does this by constricting or reducing the diameter of the blood vessels leading to the extremities, reducing the flow of blood and its inherent body heat away from the torso. As heart and lungs grow warmer your hands and feet grow colder.

In conditions of increased internal temperatures the opposite occurs, the blood vessels to the extremities dilating or expanding to allow for increased blood flow, and with it excess heat which then radiates from the skin.

So, how does the head affect your hands and feet? Is it not an extremity of sorts itself?

It is possible to consider the head as an extremity, but the body considers it as a special case, one which must be pleased whenever possible. The flow of blood carries with it not only heat but oxygen, a vital and constant need for proper brain function. Consequently, the body will not reduce the flow of blood to the brain unless forced to do so. If the head is exposed to cold temperatures which slow its blood flow, the body will automatically force additional supplies to the brain, taking that blood supply from the less vital hands and feet. Depending upon which source of information you use, heat losses of as much as twenty-five to fifty percent can be experienced through radiation of heat from the head and neck. Either way, it results in a dramatic reduction in available heat resources for the remainder of the body. Covering the head with a layer of insulation, as with a wool cap, reduces the loss of body heat, allowing it to be redirected back to the extremities.

There are numerous ways in which the body loses its body heat. Radiation is one method. Placed in an environment colder than its internal temperature the body actually gives off heat in what might be described as an effort to warm that environment to its desired temperature. By placing a layer of insulation between the body and its external environment you are actually able to maintain the level of body heat because you can quickly heat the minimized area between your skin and the insulation. The body seemingly does not care about the bulk of external temperature, only that environment that immediately surrounds it, and it will do its best to maintain an optimum temperature of that immediate environment or burn itself out in trying to do so. In that event an individual enters the initial stages of hypothermia, and unless reversed, will follow through all stages until death results.

Although hypothermia will be discussed at great length in a following chapter, it is important to know that the majority of hypothermia cases occur in seemingly mild temperatures, ranging from 30 to 50 degrees Fahrenheit. Thus, even the dayhiker must be aware of the effects of hypothermia, and the steps he must take to avoid it. Layering of clothing is one major step.

Just what is layering? It is the application of several lightweight layers of clothing, one atop the other, added as temperature and climate reduce to maintain that internal body temperature. Why several layers instead of one or two heavier layers? If you were able to determine positively the temperature and weather conditions you would find during a given backpacking trip, and could guarantee that those conditions would never change, remaining the same from the first step you take until the last, you could dress for that condition, using perhaps one bulky, heavyweight parka to serve your needs.

Unfortunately temperature and weather conditions do not remain constant. You will probably experience much cooler temperatures in the early morning and late evening hours than you will at noontime. You might, perhaps, run into a summer squall that sends temperatures plummeting for a period of time, or find yourself walking out of shady, cool forest lands into barren, sun-drenched plains. Layering allows you to add or remove clothing items as the environment dictates, without the necessity of removing more clothing than you would actually like. When changes in weather or a reduction in physical exertion demand, you can replace that clothing. For this reason your backpacking clothing should be as versatile as possible.

## UNDERWEAR

The initial consideration in layering is the choice of underwear to be worn, the primary function being the capability of absorbing and wicking away perspiration. If backpacking during the hot, arid months of summer and early fall you will probably consider your normal, everyday cotton underclothes. Cotton absorbs the excess moisture from your body, and in retaining that moisture can actually cool you by surrounding your skin with its damp, moist covering. Keep in mind, however, that if your hike extends to the cooler evening hours that cotton underwear will still be damp and moist, producing no warmth or insulation abilities whatsoever. In fact, your body will then lose body heat as it tries to dry out your garments.

There are many who will advocate the use of wool underwear when faced with the likelihood of cool or damp weather. Unlike cotton, when damp, wool retains its insulating capabilities, providing warmth as it wicks the moisture away from your body and to its outer layer. It is, however, frequently itchy, very warm, and for some produces allergic reactions, especially if it's low-quality wool. If you are going to wear wool underwear be sure that it is of premium quality. The added costs will pay for itself in the increased warmth and decreased skin problems. A

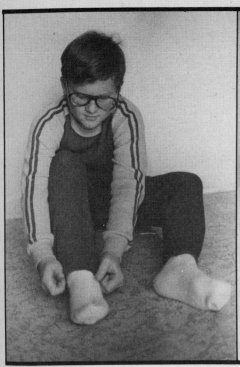

Layering begins with your underwear. For cool, dry temperatures thermal underwear is ideal, but don't get it wet, or you'll suffer a new Ice Age.

Wool shirts, a favorite for outdoors, provide warmth without unnecessary bulk. Be certain the shirt is large enough so you can stretch without bind.

Pants should be roomy in the seat and legs, without cuffs to hang up in the brush. Suspenders can replace belts for added flexibility at your waist.

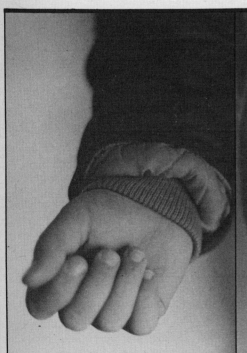

Parka sleeves should be adaptable to weather conditions. Knitted inner cuff is for cold weather, but does not allow ventilation in warm clime.

In selecting a parka, look at pocket corners for reinforced stitching, as this usually will result in much longer wear afield for backpacker.

Zipper closures should be protected by zipper flap held in place by tabs of Velcro or buttons. This should reduce cold air, entry of moisture.

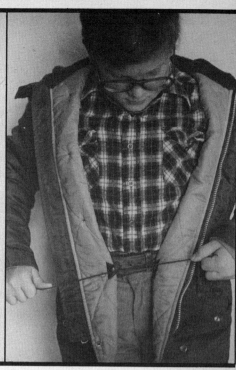

*The third layer, a parka, must be roomy to allow for added clothing beneath if needed. Look for extra storage in inside, outside pockets.*

*Note fitted waist, fully lined hood. Drawstring at waist allows parka to hang free in warmer situations, but drawn snug, eliminates cold drafts.*

*There is nothing complex about waist drawstring. Quilted nylon taffeta of lining is padded with polyester fill for warmth, yet is light in weight.*

blend of cotton and wool, in two layers, can be an excellent choice, the cotton next to the skin to absorb the body's moisture while the outer layer of wool wicks that moisture away. You might also wish to consider the fishnet or mesh underwear. Worn under a shirt, the fishnet traps pockets of dead air space, the most efficient source of insulation available, while allowing moisture to escape.

Regardless of your style of underwear, look for unrestricted comfort. Cuffs, ankles and neckline should fit closely but not tightly.

## SHIRTS AND SLACKS

Over your underwear you will want a layer of clothing that provides warmth, whether against cooling temperatures or chilling breezes. For warm weather, cotton or cotton blends make excellent shirt material. For cooler weather lightweight wool shirts are ideal, offering excellent insulation as well as water-repellency. Wool is strong and extremely abrasion resistent. Heavyweight wools are available for even colder temperatures.

Some folks prefer nylon shirts to either cotton or wool. Nylon is an excellent barrier against the cold, however it offers no "breathing" capabilities, holding perspiration inside where it can result in wasted body heat as the body's mechanisms attempt to evaporate that perspiration.

When we think about the early backpackers we think of rugged-looking men with beards halfway to their waists, dressed head to toe in buckskin. And buckskin does have its advantages, being extremely strong, and nearly impossible for insects to assault. It also makes it impossible for perspiration to escape, making summerwear as well as active winterwear most uncomfortable. Then, too, it's difficult to find buckskin these days.

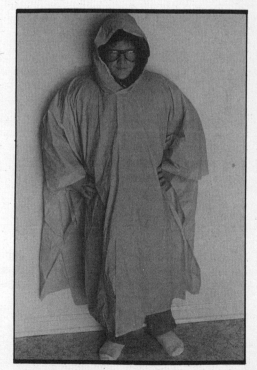

*The final layer of clothing must provide resistance to water and wind. The most economical, costing only a few dollars, is ordinary poncho style.*

*Much of the clothing one will need for backpacking may already be hanging in your closet at home. Cotton shorts or jeans are a favorite among summer hikers. There is little fun in hiking, though, if clothing is uncomfortable.*

Today's selection of fabrics are far more accommodating to the human body, and in far greater abundance. Whatever your choice of material, check your shirt's construction. Seams should be double sewn for dependability. A lap-fold seam in which junctions of material fold over each other is about the strongest construction you can buy. Your shirt should be cut full enough to allow for unrestricted movement, and long enough to stay tucked inside your trousers or shorts.

Which type of trouser to wear backpacking is a matter of temperature and tradition, many backpackers looking for ruggedness, others for warmth and/or comfort. A favored trouser for warm, summer packing is short pants. Even winter packing will find some hardy packers decked in shorts, with long wool socks reaching to just below the knees. Shorts are super comfortable — they are also short, which exposes your lower legs to the mercy of the terrain, a consideration in thick, brush-covered terrain.

Another favored trouser of today's backpacker is the denim blue jean, a strong, twilled cotton fabric. For those seeking strength blue jeans may be hard to beat, but when warmth is required they fall far short of being the answer. Subjected to wet weather jeans soak up rain like a sponge, taking forever to dry.

There was a time when all jeans were cut straight-legged, restricting stretching movements to a noticeable degree, but today jeans can be purchased with varying degrees of leg cut, with fuller seats, thighs and hips. If you should choose jeans as your backpacking trousers it would be wise to purchase a pair with that extra room in the seat and legs,

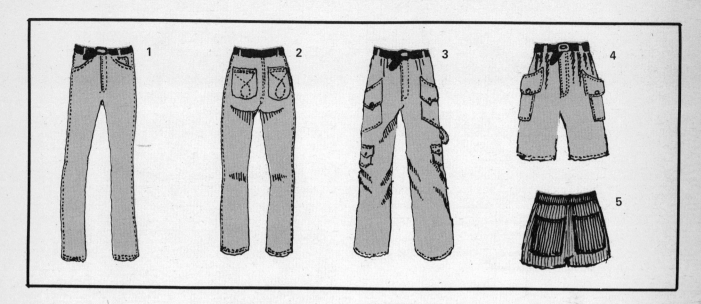

1. Straight-legged
2. Fitted style
3. Loose khakis
4. Knickers-Bermudas
5. Corduroy shorts

As an added choice you might wish to consider one of the cotton blends, such as khaki or canvas. Both are highly durable yet comfortable. Independent of the material you choose, there are some construction qualities you will want. If the legs are full length, be sure that they have no external cuffs. Cuffs have a tendency to "grab" passing brush and collect all manner of objects, from rain to berries. Look for ample pockets, reinforced stress points, double fabric knees and seats.

## PARKAS AND VESTS

As a third layer of clothing you will want to include a warm but lightweight parka or vest. There are a number of quality parkas and vests available today, making final selection difficult. You will need to consider not only the insulating capabilities of the garment, but its overall weight, durability, stowability and cost as well.

The outer shell of many vests and parkas is made of ripstop nylon, a lightweight fabric featuring reinforced threads crossing each other in a matted fashion. These threads act as a barrier against tears, allowing tears to be contained within the surrounding reinforced threads. Although hardly impervious to tears, ripstop's unique design makes it unlikely that those holes will grow in size during normal movements. The inner lining may also be of nylon or a cotton/nylon blend.

Sandwiched between the outer shell and lining is perhaps the most important aspect of quality parkas and vests — the insulating materials. For a maximum of warmth with a minimum of added weight, down is considered to be the insulating material of choice. Keep in mind, however, that down loses its loft (depth of insulation) when wet and will require an outer shell of excellent water-repellent capabilities. There are a number of synthetic fiber fills that work nearly as well, and may be less affected by moisture.

While manufacturers are continuously introducing new insulation materials there are a number that have already

and to carry along a lightweight pair of rain pants.

Wool pants are a favored choice of trouser for the experienced backpacker and mountaineer who need warmth, comfort and durability. Often reinforced at the knees and seat, wool trousers stretch with you, offering easier mobility. Being wool they, like all wool garments, will wick moisture away from the skin, allowing you to remain much warmer in damp weather.

If you are really into backpacking you may wish to invest in a pair of wool knickers. Once the curse of every adolescent aching to reach manhood, the knicker offers maximum freedom of movement, loose fit in the seat, hips and thighs, yet is snug below the knees to block out cold air. A disadvantage to the knicker may be its lack of full leg protection.

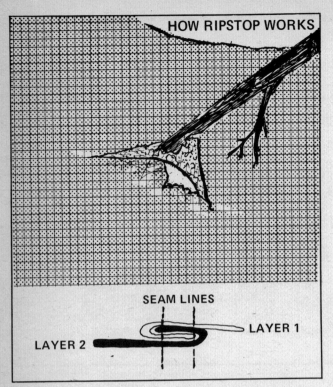

## HOW RIPSTOP WORKS

SEAM LINES

LAYER 2 — LAYER 1

*Ripstop nylon is lightweight, features reinforcing threads crossing each other in matted fashion to act as barrier against tears, which are contained in surrounding threads.*

gained respectability in the backpacking field. One such material is PolarGuard, a polyester material said to be highly water resistant. Ideal for damp climates, PolarGuard is a good deal less expensive than down. Another favored insulation is Hollofil II, a short, hollow-fibered synthetic that absorbs far less moisture than down.

Recently developed by the engineers of 3M Company is a fabric known as Thinsulate. Thinsulate absorbs less than one percent of its weight in water, yet is extremely thin, making for excellent mobility. Also developed by 3M Company is a special finish for backpacking garments called Scotchlite Reflective Finish. The Arthur Kahn Company took that finish and added it to a fabric they call Early Warning to create a reflective surface which bounces light directly back to its source. To oncoming drivers, Early Warning garments appear as a glowing silver object in the path of their car's headlights. It is a first rate safety development having no apparent adverse effects on the materials it covers.

*TR System jacket from Camp 7 is a medium-length style of nylon/Klimate outer, with a nylon taffeta liner. Water seepage is prevented by the fact that there are no seams on top. The large skirt snaps to the lining or drops to become a skirt against bad weather when it is required.*

*Gore-Tex Warm II contains 600 fill-power goose down. For added warmth, there also is a down-filled draft tube that extends back up the zipper, an added touch. In recent years, outerwear designs have come far.*

Some parkas may be coated with another substance known as Zepel. Zepel-coated fabrics offer not only water-resistance, but are especially resistant to stains as well.

Perhaps the best water-repellent material now available to backpackers is a material called Gore-Tex. Gore-Tex is actually a film which is placed between the inner and outer shells of parkas and vests. The film offers a microporous layer so minute that it resists penetration of water in drop form, yet allows vapors to pass through. Consequently, the material is said to be water-repellent yet breathable. Parkas and vests which include Gore-Tex have no noticeable increase in weight caused by addition of the film.

Whatever choice of material you choose for your parka or vest, there are a number of construction designs you will want to include. Look for light weight yet plenty of room for movement or to accommodate the addition of added layers of clothing beneath. Check the hood and collar areas. The hood should be attached below the collar to prevent air or water channeling down inside the neck. Be sure that you have unobstructed side vision with the hood in place. Many hoods offer a radical side cut to accommodate peripheral vision.

Zippers and cuffs are of great concern if you are traveling in cold or wet areas. Zippers must be protected by an added width of material called a draft flap, which covers the zipper completely to block out air and moisture. Cuffs should be adjustable to fit snugly around your wrist in cold weather, open up to allow for cooling ventilation in warmer weather. Some cuffs offer Velcro closures to provide custom fits, others have adjustable snaps.

Check for bottom and waist closures on your parka. A drawcord at the waist prevents drafts from climbing up from below. The drawcord at the bottom should fit snugly to divert drafts yet allow ample mobility.

Consider, as well, available cargo space. A parka with plenty of roomy pockets offers increased packing capabilities for frequently needed items such as maps, compasses, pocket cameras or snacks. Look for reinforced stitching at pocket corners. Avoid sewn-through seams that allow cold air and moisture to wick their way into your inner layers of clothing.

Even though your parka has an included hood, carry with you a second head covering to reduce the loss of body heat through the head. A favored style is the ski cap or balaclava, often of wool, nylon or a combination of the two. Your cap should offer protection to both the head and ears.

*Left: This versatile down parka has 10 ounces of goose down insulation within a nylon liner, dacron/cotton outer shell. Elastic cuffs, with ventilation snaps, are replaceable.*

A16 calls this their WTR or the Wide Temperature Range parka, because of ventilating systems. Note adjustable cuffs, collar; the zippered underarm vents; elastic waist and drawstring at bottom; ample storage pockets.

## RAIN/WIND WEAR

The final layer of clothing you will want to include is a water and wind resistant shell. Wind can chill your body as quickly as rain, by continually forcing you to replace the ever present layer of warm air that surrounds you. Good rainwear must do more than keep rain and wind out, it must also allow body moisture to escape. If your parka is made with Gore-Tex you should not need added rainwear. If not, consider the simple but effective poncho. For brief periods of rain the poncho offers ample protection at very little cost and is easy to stow in your pack. When needed the poncho can protect not only you but your pack as well. The loose fit gives plenty of ventilation.

If you expect to hike in wet climates for extended periods of time you may be wise to purchase a rain set of pants and hooded jacket. There are a number of styles of rainwear to choose from. Some are made of plastic, some of rubberized fabrics, others of nylon or dacron coated with Neoprene. For toughness and flexibility the nylon or dacron suit is hard to beat, unaffected by cold weather which may brittle the plastic and rubber.

Look for ample ventilation capabilities in your jacket. If the jacket has underarm, shoulder and/or back vents all the better. It should be large enough to permit you to move about freely and to allow body moisture to escape. During hot summer months you may prefer a separate rain hat to an attached hood. The separate hat offers better ventilation and increased comfort.

If you are hiking in snow-covered terrain that requires waterproofing from the knees down, consider using gaiters, waterproof sleeves that cover your legs from ankle to knee. Gaiters prevent snow and dirt from working inside your boots, yet add little weight. Gaiters make an excellent companion item to the poncho for total rain protection. Look for those that can be donned easily, with a snug but unconfining fit.

## CLOTHING MAINTENANCE

Once you have purchased backpacking clothing you will want to protect your investment with proper care and cleaning. For the most part you will receive cleaning instructions when you buy the item. There are some generalized rules to keep in mind, however.

Apparel containing goose down should be either hand laundered or dry cleaned, being sure that the dry cleaner is familiar with the cleaning of down, and uses a mild petroleum base solvent. Don't assume your favorite dry cleaning establishment knows how to clean down apparel. Ask them. If hand washing, do not wring the down garment out or you will reduce its lofting capabilities. Use mild soaps and cool temperatures.

Items containing Gore-Tex should never be dry cleaned, it can remove the water repellent capabilities of the Gore-Tex. Hand launder these items.

Do not dry clean synthetic polyester materials unless specifically directed to do so by the manufacturer. Hand or machine wash with warm water, never above 140 degrees Fahrenheit. Synthetic apparel can be dried in a dryer using "low" or "air" settings.

## BACKPACK RAIN COVER:

This backpack rain cover by Tough Traveler will fit most standard packs and has an adjustable drawstring to make the fit secure. It's of coated taffeta for maximum water repellancy.

Do not stow wet apparel away while still wet. If on the trail tie the item to the outside of your pack until it dries. If you must carry it inside your pack while wet, place it in a plastic bag to protect the remainder of pack items. Remove it from the bag and dry as quickly as possible.

Manufacturers have produced a multitude of clothing items especially for the backpacker, designed to be both functional and attractive. Most require very little maintenance, and many are ideal for everyday wear as well as in the field. When selecting backpacking clothes do not fail to check in your own home closet before you shop. You may be surprised to discover that you already own most of the needed items. But it will be a pleasant surprise.

Lightweight gaiters from A16 are made of a polyester/cotton fabric that is water repellent but still breathes. They are equipped with an instep tie as well as a lace-type hook and have full-length zippers for quick off/on.

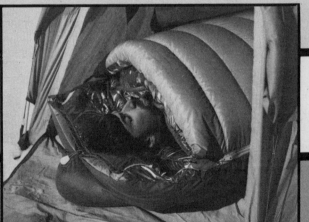

*Alaskan Wilderness bags include two separate down tops, one light, the other heavy; both are removable. This allows for a wide temperature range of uses. (Right) A special feature of bag is the collar built into bottom and heavier top shells for warmth, protection from drafts.*

# SURROUNDED BY WARMTH

## CHAPTER 5

**F**OR THOSE who take to the trails in quest of multiple days' backpacking, the afternoon of the second day — if not before — will find thoughts of camp and a good night's sleep a frequent occurrence. It's a pleasant thought: snuggling into a cozy sleeping bag knowing you've completed a good day's hike. You deserve a good night's sleep. You've earned it, your body needs it and you shall have it, provided you know a little about how sleeping bags are made, how they work and how to choose the right one for you.

A sleeping bag is designed to provide a comfortable night's sleep outdoors, to insulate the backpacker against the climate, regardless of how cold that climate might be. And it can get mighty cold, whether you're spending a summer night in the California mountains or January in the hills of Kentucky. Consequently the design of today's sleeping bag is

# After A Day Of Hard Hiking, You Deserve A Good Night's Sleep. With Today's Sleeping Bags You Can Have It.

built around the principles of insulation.

Your sleeping bag cannot generate heat itself. Its sole purpose is to retain your body heat within its internal boundaries, by holding that heat in while restricting the entry of colder temperatures from outside. It does this through use of dead air space trapped within the bag's insulation materials, termed fill. How effective this fill may be is determined by the degree of loft it displays. Loft is the thickness of the bag's insulation, or more accurately, the distance between your body and the outside air. It doesn't matter how heavy that fill might be, only how deep it is.

In theory almost any material could provide some insulating properties. It's said soldiers of Valley Forge used rags to stuff their boots for insulation against the freezing snows, and newscasters have told of men who used the only material available to them, old newspapers, to insulate themselves against arctic winds. Had these men taken that same newspaper and loosely wadded it up, it would have provided them even greater insulation by trapping dead air within its folds.

The greater the loft, the warmer the bag. In backpacking, this is most important, for it also means an equal reduction in bag weight. Manufacturers of sleeping bags look for insulating materials that provide the greatest loft with the minimum of weight. They also seek materials that are soft and clinging, that will withstand repeated use yet retain their loft. How much loft you need in your sleeping bag is dependent, to a great deal, on you.

Obviously the weather conditions you encounter will play an important role in determining bag needs. Not so obvious, perhaps, is the part your body plays in that determination. Many physical factors can influence the effects of cold, including your overall condition and mental state. If you put off your afternoon meal in favor of an early arrival in camp, or skip dinner because you're too tired to eat, cold weather may have a greater effect on you. Being tired, alone, will have its effect, as will your normal body metabolism, smoking or alcohol. Some people are simply cold sleepers and will need

*Early Winters Silver Lining sleeping bag features special reflective lining between layers of PolarGuard, meant to prevent heat loss through radiation. The tapered bag is contoured to the body shape, which means less heat loss.*

| Down | | Hollofil II | | PolarGuard | |
|---|---|---|---|---|---|
| Loft (in.) | Temperature (deg.) | Loft (in.) | Temperature (deg.) | Loft (in.) | Temperature (deg.) |
| 11.1-12 | -30/-40 | 7.1-8 | -10/-20 | 9.1-10 | -15/-25 |
| 10.1-11 | -25/-35 | 6.1-7 | 0/10 | 8.1-9 | -10/-20 |
| 9.1-10 | -20/-30 | 5.1-6 | 10/20 | 7.1-8 | -5/-15 |
| 8.1-9 | -10/-20 | 4.1-5 | 25/35 | 6.1-7 | 0/-10 |
| 7.1-8 | -5/-15 | | | 5.1-6 | 5/15 |
| 6.1-7 | 0/10 | | | 4.1-5 | 15/25 |
| 4.1-5 | 5/15 | | | 2.1-3 | 35/45 |

*Variations in figures supplied by manufacturers are caused by the differences in construction: mummy, tapered, rectangular shapes. These figures also reflect differences in individual reactions to the cold.*

more insulation than the guy who never sleeps with a cover but perspires anyway.

So how do you go about purchasing the right sleeping bag for you? You begin by honestly judging your physical condition and your reactions to cold. With that in mind you can then examine available styles and qualities of bags, looking first for the tag that indicates minimum temperature rating. All quality bags should have a temperature rating. Remember, however, that this is only intended to be a guideline, based on the "average person," a fictional fellow that never quite matches anyone, but comes close to a large percentage of us.

As the temperature chart included in this chapter should indicate, there is a variation of ten degrees or more between each lofting material and its accompanying depth of loft. This temperature rating represents a *minimum* effective temperature, the variations reflecting differences in individual people. The chart was formed by combining the individual charts of the major sleeping bag manufacturers to arrive at an average effective rating. Their individual charts will differ from these figures slightly, and it's not necessary that they be exact. As previously mentioned, these ratings are intended only as a guideline.

## DOWN OR SYNTHETIC FILL?

In reviewing the chart, you'll note a consistent variation in effective temperature ratings between the three major lofting materials: down, PolarGuard and Hollofil II. Down is recognized generally as the best insulating material you can buy, under dry conditions, offering the highest loft at the lightest weight. There is a wide range in quality of down products, and you may need the assistance of a knowledgeable salesman to determine what's best for your needs. But a bit of background information may be of benefit.

Down comes from the fine, soft plumage beneath the feathers of waterfowl, usually geese and ducks. Of the two, goose down generally is considered a better choice when comparing similar grades of down.

The quality of down depends on many factors, including the bird's diet, his age when the down is collected and the method by which it is collected. The younger the bird, the smaller and shorter the plumage will be, resulting in a lower lofting ability. The younger down will be extremely soft, but will display far less elasticity. You want a bag that is soft, but even more importantly, you want one that will return to its loft after a day's hike crammed in a stuff sack tied to your backpack.

Most major manufacturers test their down right in their plants, rating it for actual down content as well as fill power, establishing a minimum level for their bags. For instance, North Face of Berkeley, California, has set its minimum down requirements at 550 cubic inches per ounce of fill power, containing no less than eighty percent down. What is meant by "no less than eighty percent down"? In all down, there is some percentage of feathers; it's unavoidable. The challenge is to hold that percentage of feathers as low as possible for the highest possible loft.

*The A16 white goose down bag is practical mummy design for year-around use. It is cut to reduce likelihood of cold spots and is good to -30 degrees.*

*The Camp 7 Pioneer bag is excellent for summer use or as an outer shell over a Camp 7 down bag. It has PolarGuard fill and is made of nine-ounce taffeta, a PolarGuard layer on each side; 2½-inch loft.*

When you consider that good commercial-grade goose down is usually rated at 450 to 500 cubic inches per ounces, the 550 cubic inches per ounce rating is excellent.

Once considered the highest grade of down available, prime Northern goose down lofts to 750 to 800 cubic inches per ounce. The folks at Stephenson, a small but superb sleeping bag manufacturer in Gilford, New Hampshire, specializing in custom-fit bags, tells us of an even better grade of goose down used exclusively in their Warmlite series of sleeping bags. Mature L.P. (live-picked) goose down from Poland is said to fill 1150 cubic inches per ounce. As might be expected, goose down of this quality is extremly expensive, as is prime Northern goose down and all good grades of down, with good reason.

The best down — that with the longest fibers and highest loft — comes from older, more mature birds. Unfortunately geese and ducks are not normally raised for their down, but rather for their meat. And the best tasting meat comes from the young birds. Thus it is economically more feasible for farmers to look to their birds as a source of meat supply rather than down. Down has been more of a by-product of the bird rather than its primary product.

That Stephenson was able to obtain such a high grade of down is due to both luck and research, combined with the exotic tastes of the central European countries where goose liver is considered one of the finest of delicacies.

As luck would have it, the largest livers come from the older birds, and in this case the value of the livers has made raising the birds to maturity economically feasible. Also aiding in the development of this liver is the frequent plucking of the birds' down. The live-plucked down, according to Stephenson, provides the best down possible and, when taken from the large, mature birds, has the highest loft, most resilient fibers. It also is the highest in cost.

As efficient an insulating fill as down is, it does have its negative properties, not the least of which is its susceptibility to matting if it becomes wet, and the lengthy time needed to dry it out. Consequently, if you do not intend to backpack the -30-degree mountains you might consider the less expensive, more available grades of down or the several types of synthetic fills currently available, including Hollofil II and PolarGuard.

Hollofil II is an excellent insulating fill produced by

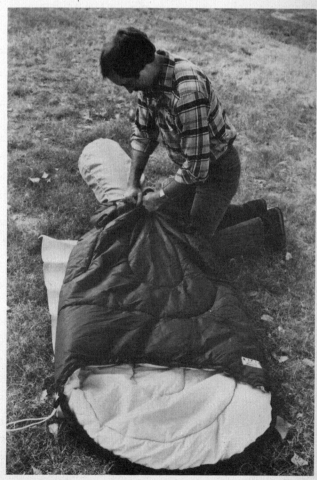

*The Peak 1 line from Coleman includes a lightweight 40-ounce fill mummy bag that is excellent for three-season use. Pack weight is only 70 ounces and it's washable.*

*This PolarGuard-filled mummy bag made by Cedar River Mountaineering has a three-way hood closure, Velcro closure for added security, full-length draft tubes, offset quilting, differential cut. Eight styles offer -35 to +35 comfort.*

DuPont. Although it requires a greater weight per volume to insulate, it is also a good deal lower in cost. Unlike down, it will not mat when wet and dries much faster. It is said to be non-allergenic, odorless and consistent in loft.

PolarGuard, a polyester fiberfill manufactured by Celanese Fortrel, is similar to Hollofil II in that it also requires a greater weight per volume to insulate. A continuous filament, PolarGuard will neither mat nor separate when wet, and is said to dry three times faster than down, maintaining eighty-three percent more loft when wet. PolarGuard is a favored fill in sleeping bags manufactured by such major manufacturers as Camp Trails and Camp 7, while Coleman and North Face prefer the Hollofil II synthetic.

Do not be misled by the claims of some manufacturers that the synthetic fills are "warm when wet." Wet is cold, unless you have the extreme good fortune of being exposed to warm-water rainfall in midsummer. The advantage the synthetics have over down in wet conditions is that they dry more quickly and retain most of their lofting capabilities while wet. But until your body is able to generate the heat necessary to dry them out, the fill closest to your skin still will feel cold.

Whatever the insulating fill in your bag, it is best not to get it wet at all. If the bag is well constructed, you should be able to avoid that. You will want to look carefully at bag construction, beginning with the overall design of the bag.

## BAG DESIGN

There are three basic bag designs: mummy, tapered and rectangular. Of the three, the mummy bag is the most heat efficient, with its fitted cut restricting all unnecessary added material and space that must be heated. Consequently it keeps you warmer and weighs less. However, it can prove restricting and thus uncomfortable for some.

*Peak 1 Model 754 is rectangular style with 2½ pounds of Hollofil. Machine washable, it is good for minimum temperatures of 20 degrees.*

*Explorer Slumberjack is modified tapered type for weather from -5 to +55 degrees. It features a triple layer top, double layer bottom. The preformed hood with extra-wide arctic collar allows maximum comfort, protection. It's filled with Hollofil II. Gross weight is 4½ pounds.*

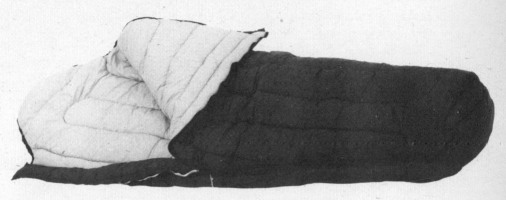

*The Glacier Big Horn is a modified tapered bag featuring a quick-release heavy-duty two-way separating coil zipper backed with anti-snag tape. With double offset construction, it has generous oval foot room, complete hood closure with hook/loop collar closure.*

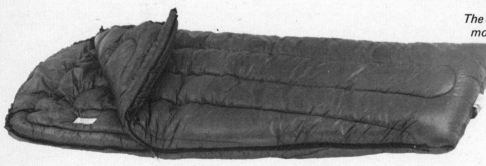

*The Slumberjack Summit series features modified tapered design, double offset construction with a full hood, a drawstring collar and anti-freeze locking device. Filled with Hollofil II, comfort range is from 10 to 65 degrees.*

The tapered or semi-rectangular bag offers a narrow but still roomy cut. Neither too large nor too restricting, the tapered cut may be ideal for most backpackers when extreme temperatures are not encountered.

The rectangular bag is the one with which most people are familiar. Loose fitting, the rectangular bag offers plenty of room to move about, but at a sacrifice. That added space is both less heat efficient and heavy. The rectangular bag does have the added advantage, however, of doubling as a bed cover when opened up.

The ideal bag will be one that allows you enough room to sleep comfortably, even if you like to roll over during the night. It also should be long enough that you need not curl into it, but not so long that you've enough room beneath your feet to store your entire wardrobe. If you've space for the next day's clothing, that may prove desirable, but that's about all.

Once you have chosen a style of bag you will want to examine its construction, beginning with the inner and outer shells. The term "shell" refers to the material that forms the bag, the insulating fill being sandwiched between this inner and outer material. Normally the shell material is ripstop nylon, a strong, abrasion-resistant, yet lightweight material seen in sleeping bags, packs and even tents.

Most better sleeping bags will offer what is termed a differentially cut shell construction. What that means is that the inner shell, or liner, has been cut smaller than the outer shell, forming a tube in which the fill can rest. Were the inner

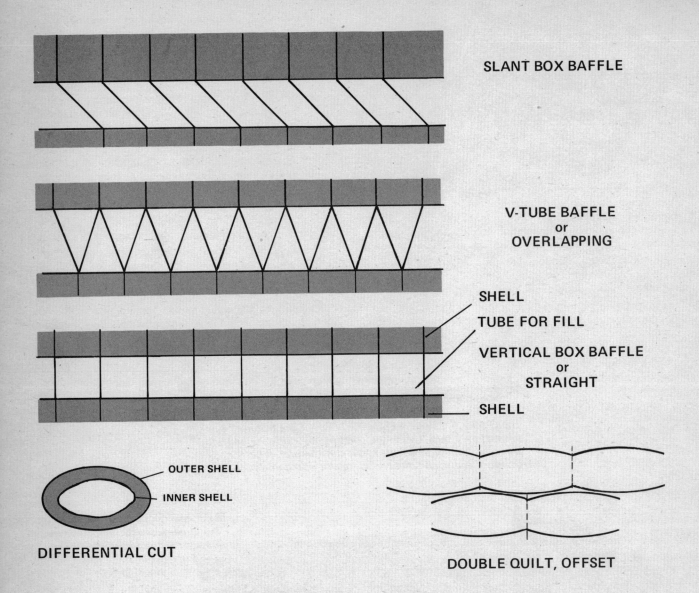

SLANT BOX BAFFLE

V-TUBE BAFFLE
or
OVERLAPPING

SHELL
TUBE FOR FILL
VERTICAL BOX BAFFLE
or
STRAIGHT
SHELL

OUTER SHELL
INNER SHELL

DIFFERENTIAL CUT

DOUBLE QUILT, OFFSET

shell to be the same diameter as the outer shell, folds of extra material would crease through the insulation, causing cold spots where the loft is reduced. To avoid these cold spots, the bag must have uniform loft throughout; the differential cut is among the methods used to provide that uniformity.

If you do not intend to do any cold-night backpacking you might consider purchasing a bag offering the more economical regular cut, where inner and outer shells are cut the same size. For moderate temperature camping, a regular cut should be sufficient.

Cold spots, as the term implies, are areas along the sleeping bag that, for one reason or another, do not have enough insulation to repel frigid outer air or retain body heat. These cold spots usually occur along seam lines, but can occur anywhere in the bag, and it may have nothing to do with the lack of sufficient insulation material. It could be that the insulation has simply slipped to one side or the other, allowing a bare spot within the bag's shells. Down is

particularly susceptible to this. It is the purpose of baffles to prevent such a problem.

Baffles are walls of material connecting the outer and inner shells and forming tubes across the bag's width, usually about six inches apart. The fill, whether down or synthetic, is placed inside these tubes, then sealed shut by stitching.

There are three basic styles of baffling for sleeping bags: straight box, slant box and overlapping V-tube. In straight box construction the baffles are sewn straight between the shells. Slant box baffles are sewn at an angle between the outer and inner shells, producing an overlapping effect. In the V-tube baffle, the overlapping is even more prominent, with triangle-shaped tubes butting against each other at two sides.

There has been a great deal of controversy over which of the three styles of baffling is best, but most manufacturers currently seem to prefer the slant box baffle. But regardless of the style, so long as that baffle contains a specified loft of insulation and is able to contain that insulation within its boundaries it should provide you the required warmth you are seeking.

Be wary of the manufacturer who has found it necessary, often because of economies, to reduce the fill within the baffles of his bags, resulting in a bag with overall size the same as his competitors' bags, but the loft of which is a good deal less than needed.

How can you tell if a bag has been underfilled? When hung up on the display racks it may be difficult. Take the bag you are interested in down from the rack. Holding it by one side, gently shake it to distribute the fill. Now lay it flat on the floor and feel the loft. You should be able to feel and possibly see the deficiencies in an underfilled bag.

In choosing a bag, you also will want to be alert to any sewn-through seam lines binding the outer shell to the inner liner. These seams will allow heat loss regardless of the insulation fill used. Keep in mind, however, that the seam must run completely through the inner and outer shells. Many manufacturers will offer bags with seams running through the inner and outer shells, but independent of each other. These "quilted" shells then are offset from one another, with one seam line placed directly over the middle of the baffle above or below it. Such offset layering prevents any cold seepage.

As previously mentioned, the insulating properties of a sleeping bag serve two purposes: to keep cold air away from our bodies and to keep body heat in. Sometimes that insulation works too well, and we awake the following morning with a damp, almost wet inner shell. If that shell has no moisture-repelling characteristics, the insulating fill also will be damp, and in the case of down may actually have matted. The moisture has come from our bodies, in the form of perspiration, a natural and spontaneous reaction to overheating.

When our bodies are warmer than the air around us, we lose heat to that surrounding air. That's why we are able to warm up our bags in a relatively short period of time. When that air, however, becomes warmer than our bodies, as it often does in the course of the night, we must rid ourselves of the excess internal heat in another manner, by perspiring. It's said that we can lose as much as four pounds through water loss by evaporation during the night.

There are several schools of thought regarding the best methods of reducing water loss through evaporation. Among the most popular is the "breathable" fabric, which allows perspiration to be wicked through the inner shell to the outer shell. And unless the moisture is trapped in the insulation and dead air between the two shells, this works well in keeping the inner bag dry.

A second method involves keeping that perspiration inside the bag, preventing its passage through the inner shell by use of what has been termed a vapor barrier. The theory behind this is that the moisture lying next to the skin serves the beneficial function of cooling the body as body heat is

*In choosing a sleeping bag, there are many considerations, including terrain, weight, but above all else, comfort. Most serious backpackers have more than one bag and thus are able to match the bag to the area they will be hiking.*

Left: Inexpensive rectangular bag has no provision for comfort above the shoulders, unless you are short enough to shrug down. Slumberjack bag (right) has integral hood that becomes padded pillow, room for stretching in comfort.

expended in attempting to evaporate it. Since the perspiration cannot pass through to the fill, there is no chance of losing loft due to matting.

Credit for the incorporation of the vapor barrier has been given the folks at Stephenson. The use of a vapor barrier — termed "VBI — is an integral part of their Warmlite series of bags, as it is in Camp 7's bags. The inner shell of these bags contains a urethane-coated, metalized yet soft fabric that repels the moisture. Stephenson has separate VBI fabric available for sale to those who wish to add it to the interior of their own bags.

As an added method of controlling internal bag temperature, most manufacturers include two-way zippers at both the side(s) and feet, allowing the packer to ventilate his bag to suit his needs.

## OVERALL CONSTRUCTION

Once you've determined that the bag has the loft and baffle construction you desire, it's time to look at overall construction, beginning with those seams that could be sources of cold spots.

The most likely area for heat loss is that full-length zipper that goes down one side and across the foot of your bag. Or perhaps the bag you are considering is one of the many that are intended to zip together, and thus have double zippers for attaching at either side.

The type and placement of the zipper in your bag deserve a good deal of attention, since it has been the source of repeated problems and frustrations in the past. Almost without exception, YKK zippers are used in today's bags. Their separating coil closure is self-repairing, smooth-working and freeze-proof. Most bags will have double sliders that

*Cold weather comfort often means keeping your head and neck warm. It is said that one can lose as much as 50 percent of the body's heat through exposure of the head.*

allow for ventilation at head or foot, as desired.

To prevent heat loss, the zipper should be backed by a draft flap, a narrow strip of insulated material that runs the length of the zipper, acting as a weather strip to block out air. Try out the zippers on the bag, looking for any possible jamming as either excess material around the zipper channels or interference from the draft tubes lap the coils. A jammed zipper is a poor way to begin a morning.

Check also the ease with which the zipper slides, and the availability to lock it into place. A zipper that slides down during the night, leaving the packer unprotected, means a disgruntled, cold packer in the morning. A Velcro tab that holds the zipper in place at the head is a nice addition to any bag, and can be easily added to yours, if it doesn't already have one.

There are those who will tell you that top zipping sleeping bags are a bad investment, offering poor insulating capabilities. Actually, it doesn't matter whether your bag zips at the side or top. If it possesses adequate draft protection it will be as warm as the remainder of the bag. Those who find frequent night movement to result in a zipper that has rolled beneath them by morning may prefer the top center zip to

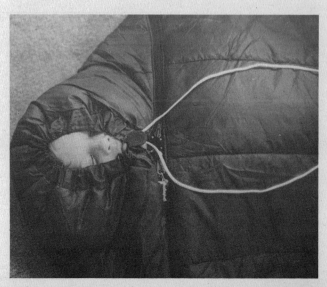

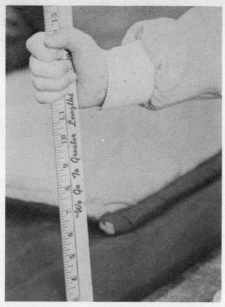

Loft is the key to warmth in sleeping bags. The two-inch loft in bag above indicates it would offer little warmth below 50 degrees. (Right) With four-inch loft, this inexpensive bag is adequate for temperatures down to 25 degrees.

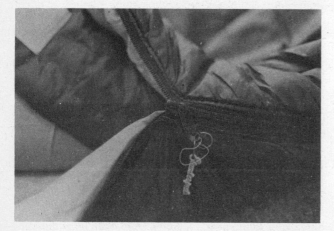

With YKK Coil Zipper and wide insulated draft tube, this is a premium bag. Zipper will not freeze or snag. Draft tube protects against cold air entry. (Right) Because of tendency to freeze up, metal tooth zippers are not often used in today's sleeping bags. Lack of draft tube means a cold spot the entire length of this zipper.

Synthetic-filled bags should never be dry cleaned as the process tends to break down the insulating capabilities. Cleaning instructions invariably are included with all of the quality bags.

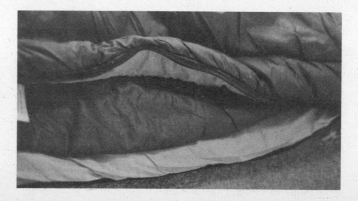

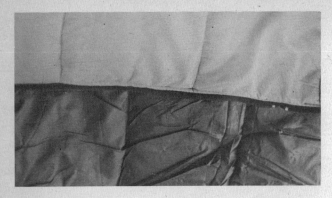

*Note the effects of the offset baffling. The seam lines offset each other, thus providing a consistent layer of insulation throughout the bag for comfort, warmth.*

instead, a dacron or dacron/cotton thread, which is much easier to sew. This means a noticeable reduction in time and labor spent in the construction of the bag, as reflected in the purchase price. Dacron is a stiffer thread, however, and much more resistant to stretching. Consequently it may draw excess stress when use of the bag pulls on those seams, resulting in more rapid thread abrasion.

## GETTING A GOOD FIT

In considering a sleeping bag, it is important to determine whether that particular bag will fit you. Not all bags will. To determine this you will need to do one of two things: either place the bag on the storeroom floor and climb into it (a feat that may cause the salesman to pale or flush, dependent on whether it causes him embarrassment or anger), or tote along a simple tape measure and use it.

If you order your sleeping bag through a mail-order outlet, they probably will insist on the inclusion of some basic measurements so they can fit you more accurately. These measurements should include your height, weight and girth. If ordering for a child; it will be up to you to gauge the child's growth rate and accommodate for it.

Height need not pose a problem, even if you prefer a sleeping bag with added space at the bottom for storage.

the side zip. The bag has to slide a good deal farther before the zipper is out of reach.

When checking your bag for sewn-through seams, look also at all fabric edges, being especially alert to potential raveling of the bag. Most manufacturers prefer ripstop nylon for their outer shell because of its high strength to weight ratio. Ripstop is tear-resistant, but will unravel, as will all other nylon fabrics. To protect against damage from unraveled seams, manufacturers use two preferred methods. The surest way to prevent unraveling is to hot cut the material, fusing the edges together. As efficient as this method is, it is also expensive. A less expensive method involves gluing the edge of the material, then turning it under before sewing. Some manufacturers will skip the gluing process, and just turn the edges in. If that's the case with your bag or you are unsure of how raw edges were sealed, it's probably a good idea to use one of the many seam sealants available through your backpacking supply store.

While examining bag seams, give thought also to the type of thread used on your bag. Cotton thread never should be used. It is too likely to break or rot. Nylon thread is the strongest thread available, and is used by those manufacturers who do not mind the added time or difficulty inherent in using this stretchable thread. Other manufacturers use,

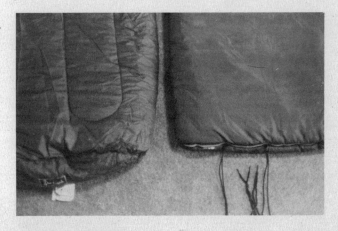

*Above: Baffled foot section allows room to move, no pressure on any toes. (Left) This traditional mummy style on right has hood, the rectangular bag has none.*

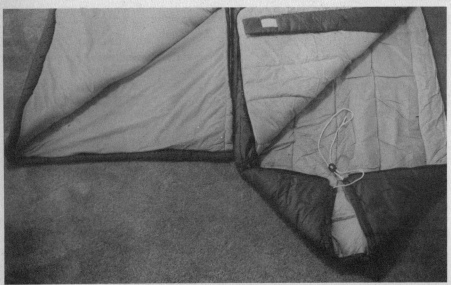

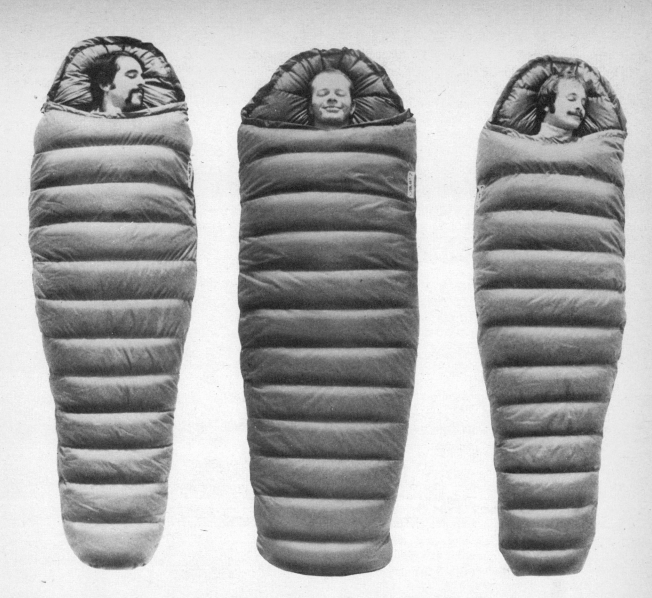

The Camp 7 Arette mummy bag at left is designed for climbers, backpackers and cyclists, who need maximum warmth from minimal weight and size. It weighs only 43 ounces, yet handles temperatures down to 5 degrees. In center is the Camp 7 Mitten model with 6½'' loft. Rectangular in design, it weighs four pounds and is equipped with a full hood. At right is the same maker's Expedition North Col model, which has 8½-inch loft, has a -20-degree warmth rating.

It's fine to have this space, provided you understand that its inclusion will mean a reduction in warmth performance of your bag, since your body cannot differentiate between the internal space it must heat to keep your body warm, and the space it will be heating to warm your stored items.

If purchasing your bag from an outdoor shop or major department store, you may find a tag on the bag giving the bag's dimensions in length, width and loft. Be alert to the fact that the length and width given may be that of the outer bag, not the actual space available to you. A bag that has four inches of loft will have an outer width eight inches larger than the inside width. That same bag may state a length of six feet, yet only cover a length of five feet eight inches, resulting in some cold shoulders if six feet was what you needed.

There is little difficulty in determining your height requirements. Most of us know how tall we are, and if anything are inclined to add an inch or so to that figure

rather than subtract from it. A girth measurement may be more difficult, and requires the aid of another person.

Girth is the circumference of our body, measured at its greatest point. Normally this will be the distance around the back and chest, including your arms. Unfortunately such a measurement has no allowance for added space required to move around in your bag, needed unless you like form-fitting sleeping bags. From the folks at Alaskan Wilderness and Stephenson come a simplified method that accommodates this added space requirement.

Begin your measurement by standing upright, elbows at your sides, forearms bent parallel to the floor, hands in a fist. A slight twist of your wrist will place the outside of your fists at a distance equal to the span of your shoulders. Have your partner then measure the distance completely around you, including your extended arms, to obtain your girth measurements.

As a final consideration in fit and comfort, turn your

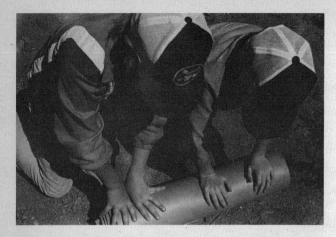

*A foam mat to be used under the sleeping bag can be rolled into a small bundle for packing, yet will pay off with big dividends in providing protection against the cold.*

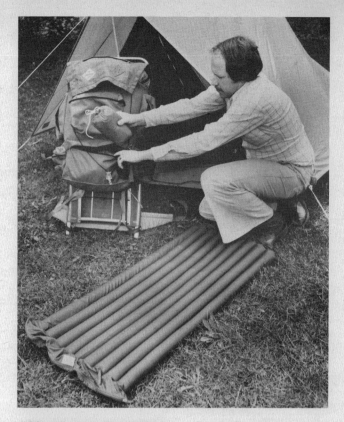

attention to the hood and foot area of your bag. If you have ever slept in a sleeping bag and felt the uncomfortable sensation of unyielding material pushing down on your toes you'll appreciate the necessity of billowed foot design now included in many bags.

If cold weather backpacking is your interest, you'll appreciate the inclusion of an insulated hood, an integral part of the bag that draws snug against your face when needed.

## SLEEPING PADS

There are a number of styles and types of sleeping pads on the market, most relatively inexpensive, especially when compared to the increase in sleeping enjoyment they provide.

Basically your pad will give support by either foam or air, both of which trap dead air space within their boundaries to provide insulation against rough, cold ground.

Foam pads come in two basic styles: open cell or closed cell. Closed cell pads are firm, dry out quickly and provide the best warmth. Open cell pads are thicker and much softer. Foam pads are considered the most durable and offer the best insulation. They are also the most bulky, adding to space and weight requirements of your backpack.

*Air Lift's Blue Wing modular mattress provides solid support with minimum weight. It has individual chambers for air; each tube has its own push/pull valve, too.*

Air mattresses are extremely light in weight, and when deflated, stow in little space. However, they are also susceptible to puncture or rupture. To combat the effects of such air loss, manufacturers now offer several styles of modular air mattresses, with individual air tubes held in place by a channeled outer mattress. The design offers better support for the rolling sleeper and reduces the tendency to roll off the mattress. Spare tubes can be carried for quick repairs in case of puncture.

When it comes to insulating against the cold, air mattresses often come in a low second with their tendency to transfer that cold. Because of this some mattresses now are being injected with down, a feat that adds immensely to the insulating qualities of the mattress — and to the cost as well.

In determining which to use, foam pad or air mattress, you must weigh the good and bad qualities of each and determine which will work best for you. As a general rule, air mattresses offer the greatest comfort for fair weather

*This Air Lift Model BW-72 can be inflated with little effort and can be used for a snooze in the sun after you've had that lunch on the trail or on a break.*

*Therma-Rest mattresses utilize a waterproof nylon coating that is bonded to the foam core. It is self-inflating; one simply unrolls the mattress and it inflates itself.*

backpacking, foam pads the best insulation for cold weather.

Some may wonder why they need a sleeping pad at all, particularly if the bag is one which offers a high loft of down already. That was one of the major reasons for purchasing the bag in the first place: because of its indicated fill weight. If that was your *sole* reason, then you are apt to be disappointed in the field.

Fill weight for any given bag includes the weight of all insulation in that bag, including that of the bottom shell. If you were to use that bottom shell as a top cover its insulating capabilities would be excellent. As a bottom shell it could be worthless. The weight of your body cannot help but crush that insulation loft to near nothing. Where it does so, insulating capabilities are lost, and the total interference between you and the cold ground must come from your sleeping pad.

To sleep comfortably you need insulation all around you, underneath included. Its inclusion guarantees you a good night's sleep, and is so important that some manufacturers are building pads directly into their bags during production.

## BAG MAINTENANCE

Because your sleeping bag is one of your most important and expensive backpacking items you will want to take care of it, both in the field and while not in use. Some basic rules will help to maintain the bag in its best possible condition.

Your bag will normally spend the entire day in a stuff sack, and will need to be fluffed to regain its loft before using. A gentle shaking is normally all that will be needed, not rough, whipping motions. Rough handling tends to force the fill to one area of the bag rather than to distribute it throughout the bag where you want it.

Never store an unused bag in its stuff sack for an extended period of time. Place it loosely folded on a shelf, hang it up or place it in an oversized sack where the fill is not compressed continuously, and will not be damaged.

Your bag should be clean and dry before you store it, whether in the field or at home. For field use, simply wipe out the inside bag, then air dry as necessary. Once at home, you'll want to clean the bag to prevent mildew or bacterial growth.

Down-filled sleeping bags should be dry-cleaned or handwashed. If dry-cleaned use only a cleaner knowledgeable in the cleaning of down products. A mild cleaning agent, such as Stoddard should be used.

To hand wash a down bag, immerse it in cool water in a large basin, such as your bathtub. Use low temperatures and mild, non-detergent soaps. Avoid any unnecessary wringing or twisting of the bag that will destroy the loft. Press the water out of the bag, then hang it up to dry, preferably out of the sun. If you feel compelled to dry your bag in a commercial dryer, do so only on a non-heat, air-fluff cycle.

Synthetic-filled bags never should be dry-cleaned, as the

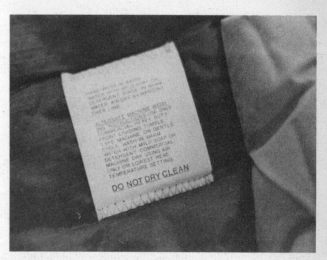

*On the better quality sleeping bags, instructions for proper care usually are sewn into a seam, easily available for the owner's reference for proper care and cleaning.*

tag that accompanies these bags will caution. Machine wash in gentle cycle, using cool water, or hand wash as you would down bags. Commercial dryers can be used if set on non-heat, air fluff cycles. Spots on down bags often can be removed by using a sponge and mild soap, while Benzene-type solvents are said to work well on synthetic bags.

Proper care in selecting your sleeping bag and proper maintenance afterward will guarantee continuous nights of comfort and warmth in the outdoors, even if sleeping under the stars. Only the threat of rain could interfere with your dreams, and a good tent will ease that threat. A good tent is the perfect companion to a quality sleeping bag.

*Layover days in a pleasant location afford an opportunity for backpackers to rest, explore the location, but a light shelter makes it more pleasant.*

# CHAPTER 6

# SHELTER, A PRIMARY NECESSITY

## Your Tent Need Not Be Large

## To Provide Adequate Shelter —

## Only Warm And Dry

C LEAR AND SUNNY," predicted the weather forecaster, "with the chance of precipitation zero through the weekend."

So how come Saturday night finds you drowning in that zero precipitation, soaked to your skin, with no shelter within miles? You've forgotten one of the basic laws of outdoor survival: Never count on Mother Nature. You listened to the forecaster, failed to remember that his is only an educated prediction, and decided a tent was just an unnecessary increase in pack weight. You made a mistake!

If you have ever found yourself in such a situation perhaps it will cheer you to know that many of us have learned that lesson in the same, hard way. Of even greater benefit will be the knowledge that it is a lesson you will not soon forget. In fact, you'll probably never forget it, making use of the first opportune moments to price and compare the many portable shelters on the market: tents.

By definition, any material that provides temporary shelter against the elements is a tent. Branches of a nearby tree, tied together, can be an emergency shelter, although most forests and parks where you will be backpacking forbid the cutting of trees today unless in an emergency situation. Expect officials to ask you to prove that emergency really did exist.

Much easier to erect and a good deal drier is the simple lean-to, formed by suspending a lightweight tarp between two trees, one or both ends anchored at the ground. Where minimum weight is essential a tarp can provide limited protection against wind and rain. For those who hike the dry, arid regions of the West, where rainfall is likely to be extremely sporadic, the versatile tarp provides an excellent means of shelter.

Depending on the availability of trees and the size of your tarp, the shelter may resemble anything from a one-sided shed to a tepee. Although such a shelter will offer little in the way of insulation against the cold, for summer packing the tarp does fill two major needs: it adds very little weight to your pack (about one pound for a six-by-eight-foot section of coated ripstop nylon) and it keeps rain away from you and your gear.

For those who do not mind a more restricted, yet drier, shelter there is the bivy sack, a unique combination of sleeping bag and tarp. Resembling a cocoon, the tarp encircles the sleeping bag, allowing just enough inside room to sleep and eat, provided you can eat in a near prone position. A bivy sack measuring seven feet weighs about eighteen ounces, and will accommodate average sized bags.

In seeking the best protection as well as comfort, most

The A-16 Half Dome has a suspension system of spring aluminum alloy poles engineered to bow the fabric. This affords more usable space. Rounded roofline offers greater strength against wet snow, too.

backpackers look to the more traditional tents of today, the A-frame, ridge style and dome-shaped tents, with four walls, doors, windows and floors to provide total protection against the elements. Tents come in all shapes and sizes, some resembling Arctic ice homes, others appearing as if migrants from a space film.

In designing a portable shelter, the tentmaker is faced with the task of creating a tent that is light in weight yet comfortable. In addition, it must be strong, easy to pitch, easy to enter, offer plenty of ventilation and provide maximum wind stability. Providing a tent that yields the optimum in all these categories has been the justification

*Eureka Mushroom uses a unique umbrella framework that breaks down for backpacking. A fly, suspended from the frame by shock cords, forms a weather-resistant cap.*

*Early Winters Pocket Hotel is a one-person unit weighing only two pounds and is extremely compact for packing. It is of Gore-Tex material, with two fiberglass poles.*

As illustrated by this showroom array, A-16 tents come in all sizes, shapes and prices to fit most outdoor needs. However, the backpacker must be careful in his choice and not end up with more tent than he can carry.

for years spent in research and design. Tent designs offered today are the closest we have come thus far to that optimum.

In selecting your tent you must weigh the importance of each category, and choose the tent that meets your needs, physically and economically. A closer look at these qualities may help you to make your choice.

Comfort implies ample space to live within the shelter, whether for brief or extended periods of time. Do not assume that because a tent is labeled as being a two-man tent it will actually hold any two men. Be sure that the internal space

*Eureka Sentinel blends design features of backpacking model with their mountaineering tent. It is spacious, strong, self-supporting with break-down aluminum frame.*

*Early Winters Light Dimension is a two-person tent of Gore-Tex. Shock-loaded poles feed from the top for quick pitching. Floor keeps out water, hood acts as eaves.*

*Moss Star Gazer has unique screened top window to act as a chimney, also producing a natural flow of air for its ventilation. Shelter can be moved after it is set up.*

tent was the most popular of backpacking shelters, deriving its name from the lightweight aluminum poles positioned so as to resemble the letter "A." Guy lines held the tent secure, and when properly positioned reduced tent flap to near non-existence. Tent sides were staked down to retain the tent's basic shape.

Today the A-frame is still among the most popular of backpacking tents. It is warm and dry, and at an average weight of six pounds for a five-by-seven, two-man shelter, is well within acceptable packing weights. Perhaps the most serious drawback to the A-frame tent is the limited head room it offers. Even with side wall pull-outs that dramatically increase usable space along tent walls, the maximum height at the highest point is only about 3½ feet. Getting dressed remains a sit-down affair. Limited head room is an unavoidable handicap to the design of the A-frame. The purpose of the sidewall pull-outs was to ease that limitation as much as possible. As an added benefit the pull-outs serve to make the tent more stable in high wind.

If you direct your attention to the parallel lines of most A-frames today you will note an apparent sway in the tent's ridge or top seam. No, the tent has not been poorly erected, the sway was built in, a deliberate arch that increases the catenary or accentuated curve of the ridge to increase sidewall tension while decreasing downward pressure on the

will hold *your* needs, including your gear.

Comfort also implies a warm, *dry* area, strong enough to withstand driving wind and rain. Not so long ago the A-frame

*Eureka Caddis is a modified hoop model. The one-man tent weighs 4¾ pounds, can sleep two people. The middle aluminum arch is greater in diameter for maneuverability. Netting attached on outside allows cross-ventilation.*

Pole boots can be used to prevent poles from sinking into wet ground. The pole sleeves attached to the skin of the tent aid in maintaining rigidity of the tent wall.

The Eave is a lightweight, versatile tent by Moss that performs well in strong winds, which tend to follow the streamlined effect of design with a minimum of damage.

guy lines. It aids stability.

Some tentmakers have taken the drive to more usable space a step further and added a self-tensioning spreader bar to their A-frames. Placed mid-point along the tent ridge the spreader bar holds the top of the tent apart, greatly increasing headroom. The result of this, and other changes, has been a much more efficient, yet still lightweight, portable shelter.

For even greater availability of internal space, however, you may be well advised to look beyond the A-frame to the more futuristic dome-shaped tents rapidly gaining in popularity. The dome tent removes most acute tent angles, giving more head and shoulder space along tent walls. Depending on the style of tent you choose, you may find an increased volume of fifty to sixty percent over the triangular tent of comparable height and width. The dome-shaped roofs offer more resistance to high winds, having less tendency to "sail"; the lower their overall height the more stable they become.

The increase in internal space is not without its tradeoff, however. Dome-shaped tents require a combination of several tent poles to provide and maintain their shape, consequently they will involve an increase in backpacking weight even if of a free-standing design which allows you to erect them without the need of tent stakes. Free-standing tents offer an added comfort capacity in that they can be moved after they are set up. The hapless backpacker who finds the ground beneath his tent not nearly as level or smooth as he first thought, or experiences a sudden shift in the wind that makes keeping windows and doors open an uncomfortable situation, need only pick the tent up and move it to a more desirable spot or direction. A five-by-seven-foot dome-shaped tent will weigh about 6½ pounds.

Due to the sectioning off of tent materials into small, more easily contained units, the dome-shaped tent is said to be much quieter than a comparable A-frame. Movements of these small sections become more of a flutter than an actual flapping. In all tents you will experience some noise, just as you will get some condensation. Limiting these problems is a major concern of designers.

Control of condensation is especially important to the

With rainfly removed, the Eave takes on a more fashion-oriented look. It's easy to pitch, requiring little time. Poles fit through tunnels, the pole tips in grommet tabs. The rainfly provides 16 square feet of vestibule space.

*The Solus model from Moss Tent Works is designed as a one-man tent, but will handle two easily. Eye-catching in design, it is effective as an ultra-light warm weather shelter and is super simple to erect in minimum time.*

backpacker, and is the reason many tents now offer a double-wall construction, either as one integrated unit or two separate walls complementing each other. Nothing can ruin your outlook in the morning like waking to wet gear.

### Double-Wall Construction

As mentioned, you will get some condensation with all tents. The advantage to the double-wall construction is in the location of that condensation. To understand how this construction works you must first understand why condensation appears at all.

When you erect your tent it is at, or very close, in temperature to that of its environment and there is no condensation. As the evening wears on, however, the air cools. This would be true inside your tent, as well, if you were not in it and all doors and windows were left open.

As discussed earlier, your body gives off heat, warming not only the dead air space around your sleeping bag, but that within your tent. You also give off moist heat, in the air you expel.

If you cook inside your tent, moisture from that cooking will add to the tent's internal humidity. Wet gear brought into

*Partially erected in cut-away fashion, this view offers a look into the manner in which the Solus is constructed.*

*The Trillium model from Moss Tent Works boasts a covering fly that keeps the model from becoming overly warm when the sun is high. A floor makes it easier for camping.*

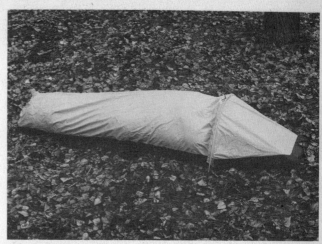

*Marmot Mountain Works' Burrow Bivy Sack packs to length of only 15 inches. Fiberglass pole keeps the hood off your face. Made of windproof Gore-Tex, it is warm.*

*Stable parabolic design of Tuka Tent from Marmot Mountain Works dispels fierce winds, withstands heavy snow. It has 45 inches of headroom and measures nine feet in length. Tuka is an Alaskan Indian word for a glacial wind.*

the tent adds even more, as does any sweating you might be doing. Moisture accumulates on the tent where, upon contact with the cold walls, it condenses. Unless you are aware of what is happening you may misinterpret this condensation as being a leak in the tent walls or floors.

The purpose of double-walled construction is to keep moisture off the inside tent wall. It does this by placing a layer of insulation, that same dead air found inbetween layers of sleeping bags, between the two walls. The inner wall is generally considered to be the tent, itself, the outer wall is the rainfly. The layer of dead air serves to separate the cold outer wal¹ from the warmer inner wall, thus preventing the

formation of condensed moisture.

Some tentmakers make their inner tents exclusively from "breathable" ripstop nylon. The tern breathable refers to the characteristic of the material that allows the passage of vapor through it while barring the passage of actual liquids from the outside in. As a result, moisture passes through this inner tent, crosses through the layer of insulation and on to the inside surface of the outer tent, made of non-breathable nylon. Once it comes in contact with that colder tent layer it then is transformed into condensed moisture and runs harmlessly to the ground. Although the outer wall must be dried before packing up, contents of the inner tent, including

New from North Face, this is the Skeeter 23 model, with a zip-up rainfly. It also can be opened up, with built-in netting screens for ventilation, if the weather is warm. Geodesic design offers high strength/weight ratio.

you and your gear, remain dry.

Tents with an integral fly provide the same layer of insulation. However, because the walls are joined as one unit, material used in the inner wall is normally coated to prevent the passage of moisture through it. Since the integral double-wall serves as a single unit, it is extremely difficult to remove moisture accumulated between the two layers. The only reasonable approach, then, is to prevent moisture from entering the insulating space. Should condensation form within such a tent, as well it might when cooking inside, it cannot wick through the wall to the outer tent and will instead appear inside. To avoid this you must limit the introduction of unnecessary moisture.

It might seem as if the separate fly/tent construction is the construction of choice when considering control of condensation and it does keep moisture from forming inside the tent so long as the layer of dead air is able to keep the tent wall warm. However, a separate fly can have its problems, especially in high wind or storm, where a dislodged fly can leave you wet and miserable. Because the integral fly is already a connected part of the tent, the problem of anchoring it into proper position, and the possibility of losing it to a high wind or storm is removed.

Not all moisture may enter your tent from tent walls. Occasionally it comes from below, seeping through tent flooring or seams while you sleep. To prevent this most

manufacturers now make their tent floor from waterproof coated fabrics such as urethane coated ripstop nylon or taffeta. Only that first overnight in rainfall will tell you whether the floor is indeed waterproof but there are some things to look for and to do to keep your tent floor dry. Take along a waterproof ground cloth. The cost and weight is negligible, and the benefits huge. Look for bathtub style design in the flooring, with the floor material extending several inches up the side wall before it is sewn. This keeps the floor seams off the ground, where they may wick up water.

A second, and equally effective method of reducing condensation on internal tent walls, and one which works well with tents having only one layer, is the placement and proper use of vents. Moist warm air, pushed by cooler air, will rise and if offered an escape vent, will continue to rise. If your tent can offer the continuous entry of cooler air from below, ideally at ground level, and an exit for moist air above at least mid-way up the wall of the tent, there usually will be little or no condensation within the tent.

Regardless of the style of tent you purchase, you will want to be certain that it offers ample means of ventilation. Frequently this is achieved through tent doors and windows, zippered closures allowing you to adjust circulation as need dictates. More and more you will see tentmakers adding additional vents, either along the upper side walls or at the apex of the tent.

*North Face's Westwind model retains many of the basic design facets of the Skeeter 23, but has greater length. Poles interact to form a series of triangles to form framework beneath the skin.*

In examining your tent, check to see that these vents offer protection against intrusion of either animals or, more commonly, insects. And while you are checking, look into the capabilities for continued ventilation when tent rainflys are in place. A vent that is blocked by a wall of nylon is of no value whatsoever. Most well-made tents will match tent vents to compatable fly vents.

While examining the venting capabilities of your tent's rainfly, also called a flysheet or fly, ask the salesman to show you how it is to be positioned. Does it offer full waterproofing, from the top to the bottom, or just partway down the side? To provide the best insulation it should cover the entire inner tent.

When the rainfly is in position can you enter your tent with reasonable ease? Some tents have a built-in veranda to shelter the open door or to provide a sheltered area for cooking. It's a nice option but may present problems for entry and exit.

Check to see how your rainfly is anchored. Does it require separate stakes or does it attach directly to the tent poles? If attachment is directly to the poles, does the fly include tiedowns or does it, perhaps, have sewn on shoes that fit over or around the tent poles? All means of attachment should present reinforced sewing, and the fly itself, should be both waterproof and strong. Most flysheets are currently made of coated ripstop nylon, and can withstand the brunt of what nature has to offer. Nylon, however, expands when wet. Because your rainfly must be taut in order to be quiet, you may want to invest in shockcord tiedowns if they are not already a feature of your tent. The shockcord line automatically adjusts to any changes in the fit of the fly.

### Easy to Pitch

Remember the "good old days" when pitching a tent required a huge serving of patience and perhaps a degree in engineering? Fiberglass poles came in varying lengths and sizes, and unless combined correctly would never resemble their intended shape. Today pitching a tent can be as simple as putting up an umbrella. In fact, some tents do offer umbrella construction, with top center poles permanently joined to each other while side poles slip in and out of the pole sockets, all joined by shock cords. Tents that have

*North Face's Model 01-22 also takes advantage of geodesic design. Sag and flap are reduced, because tent skin is supported equally, with stresses distributed equally.*

individual poles solve the problem of pitching by keeping all poles of the same size — they can be used in any position — or by color coding the poles. One tentmaker even sews the instructions for pitching his tents directly to the inside tent wall, making it impossible to lose them.

The material of choice for tent poles today is anodized aluminum, the same type of aluminum used in aircraft, extremely strong yet much lighter than the fiberglass poles. Placed outside the tent walls, anodizing protects the poles from the weather. Added protection is found in those tents that offer continuous pole sleeves which serve the dual role of maintaining tent shape while evenly distributing stress along the tent walls. If your tent does not have these pole sleeves, but is instead held in place by rings or loops spaced along the length of the poles, you'll want to check these loops frequently to be certain there is no separation.

To compensate for expansion of the nylon tent walls when wet, your tent may offer inside tension adjustment which allows you to tighten the tent without leaving it, an especially appreciated benefit midway through a cold wet night.

### Ease of Entry

Getting in and out of a tent should be no problem but check your tent to be sure of that. If construction places a tent pole squarely in the middle of the doorway there could be difficulties, especially if you are in a hurry to get inside, or are not paying attention to what you are doing. Look for doors that are of ample width as well as height. Does your tent have both a storm door, made of the same material as the tent walls, and a screen door, usually of a material called "no-see-um" netting, an ultralight, fine monofilament knit? Preferably the screening will be on the outside of the tent wall, which allows the packer the luxury of adjusting the main door for ventilation without opening the screening to uninvited guests.

In tent windows look for screening as well. Windows should be adjustable for ventilation, preferably extending high along the tent wall to allow moist warm air to escape the tent.

### Construction

As with all backpacking equipment, your first indication of the product's worth will come in the outdoor shop where you can examine your tent for construction qualities. But what do you look for?

In tent materials look for strength as well as resistance to abrasion, especially of the tent floor. Ripstop nylon is favored because of its light weight coupled with its durability. However it does stretch when wet and is subject to

*At first glance, the parts of the Instadome geodesic models might prove to be a bit frightening, but that should not be a discouragement. The author found that putting up the tent was simple, following the directions supplied by maker.*

deterioration from prolonged exposure to the sun. Dacron is not quite as strong as ripstop but is less expensive, suffers less from ultraviolet light, and does not stretch.

Many tents will feature coated nylon taffeta because of its greater resistance to abrasion. And for those who do not mind the weight factor or can split the load of tent and poles, cotton can be considered. It is both economical and durable. Cotton is also hot and heavy and not normally included among backpacking tents.

You should find that most of the seams on your tent are lap-felled, the material folded over before sewing to aid in water repellency. All seams should be double sewn, with stress points reinforced with either extra material, bartacks or webbing. Polyester core, cotton-wrapped thread is used by most major manufacturers because of its extreme strength and durability. The cotton-wrap has the added advantage in that it will swell when wet, closing off needle holes.

As with most other backpacking gear, zippers used in tents are almost exclusively YKK self-mending polyester coil zippers. These zippers will slide easily in wet or cold weather, and should neither rust nor corrode. Most tents feature two-way zippers, allowing you to open them from either end. Frequently you will find a rain shield over the outside of each entry zipper.

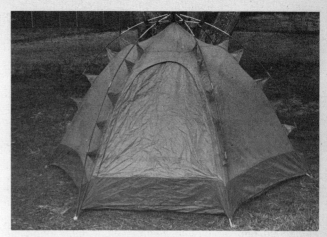

*The final step in tightening the skin or fabric of the tent is simply to push down on the top center pole, while pushing up from inside the tent. Frame snaps into place.*

*The first step in erecting the tent is to unfold integral tent and the frame. The shock-corded poles then are set properly in place. The next step, she learned by doing, is to draw the poles out and arrange them teepee fashion.*

*Bivouac shells by Cedar River Mountaineering are a far cry from the modernistic, roomy designs, but they also require something less in the way of time and effort, as they need not be erected. A fiberglass arch keeps the face free.*

*A nearly full-length rainfly is contoured to the shape of the North Face tent frame. It is held in place by ties at the pole shoes. Zipper conceals the tent door.*

### Optional Features

A place to hang your lantern, storage pockets for special goodies, clothesline rings; all are hardly necessary items but they can be most appreciated. You'll find them in most quality tents.

Among other popular accessory features is the inclusion of top windows for inner tents, for star gazing or just for increased ventilation. The top window acts as a chimney flue for in-tent cooking as well.

*Regardless of the tent you may purchase, it must have ample means of ventilation. This frequently is achieved by incorporating windows as has been done with this Instadome III.*

A cookhole is another unique tent feature. Cookholes are areas within the tent floor which can be withdrawn to provide a bare ground for cooking. At least one manufacturer offers a fifteen-inch-wide cookhole that opens and closes with a drawcord and fixlock.

*An important note:* You'll find most tents have a tag attached to them indicating a CPAI-84 rating for flame retardancy. Most manufacturers will meet this minimum fire rating. This does not, however, mean that your tent is *fire proof.* Tent fabrics will still burn if placed in contact with

open flame. The use of a backpacking stove involves open flames, consequently you may be wise to restrict your cooking to outside your tent whenever possible, or consider a tent with an attached vestibule.

A vestibule is a form of awning or entryway extending beyond the door. The protected space within it is not only ideal for cooking but also for changing out of wet clothes or stowing extra gear. For those who like the idea of having a protected cooking area outside their tent, but do not want the added weight of a full vestibule, there are tents with

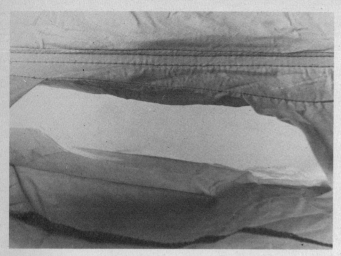

*Controlling condensation in double-walled tents is done by placing a layer of dead air between the inner and outer walls. This is the most effective insulation available.*

built-in awnings over doorways and windows. Often they are a part of the rainfly, and serve to provide limited protection against rain and wind.

### Sealing Your Tent

Tents are designed to be as waterproof as possible but you will still want to seal the seams of your tent before you take it into the field. Attention must be given to all outside seams, where needle holes leave openings for moisture to intrude.

Sealing should be done with the tent erected and taut. Seal all seams that go from outside to inside, following the directions on the sealant. Normally you brush the sealant on, working the sealant into the seams. It's the sealant inside these needle holes that does the trick, not the sealant covering the outside of the seam, so apply it wisely. Don't forget to pay special attention to the floor seams. Although your tent probably has a bathtub design floor, which places the floor seams several inches above ground level, it too must be sealed.

You can usually purchase seam sealant from the manufacturer of your tent. Often as not a supply of sealant will accompany the tent at purchase. If not, all major backpacking and outdoor shops handle it. A vinyl sealant currently popular and most effective is K-Kote. For those who prefer the cotton tent, beeswax works well.

When sealing your tent give considerable attention to that

*In checking out tents for possible purchase, be sure to look for a storm guard along the door and window closures. This device, usually covering the zipper, is designed for the purpose of preventing rain from seeping into the tent.*

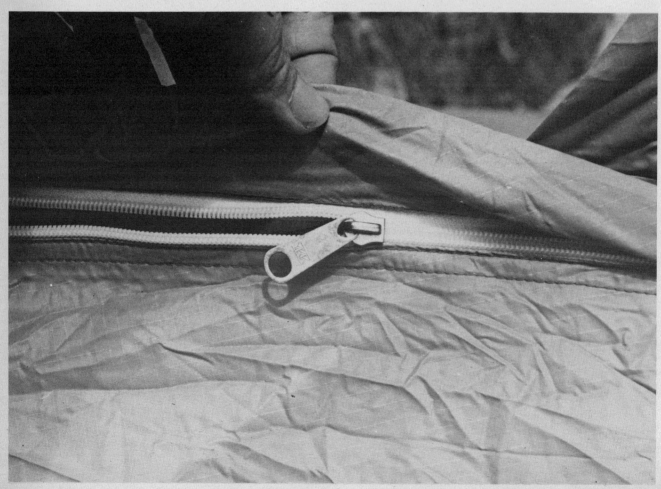

*Internal side pockets are hardly a necessity for tenting, but they are nice to have, providing extra security for items you would hate to lose. (Below) In examining your tent, check for ventilating capabilities when the rainfly is in place. Ample air is allowed at door of Instadome, but there is no provision for removal of moist air.*

rainfly. Its sole purpose is to provide maximum protection against rain and wind, a task it performs well provided needle holes have been sealed.

### Care And Maintenance

You can reasonably expect today's tents to last you as many as twenty years with proper care. Applying a good sealant not only keeps water outside your tent but protects the threads that keep it together. It does not, however, prevent all moisture from entering the tent.

As mentioned, all tents will experience some formation of moisture. Left on tent walls when they are folded up and stowed this moisture can turn to mold, and is a natural breeding ground for mildew and other fungus. Your immediate task, then, is to limit moisture as much as is possible. You cannot control the moisture given off by your breathing but if moisture comes from your sweating, you can dramatically reduce its level by avoiding overheating. Within your tent dress warm enough to prevent chilling without overheating.

Place a ground cloth beneath your tent floor to prevent the wicking of moisture from the ground beneath you. The ground cloth also reduces the abrasive effects of rough ground on the bottom of your tent. Inexpensive, lightweight plastic tarps work well.

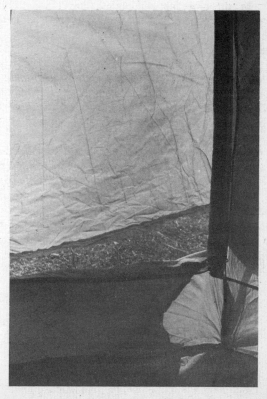

*North Face VE 23 utilizes the Geodesic design pioneered by Buckminster Fuller. This is a three-pole tent, with contour-fitted flysheet of urethane-coated ripstop nylon. Since nylon expands and contracts with changes in temperature and humidity, the shock cord incorporated in the design insures constant tautness; it weighs 7¾ pounds.*

Use a rainfly over your inner tent if you expect the night to turn cool or damp. It's a lot easier to dry a rainfly than it is to dry the tent. Most flies will lie flat, allowing you to towel dry them, or they can be hung up to the breeze clothesline fashion.

Avoid bringing unwanted moisture inside the tent in the form of water collected on your raingear. If you must remove your wet gear inside the tent, do it immediately inside the door, folding wet layers against each other, dry sides out. Wet clothing is better placed in a plastic bag until morning, then laid outside or perhaps hung from the outside of the backpack until dry.

If you must cook inside your tent, be sure that you have ample ventilation for steam. Keep lids on pots as much as possible and steam will not only be reduced, but the food will cook noticeably faster. After you've eaten, allow your cookstove to burn a few minutes longer to dry the air.

Statistics tell us that you will probably use your tent an average of four weeks or less per year. For the remaining forty-eight weeks it will be stored somewhere, preferably in a dry, cool storage room, loosely folded. Before stowing, check to see if the tent needs to be cleaned.

*In selecting a tent for backpacking purposes, one always must take into consideration the weight and the bulk of unit, although some can be divided into separate loads so that several members of the party can help carry it.*

You should be able to wipe out most soil inside your tent, using a mild soap and damp cloth. Shake out all loose dirt before cleaning. If extremely dirty, as when rain turns your clearing into a mud bath, you may need to spray out the tent with a hose and plain water. Don't forget the tent bottom. Do not attempt to wash your tent in a washing machine. You're liable to remove the water-repellent coating of the tent walls as well as damage the tent or the machine. Tent straps have a habit of jamming inside the tub.

To prevent mold and mildew your tent must be thoroughly dry before prolonged storage. Be certain to check seams. The double or four-layer sewn seams will take much

*A feature of North Face's VE 24 is the full-coverage flysheet, which clips directly to the ends of the poles and completely encloses the tent. This offers not only super protection, but a layer of dead air that helps prevent condensation on the tent skin. This particular model is designed for two people and weighs 8 pounds 13 ounces.*

longer to dry than does the single layer tent wall and flooring. Hang your tent outside to dry if weather permits but keep it out of direct sunlight as ultraviolet rays may damage it.

Treat smooth-sliding coil zippers and tent poles with a silicone lubricant to keep them smooth-sliding. If minor repairs are needed, do them before your tent is packed away. If repairs are of a major nature ask the tentmaker for advice. If you have cooked or eaten inside your tent, be sure that all traces of food are gone, or you're liable to find, months later, that your temporary shelter has become a permanent residence for mice and insects.

Once the tent is clean check those seams again. You may need to reapply seam sealant, depending on how extensive the cleaning has been.

### Selecting A Campsite

Give thought to the location of your campsite and the cleaning needs of your tent can be minimized. A sudden storm should not be a problem, provided you have chosen a site that offers good drainage. Do not rely on a trench around your tent. It rarely works as intended, and most campgrounds will not want you digging up their land. Place the tent on high ground, or on sand or gravel that offers a natural drainage. Clear the ground beneath the tent to avoid punctures. Remember to use a groundcloth.

If you intend to camp in one spot for several days, try to place your tent in a shaded area, out of direct sunlight. Be certain, however, that the trees have no dead limbs to collapse on you during a storm.

Position your tent so that the morning sun will greet you at the door and you'll not only wake up warm and refreshed but eager to enjoy the morning meal and a new day.

*The Instadome III is carried in a stuff sack measuring 22 inches in length, six inches in diameter. When pitched, it is 50 inches high and offers 45 square feet of space.*

Rest stops can be frequent, especially when water is at hand. A cup hung on the pack or belt makes drinking easy.

# CHAPTER 7

# FOOD, FIRE & FLUIDS

## Frequency With Which You Need Each Differs, But A Proper Supply May Mean The Difference Between Success And Misery

NEXT TO OXYGEN, water is the most immediate need of the body. Three minutes without air and one suffers the possibility of permanent brain damage. Three days without water and the body is in serious danger; dehydration begins, and thirst becomes an obsession for even the most physically fit of backpackers.

Your best defense against dehydration is avoidance of the conditions that cause it: lack of fresh liquids. Fortunately dehydration is a gradual debilitating condition that lets you know its presence long before it reaches the acute stage.

Although its doubtful you've ever experienced severe dehydration, you've probably seen the early signs portrayed in countless movies and television programs, even in commercials. Your mouth becomes dry and foul tasting, legs weaken and the lips dry to the point of cracking. While these conditions do not, in themselves, disable you, they do make the going rough, and panic is hard to avoid.

Two-thirds of the human body content is water. Since exercise and the environment continually drain that level, it must be replenished. During an average exertion day, the body requires an intake of about one pint of water. Increased exercise, such as hard backpacking, increases that level, while a day spent resting or fishing probably would decrease it slightly.

Depending upon your day's itinerary, you should plan on carrying at least a full quart of water with you each day. Refill your water bottle every chance you get, especially if you are unfamiliar with the country and unsure of the location of the next fresh water supply. Remember, too, that you must have enough extra water to use in cooking, since most of your food probably will be of the dehydrated type.

In choosing your evening campsite, look for an area that offers fresh water. If you are packing high into the mountains, where population is minimal, the chances of finding acceptable drinking water are greatly increased. You've probably heard it said that spring water bubbling out of the ground is the purest water you can drink. And there's a good chance such water is pure, but there is no guarantee of that. There's no visible way to be certain water is pure — only a chemical analysis will prove it so. As a

With careful selection, there are backpacking foods to meet the needs of all members of the outdoor family.

general rule, however, water that is contaminated normally will be free of vegetation. It may have a peculiar odor or taste. In the more heavily traveled national forests, contaminated water often will be posted as such. If in doubt, don't take a chance. Take the extra few minutes required to purify that water.

The closer you camp to civilization, the greater the likelihood that streams and rivers will be polluted. This water *must* be purified, either with water purification tablets or by boiling.

Boiling water for a minimum of ten minutes will kill germs. It usually will leave the water with a flat taste, but you can live with that. Most water purification methods do leave the water tasting far from the dreamed-of crystal-clear-mountain-spring stuff you had in mind.

It's a good idea to invest in a bottle of purification tablets prior to your first backpacking trip. Develop the habit of carrying the tablets in your pack every time you backpack, even in known terrain. A bottle of fifty tablets weighs just a couple of ounces, is available at a reasonable cost and will purify several quarts of water.

If you prefer not to use the more traditional water purification tablets, or are unable to purchase a bottle

*The Salewa Bivy Stove from Robbins Mountaingear, is a simple lightweight unit, complete with a one-liter pot, a lid, pot lifters, the stove and a cartridge of fuel. Cartridge will burn for three hours with sufficient heat.*

before your departure, do not leave home without some type of purification system in hand. Several chemicals used in water purification are probably in your home. A small container of household chlorine bleach has been successfully used by many backpackers for water purification. Eight to twelve drops per gallon, depending on the cloudiness of the water, is the recommended dilution. Keep in mind that while a few drops of bleach can prove beneficial, a large dose may prove fatal. Stick with the recommended dilution.

Tincture of iodine, the kind you find on the first-aid shelves of most drug stores, also can be used for water purification. The suggested dilution is sixteen drops per gallon of water.

Once you have used any of the above purification treatments, give them time to work. Usually a half hour or so is ample, but it doesn't hurt to wait longer. To hide the flat taste, add tea, coffee or powdered fruit flavoring to the water before drinking.

As vital as water is to your successful hike, you must learn where to look for it. A good topographic map will indicate water sources. These maps are inexpensive and take up little pack space. If you choose not to carry a map, you will need to "read" the terrain for water sources. Water seeks low lands. Look for it near the bottom of mountains or in pockets along the side of the mountains. Clumps of vegetation, or unusually heavy foliage are a usual indication of the presence of water. Check for game trails. If there is water anywhere within your area, the animals will have already sought it out.

If hiking arid desert areas it will be even more important that you carry your water supply with you. However, small amounts of water can be found in some varieties of cactus, especially the barrel cactus. Some wild berries provide water, but be sure that you know what you are eating first, lest dehydration relief turn to poisoning.

TO PURIFY water by boiling you must have a heat source, either a portable stove or, more than likely, a small

Several field expedients can be used in cooking, heating water. (Top) This simple rig can be constructed with poles. (Left) Heated rocks can be used or a bucket can be placed in a bed of coals or even a fire. (Below) This system has been used with great success by generations of Boy Scouts.

Illustrations by Dana Silzle

*The Precise Phoenix lightweight camp stove for backpackers is made in two models. The compact 625 (above) has a two-hour burning capacity, weighs less than two pounds. The larger Model 625 weighs three pounds, burns for four hours.*

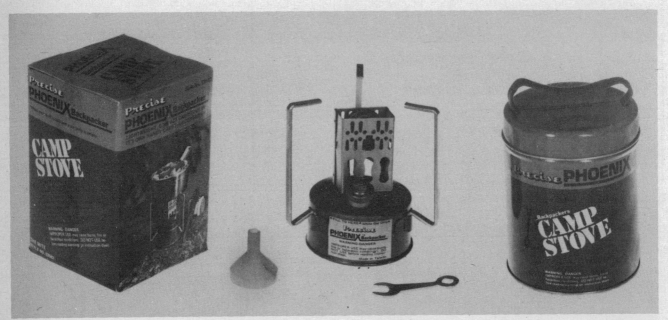

fire. As mentioned, fires are an important part of camping, providing not only a source of heat for cooking and body warmth, but a consoling mental environment. It's hard to beat the soothing effects of a campfire, and unless forestry regulations forbid its use, most packers enjoy such a fire. You must, however, be aware of the dangers of open fires and avoid them.

To burn, a fire must have air and fuel. Remove either of these elements and the fire dies. To control the fire, you need only control the supply of these two items. By clearing the area beneath and around the site of the fire of all flammable brush, you limit the spread of the flames. Fuel then is added as you need it. The clearing should be at least ten feet in diameter. Remember, too, that your fire must be free of combustibles above as well as around it. A frequent cause of forest fires is a campfire that spits sparks into overhanging tree limbs.

Never leave a fire unattended, even for a few minutes. A sudden burst of wind can carry live sparks well beyond your cleared area, turning foliage into an inferno before you have time to react.

Try to keep your fire small. Not only will this ease the draw on the fuel supply, but it minimizes the possibility of the fire getting out of hand. By building a stove around the fire with rocks, you then can place a small grill over the fire, if you have it, or perhaps improvise one using green

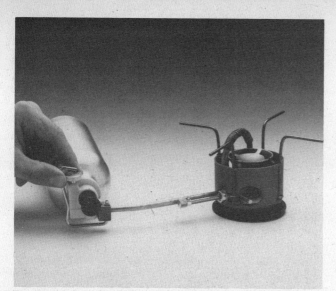

The Model G/K stove from Mountain Safety Research will burn white gas, Balzo, kerosene, Stoddard solvent, diesel fuel and stove oil. It will boil 24 quarts of water with a pint of fuel, and performs well in wind as well as cold.

tree branches. If you have placed the rocks close enough together, your cooking pot may span the fire, resting atop the rocks at the sides. In this case you do not need a grill.

If no rocks are available you might consider using a stick. The stick must be long enough to angle over the fire when anchored to the ground. A pot then is suspended from the upper end of the stick, over the fire. You may have heard veteran packers refer to this as a dingle stick. The system has been used successfully for many years by the Boy Scouts.

A quick word about the environment: if you alter the lay of the land in any way during your stay, be certain you return it to its proper condition before you depart. That means erasing all signs of your campfire. Above all, be sure that the fire is out completely before you leave the area. If at all possible, drown the fire with water, then cover it with dirt. Do this before you pack your gear and, after you have finished packing, check once more to be certain there are no live coals still smoldering.

For ease in cooking, you may prefer a backpacking stove to prepare your meals. If you are backpacking areas that forbid the use of open fires — and there are more and more such areas yearly — the camp stove will be your only means of providing a hot meal, and you should enjoy at least one such meal each day for the sake of morale as well as your health.

There are a number of styles of camp stoves currently on the market. Among the three major types are those that

Even a watched pot on a Peak 1 stove from Coleman boils water in less than four minutes, is excellent for one-pot meals. This stove (right) is compact as well as efficient and is being marketed in its own stuff sack.

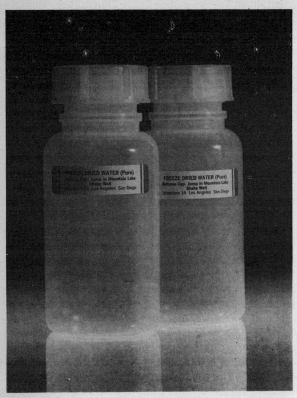

*A16 Triple Seal bottles have one-liter capacity and are made of unbreakable linear polyethylene. They will not impart any foreign odors or tastes to foods or liquids.*

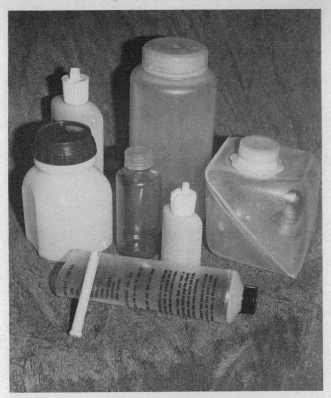

*Plastic bottles and containers are available in numerous sizes and shapes, thus making it easier for one to use in the backpack, conforming to shape, space available.*

burn gas, those that burn wood, and the lightweight, compact primus stoves.

Perhaps the simplest cook stove is the Sterno, a seven-ounce can of wax-like cooking fuel that burns right inside its container. To use it, you simply remove the cover and light the contents. Although it can be difficult to cook fresh-caught trout over a small can of Sterno, for boiling water or warming food, it works well.

For campers who like a full course meal, the gas stove is ideal. For the backpacker who camps nightly in the same area, but likes to take day excursions, the stove is a natural. But for most backpackers it is inconvenient; size, weight and fuel requirements making it a poor choice for a lengthy or difficult backpacking journey.

A popular gas-burning backpack stove is the Peak 1 by Coleman. Capable of providing more than three hours of heat with one ten-ounce fill of white gas, the Peak 1 weighs only thirty-eight ounces when full. The stove is adjustable from full flame to simmer, and will boil a quart of water in less than four minutes.

The folks at Precise International have a new line of camp stoves available, one of which will supply two hours of heat on a nine-ounce fill of white gas. The Phoebus 725 backpacker's model weighs two pounds, and has its own carrying container.

Relatively new is the MSR Model G/K by Mountain Safety Research, Incorporated. This stove burns a variety of fuels, from white gas to stove oil, and will boil a quart of water in 3½ minutes. The stove weighs fifteen ounces, when empty, and requires a separate fuel bottle.

*Robbins Mountaingeer Kettle Flask is a multi-purpose container, a 1.2-liter canteen, complete with carrying case, it has a folding, heat-resistant pouring handle to allow it to be used as an efficient water kettle afield.*

Many manufacturers now offer stoves using pressurized canisters. The canisters are easy to use but expensive. Gauging the amount of fuel remaining is difficult and you need to carry a spare canister. But you'll need to carry spare fuel, regardless of the type of stove.

Avoid using your camp stove inside your tent if possible. Although the design of today's stoves has put heavy emphasis on stability, it is still possible to upset a stove. You also must be certain of adequate ventilation, as stoves can give off poisonous gases.

HOW MUCH FOOD you will need on your journey is dependent on your metabolic requirements and the physical stress of your journey. While you do not want to overeat, you should be certain to maintain a nutritional level that will allow you optimum strength. That means making sure your daily intake includes those three vital ingredients you've heard so much about: proteins, fats and carbohydrates. If in need of dieting while at home, one of the first things you probably will take out of your diet is the carbohydrates. In backpacking, you need that to provide you with the instant energy. The body does not store carbohydrates, therefore the supply burnt up by the body during a day's hike must be replaced.

Of the three classifications, carbohydrates are the easiest to secure for backpacking foods. You simply make your own supply, by combining ingredients found at all local grocery stores. Primary sources of carbohydrates are raisins, chocolate and cereals, so take along a few candy bars. An

Individual meals can be prepared before the backpacking trip begins. They are sealed with this Seal-A-Meal unit and stay sealed in your pack until ready to be utilized.

The best way of preparing for the field is to pre-measure all of the ingredients for the various menus you plan. Thus there is no need for a cookbook and the meals can be put together simply, efficiently, with minimum waste.

It is possible to come up with a balanced diet mixing various dried fruits, nuts that will supply the protein needs and energy for at least one of your day's meals.

If the fruit and nut mixture is taken along, it can be put into bags of various sizes so that, as the mixture is used, the bags can be discarded, reducing pack bulk.

excellent trail snack that provides instant energy at negligible packing weight is what some have referred to as "gorp." Gorp is the combination of the above foods, placed in plastic sandwich wrap bags of single-day servings. Chocolate that is coated works best, since it has less tendency to melt. You'll find the raisins taste unlike they have ever tasted when eaten high among the hills.

Proteins are essential to the maintenance of body tissue. Unfortunately they also are more difficult to digest than

*Freeze-dried strawberries look like pink cardboard as they come from the package, but when soaked in water for ten minutes, they revert to their natural state.*

are the carbohydrates, and should be eaten sparingly along the trail. Better to enjoy your intake of proteins once you have reached the evening campsite. Meats and nuts are excellent sources of protein.

Fats are the most concentrated form of energy, and function as a fuel storage reservoir. The average male will have a fat reserve of about fifteen percent of his body weight; for women the figure is closer to twenty percent. This is the normal level of reserve, and contains enough stored energy to maintain a person for a month or longer.

So what does all this mean in terms of how much and what type of food you should carry with you? For normal, active backpacking, you probably will require about 4000 calories to maintain your optimum level of effectiveness. Of that 4000-calorie daily requirement, medical experts tell us you should have a balance of about fifty percent carbohydrates, twenty-seven percent protein and twenty-three percent fats.

Dependent on your source of information, these figures may vary slightly. This does not mean that you must religiously consume 4000 calories daily, or that the intake percentage will be those exact figures. You may find that on a given day you don't want to eat 4000 calories worth of food. Or you may find yourself running short of food during the last days of your journey, and that you must begin rationing your foodstuffs. In that case, the energy

*Backpacking need not mean roughing it, especially where food is concerned. With freeze-dried and dehydrated food now available a packer can dine in style on items ranging from scrambled eggs through turkey tetrazzini.*

stored within your body should easily take up the slack. But do not make the mistake of skipping meals altogether, or trying to eat only one meal each day. The lack of normal nutritional level may cause you unnecessary problems in the form of cramps, mental unrest, fatigue, any of which can take the fun out of backpacking.

WHAT TO EAT on a backpacking journey can be as difficult a decision as determining clothing needs. It's difficult to know just how hungry you might be in the mountains while standing in your living room. Naturally you want the food you carry to be as lightweight as possible, but you also want to carry enough to meet your needs throughout the trip.

To decide your needs, plan a daily menu. Actually sit down with pad and pencil and begin with Day No. 1. You'll probably have eaten breakfast before you leave home, so begin with the noon meal. Include in your menu all items you will want, from drinks to desserts. In a separate listing include the cooking and eating utensils you will need for that meal. As you go from day to day, if you find you need an additional item, simply add it to that list. When you have listed every meal you will need, add one full day's extra menu items. The added meals function as a backup, in the event your trip is unexpectedly extended, as in an emergency.

If yours is a dayhike, or an overnighter, you can include just about anything, and may not need to worry about extended preparations. For lunch, you can pack a sandwich, a piece of fruit, cookies, and perhaps powdered hot chocolate.

For dinner, you might want a hot meal. Not only does hot food taste good, but it's mentally satisfying. How about a steak and baked potato? It's not impossible, if you have planned your meal well. Freeze the steak, then pack it in a sealed, waterproof bag. There are a number of excellent

*Turkey tetrazzini, in its still dried state, resembles a handful of pebbles, but preparation is relatively simple.*

*After ten minutes of soaking in boiling water, the turkey tetrazzini has regained its original composition, flavor. One need not worry about dishes, as the mixture can be eaten directly from the plastic container. Then in keeping with ecology measures, the bag is simply burned in your campfire. Thus, as you move on, your load is still lighter.*

methods of sealing food. Seal-A-Meal is just one of the many available that works well. During the day's hike the steak will thaw, and by evening will be perfect for cooking. If you like steak sauce on your meat, you can have that, too. Just seal what you will need inside another bag.

A baked potato can take just short of forever to cook over an open fire. Instead, pre-bake your potato before you leave home, then wrap it in aluminum foil for quick warming before you eat it. If you like butter on your potato, try substituting butter salt. The taste is strikingly similar, and the salt requires no refrigeration.

As appealing as the thought of a thick, juicy steak may be at the end of a long day's hike, if yours is a trip of more than one day, to carry along frozen foods is neither realistic nor feasible. The obvious substitute is the myriad of today's freeze-dried or dehydrated foods.

Most sporting goods stores now carry a complete line of dehydrated foods for the backpacker, or you have only to look as far as your local grocery store for alternate foods.

For breakfast you can prepare powdered eggs or oatmeal by just adding boiling water. For lunch and dinner there are soups, stews and even Chinese dinners. Again, you simply add boiling water. For meals requiring milk, simply substitute powdered milk for the whole variety. If butter is needed, again try the butter salt. For rice with your meal, use the instant versions.

For meats, you probably will have to turn to the backpacking food supply companies, but demand for such foods has driven the price well above the original market prices.

*Several manufacturers are creating snack packs for the trail, utilizing high-energy foods that can be consumed on short breaks or even while hiking. (Below) For major meals freeze-dried items are packaged in cans suitable in size for storing in your pack with the reduced weight.*

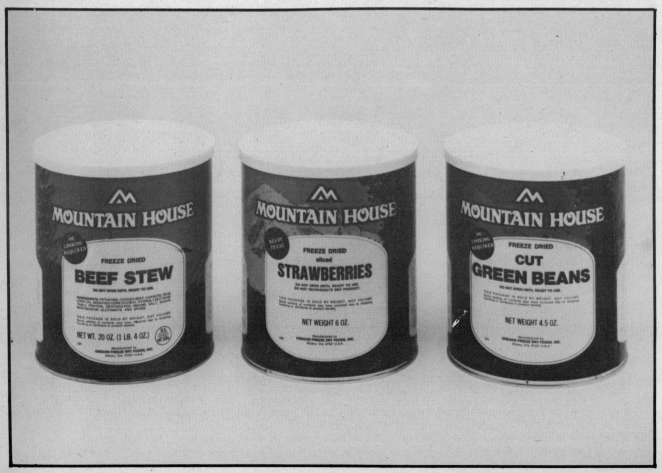

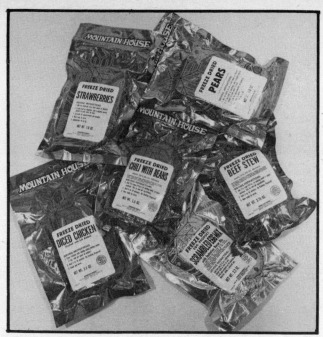

With the wide variety of freeze-dried foods available, the choice of foods is almost endless. No cooking is required; just boiling water. Packed in special oxygen barrier bags, the food will keep for years if unopened.

The variety of dehydrated foodstuffs currently on the market has grown so broad that a hike of a week's duration need not require any one meal being repeated. From turkey tetrazzini to sliced strawberries, you'll find foods rich in each of the three food classifications. Because they are freeze-dried, you'll also find that a seven-ounce serving of tetrazzini weighs only 1.6 ounces. A half pound of strawberries, freeze-dried, converts to a packing weight of less than one ounce. In its dried form, you may be hard pressed to recognize the turkey, but add a cup or so of boiling water, wait five to ten minutes, then let your taste buds tell you whether it is real or not. You'll be delighted at both the flavor and the staying capacity of freeze-dried foods.

HOW DOES freeze-drying work and why? From the folks at Oregon Freeze Dry Foods, producer of the Mountain House line of foods, comes this explanation:

*Drying of food is the oldest form of food preservation known. Centuries ago it was discovered that varieties of food could be harvested, laid out in the sun to dry, then stored without spoiling, to be eaten during the winter months when food supplies were less plentiful. It was later discovered that by applying heat, foods could be dried more rapidly and more effectively.*

*The technical term for the freeze-drying process is vacuum sublimation. By this process the water contained in foods is converted from a solid (ice) to a gas (water vapor), while in the vacuum chamber.*

*Freshly prepared food is flash frozen to a very low temperature. The food is then placed in a chamber where an almost complete vacuum is drawn. By obtaining this vacuum under carefully controlled conditions, the ice in the food is converted directly to a gas which is then removed, leaving completely dry products.*

FREEZE-DRIED FOODS are placed in oxygen-barrier containers immediately after processing. Looking a lot like dense pieces of aluminum foil, the containers preserve the foods without the need of preservatives, yet will keep indefinitely if the seal remains intact. Packing weight of freeze-dried foods may be reduced by as much as seventy-five percent of that of the food in its original form.

If including food items that you have packaged yourself, be sure to remove the items from their original containers. You should have no canned goods in your pack. Although a terrific method of preserving foods for home storage, the can makes a terrible backpacking item. Its weight and room requirements are prohibitive. The same eight ounces of instant rice in a Seal-A-Meal bag will weigh half as much, and requires one-fourth as much storage space as it would in its original box. Bags will lay flat atop one another, whereas cans will not.

With foodstuffs that you have packaged, be sure to test cook them in your home before your trip. Use the same measuring cups you will use on your journey. A collapsible drinking cup works fine as a measuring device. Simply fill it with specified amounts of liquids, then mark these comparable measurements on the outside of the cup. Be sure the markings are of a permanent nature. For metal cups, you can simply scratch the measurement into the side. For plastic cups use a label maker or permanent paint.

Freeze-dried foods also have found favor with the horsey set, as they can be carried on the trail in saddle bags.

Try out one of the menu items at home, using these measuring utensils to determine whether your markings are valid.

Try to package as many items together as you can, if you intend to eat them together. Peanut butter and jelly can go into one container, as may salt and pepper. Reduce your packing weight to the absolute safe limit and you'll find backpacking a lot easier, with no reduction in meal enjoyment. Include the directions for cooking each food item inside, written on a piece of paper, or printed on the outside of the bag. Package breakfast, lunch and dinner meals separately. Try to provide yourself with as much variety as possible; it will make your meals more enjoyable.

In the field, try to limit your cleanup to as little as possible. This is easy, if your food is contained in boilable bags. Simply eat from them. For cooking, use as few pots as possible. Often you can get by with one pan. Carry only lightweight aluminum pots. If they fit inside one another

*Hope's three-man cooking set consists of one large cooking pot, with folding handles, plate-lid; handled medium pot, with plate-lid; tea pot; pot scrubber. All pots nest, are held secure by an elastic belt. With nylon case, unit weighs only 28 ounces.*

For the backpacker who prefers natural foods, AlpineAire packages foods without preservatives, sugar, artificial flavoring or coloring. (Below) Stow-Lite foods come in individual servings or in full course dinners that serve four people. These packaged dinners include everything from drinks to dessert, including a disposable measure.

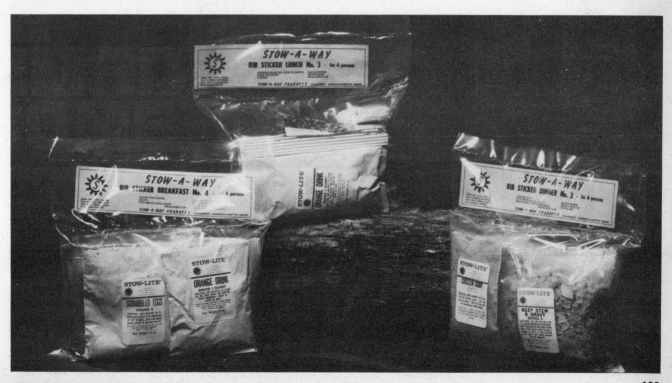

One may not need a set of traditional silverware in the field, but a good knife is a must for all backpackers.
The knife not only must serve as a cooking aide, but will function in emergency and routine backpacking chores.
Designs vary with the various makers, but your knife should have at least two blades and should be sharp on departure.

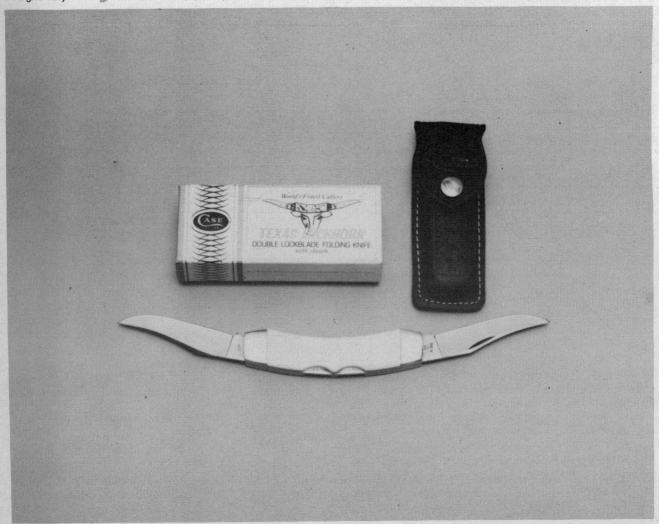

*Utilizing the Swiss Army knife concept, Precise imports their Backpacker model, which features a standard blade, backed up by all sorts of additional useful field tools.*

for minimum space requirements, all the better.

When you wash your utensils use only biodegradable soaps. If you cannot buy these at your local grocery store, look for them in sporting goods sections of variety stores and backpacking specialty shops. If necessary, sand will work as an occasional cleaning agent. Be sure to rinse your utensils well.

Use plastic silverware when possible, but be certain to have along a good knife. It makes fixing meals a lot easier, and comes in handy a thousand different times; for setting up tents, opening plastic food bags, repairing gear.

There are all kinds of knives on the market today, ranging from those with two blades and a cork screw to

those with as many as twelve different tools from can openers to nail files. You will need at least two blades, if for no other reason than to back up one another. The added items can prove a blessing in an emergency. Choose a knife that fits your expected needs and weight restrictions. Then be sure to keep those blades sharp.

As with all aspects of backpacking, the lists of utensils available seem endless, and make limiting your selections difficult. What you decide to carry along will be a matter of personal need, and the space available to you for packing. A good rule of thumb is to carry along only those items that are necessary — but those necessary for an enjoyable trip, not simply for existence.

# CHAPTER 8

*Carabiners, pitons and ropes are the paraphernalia of the climber, along with a soft pack such as the Peak 1 which will hug the body, leave the arms free. However, for the casual backpacker in mountain terrain it isn't needed.*

# THE MUHAMMAD SYNDROME

## The Basics Of Mountain Backpacking Require New Thinking For Health And Safety!

IN THINKING OF mountain climbing in conjunction with backpacking, one should keep in mind that mountaineering is a hobby — or an avocation — in itself. Those who choose to go in for serious rock climbing should receive specialized instruction in this sort of endeavor. Inasmuch as entire volumes have been written on mountaineering and rock climbing, we will not attempt to go too deeply into the subject. Instead, we will offer in this chapter some of the basic information that the backpacker may find of use in a mountain environment.

The Marine Corps has done a great deal of research adapted to practical training at the Marine Corps Mountain Warfare School located in the High Sierras near Bridgeport, California. The personnel at the school have been of a great deal of help with our research in this facet. Many of the tips passed on here are born of their experiences in day-to-day training.

It has been found that training of individuals in mountains of low or medium elevations doesn't require any special conditioning or acclimatizing. However, at altitudes of more

*Mountain climbers practice the self-arresting position, when slipping down a steep slope that is snow-covered.*

*Climbers practice rescue from a crevasse. Note the manner in which the climbers are tied together for protection.*

than 2500 meters (8000 feet), there is a required acclimatizing period needed. This consists of gradual physical exercise, including short walks with appropriate rest periods. No matter what the physical shape of the backpacker, in moving through mountain terrain, he will find a new group of muscles being taxed. If there is enough of this type of exercise, of course, these muscles will be developed and hardened. Under any circumstances, though, mountain hiking is tiring and arduous.

At altitudes of more than 2500 meters, it has been found that time must be allowed for the red blood count to increase to augment the oxygen-carrying capabilities of the blood. Thus the Marines at the Mountain Warfare School take things slow and easy in the beginning, since most of the troops being trained are from sea-level amphibious bases. At the same time, according to instructors, they tend to develop increasing confidence in their individual abilities to negotiate terrain that they probably considered impassable the first time they looked at a mountain canyon.

While it has been found that the air above 4500 meters (14,800 feet) is virtually germ-free, altitudes can produce a number of specific maladies and afflictions.

First, it is best to bring along your own water and not depend upon mountain streams. Tests have shown that many of these streams are polluted to a degree, especially where sheep are summer grazed and melting snow carries feces into the streams.

Under conditions of extreme cold, it is the tendency for one to allow himself to become constipated; don't allow this to happen. In such temperatures, don't neglect personal cleanliness. If water is not plentiful, one can rub briskly with a rough towel to hold down possible skin infections.

The feet, needless to say, are most important and one

*Areas such as Mount Rainier, while popular, are alive with crevasses and avalanche areas, requiring care to cross. It is good practice for one person to cross at a time.*

Climbers may encounter many obstacles such as these spires known as nieve penitentes. They are created by abnormal melting of snow due to dust settling on the surface of the snow. It is easier to go around than through them.

Extreme care should be taken in crossing mountain streams, choosing a good ford. The clear water often is deeper than may appear. A pole to measure depth is a good idea.

should take extreme care in high altitudes to keep the feet dry and to change socks daily. Should you have boots that utilize removable inner soles, these also should be changed daily.

A malady known as mountain or altitude sickness can affect the novice or even the experienced mountain climber at altitudes as low as 2500 meters. The cause, study has shown, usually is poor physical condition or too short a period of acclimatization. Or both. Symptoms include violent headaches, nausea, vomiting, lack of appetite, insomnia and an irritable nature. This condition usually can be relieved by rest, but in some rare cases, it is necessary for the afflicted one to be taken to lower altitudes.

At the opposite extreme is valley disease, which occurs when an individual acclimatized to the higher levels comes down to low altitudes. In short, it is the opposite of mountain sickness, although the symptoms can be similar. The one afflicted may experience lassitude, increased sweating, loss of

This broken, uneven snowfield is evidence that slide conditions prevail. Such areas should be crossed early in the morning or late in day when there is no thawing.

*Utilizing compact tents, this group of mountain hikers has established a base camp where they can acclimatize for a few days before moving to higher elevations. The site could be better, however, as rain in the mountains could create flash floods that would sweep through the old streambed in which backpackers have set up the camp.*

weight, forgetfulness, headache, noises in the ears, indigestion, depression, or neuralgia-like pain. One or more of these symptoms may be present at the same time, along with an irritable nature, but such a conglomerate of symptoms should be enough to arouse a foul humor! However, all is not lost. The symptoms usually disappear within a few days.

This particular malady is caused by the abnormal increase in the number of red blood cells created to augment the oxygen-carrying capabilities of the blood. Needless to say, the overage is not needed at sea level.

*Even on cloudy days, snowblindness can occur, and it is a likelihood, too, if the hiker does not wear glasses having lenses that are sufficiently dark for glare.*

*Four inches of snow fell on this base camp during the night, but the tents shed the moisture, keeping the occupants warm and dry. Snow sublimed later in the day.*

Photos by Geno Echevarria

*Climbers from two expeditions reach the top of Mt. Aconcagua, the 22,800-foot peak in Argentina, to plant their flags. This type of mountain climbing is beyond the capabilities of casual backpackers, but many of the rules apply. (Below) During a break for acclimatization, sleeping bags are spread on tent in sun to dry out condensation of the night.*

Another malady of the mountain hiker may be what is known as glacier or snowfield lassitude. This is a transitory physical weakening condition that often assails the climber on warm days.

The physical factors producing this sickness are hollows into which the sun beats directly, reflecting the light and stagnant or excessively still air. It is the belief of physiologists that the factors producing this feeling of weakness in the individual are due to a disturbance in the individual's circulatory system. The best cure, it has been found, is to move into an area where there are moving air currents.

Another problem that can overtake the backpacker in mountain terrain is snowblindness. This is caused by failure to wear dark glasses during brilliant sunshine reflecting off of snow or ice. In addition to not being able to see, there usually is an aching sensation in the eyes and they become badly bloodshot.

The immediate treatment is to apply cool, wet compresses to the eyes, then have the afflicted individual don a pair of sunglasses, the darker the better. Eye ointments usually will relieve the burning sensation and other accompanying pain, but they do not aid in the individual regaining vision.

Recovery can take up to three days and it may be necessary to lead the afflicted climber out of the area. The eyes should be covered to avoid further damage, if this is the case. It goes without saying — or should — that hikers should not venture into the mountains alone.

*For the individual serious about making rock climbing a part of his backpack outing, a climbing helmet protects against falling rocks from above. (Below) If a number of packers are involved, planning sessions are necessary.*

Photo by Geno Echevarria

*Rock climbing requires special skills, training, as well as equipment. Shown here is Peak 1 soft pack made by Coleman. If the casual backpacker wishes to try this outdoor facet, go with one who's experienced.*

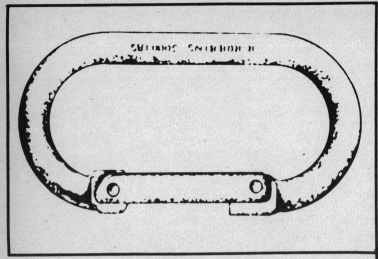

For use in rock climbing, carabiners such as those from Robbins/Salewa are designed for weights up to 4000 pounds. This means more safety, if you should find yourself hanging from a rope that is threaded through one of these units.

The Stitch belay plate is lightweight and effective for controlled belaying. It is adaptable for use in climbing in rocks, snowfields or over ice. While it and other items are designed for serious mountain climbers, a hiker who finds himself in such environs can use them to advantage for his safety.

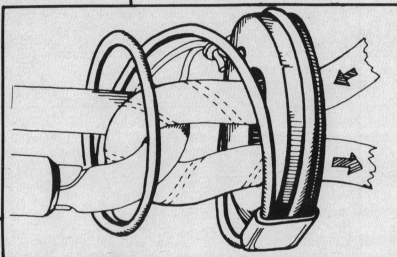

Called the Guide Harness by Robbins Mountaingear, this harness is ideal for the neophyte, who wants some safety device, when he is in the rocks or crossing a snowfield.

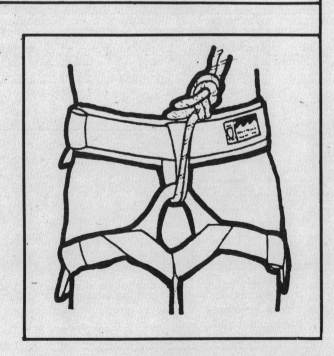

Robbins' Pro Harness is for the advanced mountaineer and features a three-inch belt. However, such safety devices can be used to advantage in negotiating dangerous terrain.

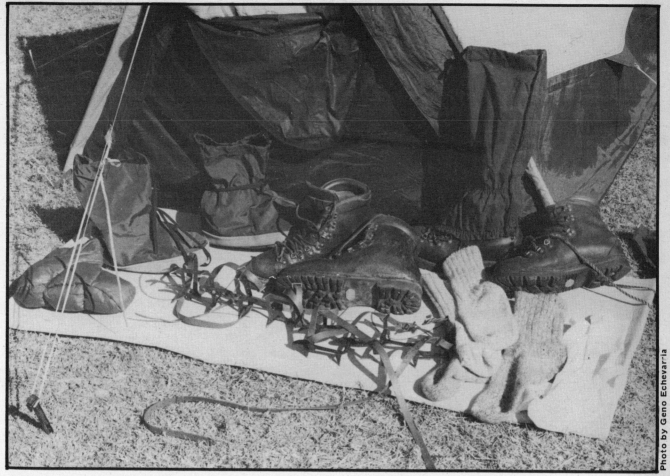

*If one expects to be backpacking in snow or ice, good boots, protective coverings, the right type of socks and ice cleats which can be adjusted to the foot are necessities, if you are to travel with ease and safety.*

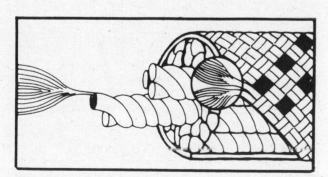

*Ropes can be an important part of one's equipment in the mountains, when backpacking. Pick a good one such as the Edelrid, which has 2200 miles of threads in 150 feet.*

Although exposure is discussed at length in another chapter of this volume, we would be remiss in not making additional mention here.

Hypothermia, of course, is the direct result of loss of body heat from prolonged cooling. In the initial stages, heat production in the body is increased by shivering; this tends to increase the individual's oxygen consumption and metabolism by a factor of four to six. It is the available carbohydrate reserves that determine just how long this particular phase may be extended.

When body temperature goes below ninety-two degrees,

the individual no longer can produce enough body heat for recovery. In this particular stage, the victim has developed mask-like features, a glassy stare; if able to talk, he mumbles, and he invariably suffers from apparent mental confusion. Blood pressure and the heart rate are reduced, too, at this point. From here, the victim develops a slow, irregular heartbeat quite soon and slips into death if some corrective measures are not forthcoming.

Treatment of exposure is aimed at supplying heat to the victim until such time as his metabolism allows him to regenerate his own body heat. If at all possible, he should be wrapped in prewarmed garments, sleeping bags and even hot, wrapped rocks can be used. Whenever possible, a fire should be built on each side of the victim and two persons, if present, should lie down beside him, all three wrapped in ponchos, tent canvases or other coverings that will hold in the heat. Warm fluids laced with sugar also can be of help in increasing the victim's body temperature.

A hazard that can quash your worries about mountain sickness, valley sickness or even exposure is the avalanche. In many areas of mountain terrain, the avalanche presents a constant hazard in winter months and often far into the spring.

One of the chief causes of avalanches is rapid accumulation of new snow. Ten inches of snow falling at a rate faster than an inch per hour, then driven by a wind of

*Students at the Marine Corps Mountain Warfare School in California's High Sierras learn the basics of climbing at low levels, then work their way to greater heights. Their methods can be adapted to learning by backpackers.*

*This means of crossing a canyon may well be beyond the capabilities of the average backpacker. Marines use it as an exercise to teach trust in their fellow climbers.*

*At the Mountain Warfare School, Marines learn basics of seeking out hand and footholds on steep faces. This is a specialized facet that anyone can use in such terrain.*

fifteen miles per hour or so tends to create a dangerous situation. However, avalanches also can occur during fair weather, when there are strong winds, when the surface is melting from sun heat or deep thawing results from rain or prolonged warm temperatures.

Rapidly rising temperatures even without sunlight can cause what are called wet surface slides or damp slab avalanches. In these, the upper layers of snow become heavier than that beneath because of the melting and resulting moisture content. At the correct angle, these wet slabs will slide across the surface of the unmelted snow beneath.

Temperatures that are above freezing for thirty-six hours or more can cause these large wet slides. Rain also adds weight to snow, thus creating a danger.

If it is necessary to travel in avalanche country, one should consider the danger signs, including prevailing winds and storm data. Hazardous slopes should be avoided. Wherever practical, one should stick to the crest of the ridge, thus avoiding the dangerous snowfields. Trails should be chosen through heavy timber; through areas heavy with rock

The Marine students must take the business of climbing seriously, as their lives may depend upon it someday. (Below) Marines also are taught how to use the mountains and equipment at hand for the evacuation of casualties.

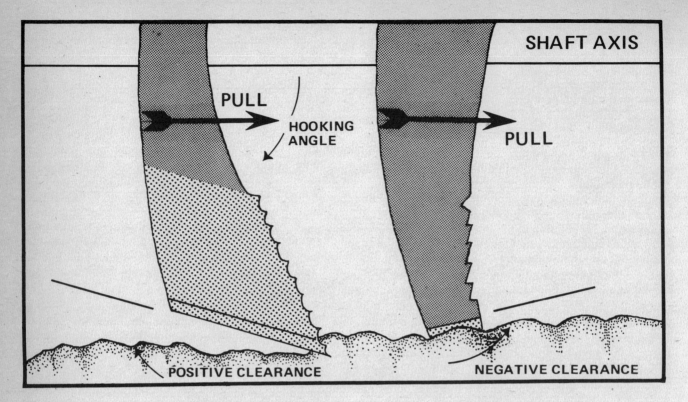

SHAFT AXIS

PULL

HOOKING ANGLE

PULL

POSITIVE CLEARANCE

NEGATIVE CLEARANCE

*Ice ax at left has better design, since the cutting edge goes into the ice. One at right has less edge exposed to the ice. (Below) Ice axes are made of steel or aluminum and are available in various configurations to suit need.*

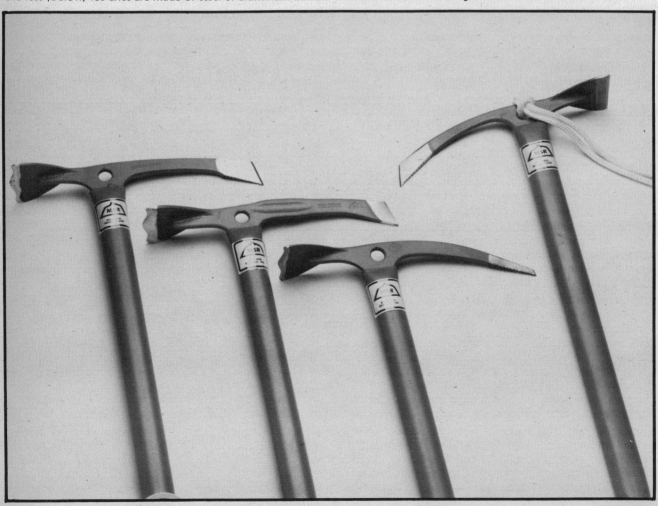

outcroppings; where there are other terrain barriers or across wind-blown slopes where snow does not pile up as deeply.

In the event of a snowstorm, travel usually is possible for the first few hours. This time certainly should be used to get clear of avalanche areas. After a storm, if possible, it is best to remain holed up until the snow either has had time to settle or to slide. Incidentally, during the spring avalanche season, the period between 10 a.m. and sundown is considered the most dangerous. The early morning hours before sunup are considered the most safe in a less-than-safe avalanche environment.

Observation and testing should be a part of the backpacker's technique should he be caught in avalanche country. Snow conditions should be tested as one travels, especially if off of normal trails. For example, before moving across a big slope, one might check the snow movement on a small slope of the same general angle and exposure. One also can roll a rock or small boulder into the snow to determine whether the snow is solid or will move when disturbed. If the path of an avalanche can be seen on an adjoining slope, it should be considered that other slopes in the immediate area offer the same danger. All of this may seem like a good deal of trouble, but it obviously is better to take the time to be safe, than to become a physical part of an avalanche!

Another way of testing a slope, if you are in a party of hikers and you are equipped with ropes and belaying equipment is to rope one of the hikers securely, then have him move out onto the slope to test it. The military mountaineers deliberately attempt to start slides to determine the safety, but I'm of the opinion that this is a bit too much for the individual without a lot of specialized training. If the slope is found to be relatively firm, crossing it should be done one at a time, not as a pack. If possible pack straps should be loosened so that the pack can be dumped in a hurry should one find himself in trouble.

As mentioned earlier, with a bit of training, one can

*MSR is one of the organizations that builds an aluminum ice ax for ease of carrying by the backpacker. It is compact, easily attached to a pack.*

| NO. | MESSAGE | CODE SYMBOL | NO. | MESSAGE | CODE SYMBOL |
|-----|---------|-------------|-----|---------|-------------|
| 1 | Require doctor-serious injuries | I | 10 | Will attempt take-off | ▷ |
| 2 | Require medical supplies | II | 11 | Aircraft seriously damaged | ⊡ |
| 3 | Unable to proceed | ✕ | 12 | Probably safe to land here | △ |
| 4 | Require food and water | F | 13 | Require fuel and oil | L |
| 5 | Require firearms and ammo | ⋁ | 14 | All well | LL |
| 6 | Require map and compass | ☐ | 15 | No | N |
| 7 | Require signal lamp with battery and radio | ⌇ | 16 | Yes | Y |
| 8 | Indicate direction to proceed | K | 17 | Not understood | ⅃L |
| 9 | Am proceeding in this direction | ↑ | 18 | Require engineer | W |

## VISUAL EMERGENCY SIGNALS

If you are able to attract the attention of the pilot of a rescue plane, these body signals can be used to transmit messages as he circles over your location. Stand in the open when you make the signals. Be sure that the background does not obscure your signals.

Need medical assistance URGENT lie prone

All OK don't wait

Can proceed shortly wait if practicable

Need mechanical help or parts-long delay

Pick us up-plane abandoned

Do not attempt to land here

Land here

Our receiver is operating

Use the drop message

Affirmative-yes

Negative-no

*The emergency signs and signals at left are universal in the present day, thus can be of use in any country.*

develop a steady rhythmic pace that allows one to travel faster and with less exertion than would be the case with the hiker who never has packed the mountains. One learns to conserve his strength, decreasing speed with the steepness of the slope. When climbing, one should attempt to maintain the normal length of his pace, but the feet should be kept flat and obstacles in the trail should be avoided where possible to bypass them rather than climbing over them.

In moving up a steep trail, one should not walk on the balls of his feet. The knees should be locked with each step and footholds selected carefully. In traversing steep slopes on soft ground, it may be necessary to kick footholds in the ground and to take advantage of naturally flat hummocks. If the ground is hard, in traversing such a slope, the feet should be flat, the ankles rolled with the slope, while avoiding logs, sticks and rocks.

In descending a hill or mountain, the continuing jar of the body can cause muscle fatigue. The weight of the pack can

*This backpacker has yet to learn that it saves wear and tear on the body to go around an obstacle rather than over it. Climbing up a rock is hard on back and the legs.*

| WIND SPEED | | COOLING POWER OF WIND EXPRESSED AS "EQUIVALENT CHILL TEMPERATURE" | | | | | | | | | | | | | | | | | | | | | |
|---|---|---|---|---|---|---|---|---|---|---|---|---|---|---|---|---|---|---|---|---|---|---|---|
| KNOTS | MPH | TEMPERATURE (°F) | | | | | | | | | | | | | | | | | | | | | |
| Calm | Calm | 40 | 35 | 30 | 25 | 20 | 15 | 10 | 5 | 0 | -5 | -10 | -15 | -20 | -25 | -30 | -35 | -40 | -45 | -50 | -55 | -60 |
| | | EQUIVALENT CHILL TEMPERATURE | | | | | | | | | | | | | | | | | | | | | |
| 3 - 6 | 5 | 35 | 30 | 25 | 20 | 15 | 10 | 5 | 0 | -5 | -10 | -15 | -20 | -25 | -30 | -35 | -40 | -45 | -50 | -55 | -65 | -70 |
| 7 - 10 | 10 | 30 | 20 | 15 | 10 | 5 | 0 | -10 | -15 | -20 | -25 | -35 | -40 | -45 | -50 | -60 | -65 | -70 | -75 | -80 | -90 | -95 |
| 11 - 15 | 15 | 25 | 15 | 10 | 0 | -5 | -10 | -20 | -25 | -30 | -40 | -45 | -50 | -60 | -65 | -70 | -80 | -85 | -90 | -100 | -105 | -110 |
| 16 - 19 | 20 | 20 | 10 | 5 | 0 | -10 | -15 | -25 | -30 | -35 | -45 | -50 | -60 | -65 | -75 | -80 | -85 | -95 | -100 | -110 | -115 | -120 |
| 20 - 23 | 25 | 15 | 10 | 0 | -5 | -15 | -20 | -30 | -35 | -45 | -50 | -60 | -65 | -75 | -80 | -90 | -95 | -105 | -110 | -120 | -125 | -135 |
| 24 - 28 | 30 | 10 | 5 | 0 | -10 | -20 | -25 | -30 | -40 | -50 | -55 | -65 | -70 | -80 | -85 | -95 | -100 | -110 | -115 | -125 | -130 | -140 |
| 29 - 32 | 35 | 10 | 5 | -5 | -10 | -20 | -30 | -35 | -40 | -50 | -60 | -65 | -75 | -80 | -90 | -100 | -105 | -115 | -120 | -130 | -135 | -145 |
| 33 - 36 | 40 | 10 | 0 | -5 | -15 | -20 | -30 | -35 | -45 | -55 | -60 | -70 | -75 | -85 | -95 | -100 | -110 | -115 | -125 | -130 | -140 | -150 |
| Winds above 40 have little additional effect | | LITTLE DANGER | | | | | | INCREASING DANGER (Flesh may freeze within 1 min.) | | | | | | GREAT DANGER (Flesh may freeze within 30 seconds) | | | | | | | | |

DANGER OF FREEZING EXPOSED FLESH FOR PROPERLY CLOTHED PERSONS

*Mountain walking is a technique all its own. One learns to pick the spot in which to place his foot, rolling the ankle so that the remainder of the body is vertical.*

increase such effects, causing strain in the legs, pelvis, spinal column, heart and lungs.

Keep in mind that time and distance required to reach specific destinations usually are underestimated. This often is due to the optical illusion of nearness caused by clear air and the perspective gained when looking down from a great height or across canyons and valleys. So select your objectives with this in mind and try not to be caught on a mountain trail at night. Such movement is difficult, dangerous and tiring. Also, moving in clouds or fog presents the same difficulties. Keeping a sense of direction is difficult, since clouds often are so dense one can barely see the ground.

The dangers have been pointed out here, of course, but if you give the idea of mountain backpacking a bit of thought, you will note that most of the dangers become minimized with the application of ordinary common sense. So think out what you intend to do before you place yourself or your friends in a situation that is potentially dangerous.

The ideal situation, of course, if you are venturing into the mountains for the first time is to have someone with experience and training along. This way, you can learn the potential dangers and ways of solving them without the pitfalls of personal experimentation.

# CHAPTER 9

# MAPS & COMPASSES

*Learning the use of a compass in conjunction with a map can prove a boon when you're out in the wilderness. Proper knowledge can aid you in knowing where you are and, equally important, help you get where you're going.*

## To Get Where You're Going, Learn To Use These Tools To The Outdoors!

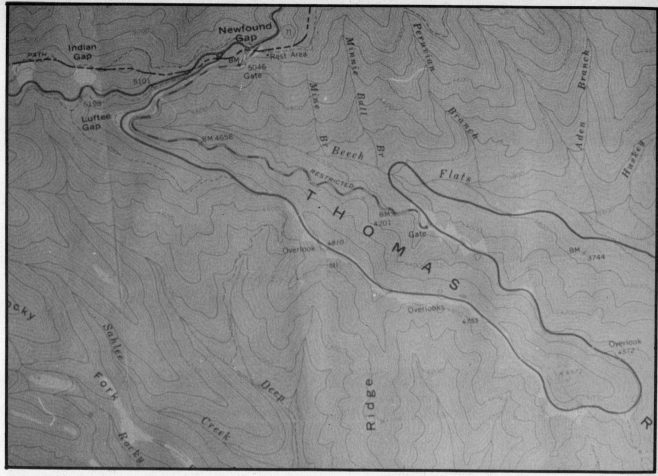

*Topographical maps show the location and shapes of plains, valleys and mountains, as well as the network of streams and rivers; in addition, the principal works of man are indicated. (Below) Maps invariably offer a distance scale, which allows one to visualize map inches as the true distances on land, interpreting natural obstacles enroute.*

**F**OR THE backpacker who travels unfamiliar terrain, especially in isolated areas, a map and a compass are vital. Even the knowledgeable packer, who alleges to know the area "like the back of his hand" would be wise to carry both. Failure to obtain and use them could mean the difference between reaching your destination and becoming an air rescue statistic; to journey into unknown terrain without these tools is not only foolish, but dangerous.

It does little good, of course, to carry along the finest of maps and compasses if one does not know how to use them. While the following information will fall far short of making you an orienteer, it will give you the basic knowledge necessary to locate your position, determine the distance between your location and your destination with reasonable accuracy, and the direction you must travel to reach that destination.

There are various types of maps available, ranging from simple road maps to topographic maps. Many are the product of the United States Geological Survey (USGS), a federal organization whose responsibility it is to collect, analyze and publish detailed information about the nation's mineral, land and water resources. While the USGS does publish a number of different styles of maps, for the backpacker the map to request is called a topographic map. These maps illustrate natural and selected man-made features of a section of the earth. Topographic maps show the location and shape

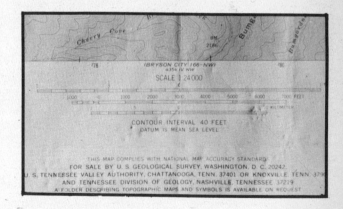

of mountains, valleys and plains; the networks of streams and rivers; and the principal works of man. Everything you need to know about the land you are packing is there, if you know how to read it. And, it's not difficult to read.

Each map has its own scale, a consistent comparison of the features as they appear on the map and as they exist on the earth. In the margin around the map, itself, you usually will find the scale used for that map. An example of a map scale would be 1:24,000. What that designation means is that any one unit (inch, centimeter, foot, etc.) viewed on the map is equivalent to 24,000 such units in reality. An area one inch in diameter would in reality encompass an area 24,000 inches

(2000 feet) in diameter. If you wanted to travel a map distance of one inch to reach a destination, you would have to travel 2000 feet on land. The purpose of the scale is to allow you to gauge the distance, thus enabling you to determine whether or not your destination is within your capabilities.

Included in the legend you will find a distance scale for converting map inches to miles, feet and kilometers. This scale allows you to determine the distance you must travel to a particular location. To use the scale you need only mark the distance as it appears on the map, then compare the mark to the conversion distance on the scale. Be sure to consider loops and switchback trails. A string is an easy method of gauging this distance. Simply line the string along your route, following the turns as they come. Mark the spot at which the string crosses your destination, then compare that length to the distance scale.

You will find a good deal of additional information within the margins, commonly termed the map's "legend." All information needed to read your map should be included here, including all color designations, contour intervals, conversion charts and symbols.

Symbols are the language of maps, and on USGS maps the colors of the symbols indicate the features they represent. Symbols for water features are blue; roads are red; green indicates wooded areas; contour lines are shown in brown. For the backpacker, contour lines are especially important, for the ability to read them correctly means the difference between hours spent climbing over steep terrain or minutes spent crossing nearby saddles.

Contour lines are used to indicate the shape and elevation of the land surface. Every point along a given contour line will be at the same elevation, the brown lines swirling in a zigzag

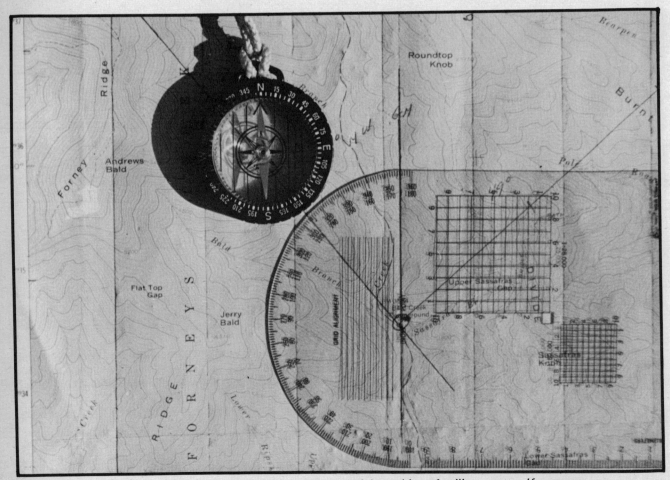

*The compass, a protractor and a map are the three tools to successful travel in unfamiliar country. If necessary, one can do without the protractor, using the compass dial, but readings will be less accurate using this method.*

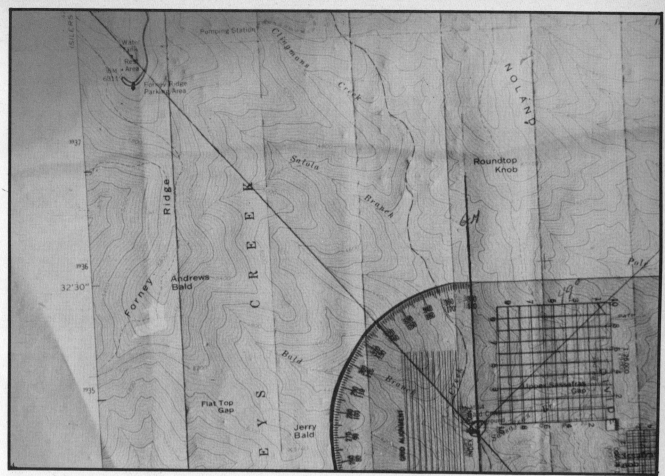

Draw a straight line, running north from your current position. Place the protractor so the "0" is over
the guideline, 180 degrees across the southern end of the line. This particular protractor has only half a circle.
For angles of more than 180 degrees, one must turn this protractor 180 degrees to read the second, greater reading.

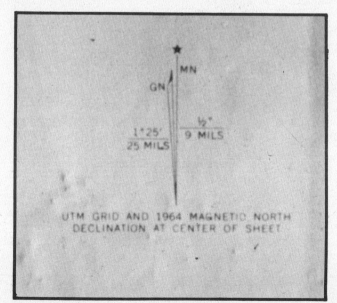

The difference between magnetic, grid and true north is
given in the declination scale found within the legend. If
the grid azimuth is greater than the magnetic azimuth (as
it is here), one must subtract the magnetic azimuth from
the grid azimuth to achieve the proper conversion factor.

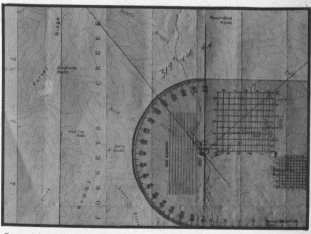

Record your measurement to within one-half degree. Your
reading is your grid azimuth. To convert this to the
magnetic azimuth, add the difference of your conversion.
In this case, a 319-degree grid azimuth becomes 320
degrees, when it is converted to the magnetic azimuth.

circle to maintain that elevation. Within the map legend can be found the interval between these lines — forty feet in the case of our sample map. This interval also will remain the same, for all contour lines regardless of their apparent visual proximity to each other. In reviewing a map, note that every fifth line is much heavier than the four in between. This is called an index contour, and is intended to aid you in reading elevations. Figures along these index lines indicate the elevation at that height, allowing you to determine the elevation for all other contour lines by either adding or subtracting the designated interval between lines (forty feet).

You also will notice that the elevation of certain additional points have been given. Usually these points will indicate the top of a hill, a road crossing, or other visible feature. But the most important function of the contour line is to indicate terrain features. Bear in mind that all contour lines from a hilltop to the ground go downhill, in all directions. To determine whether the drop (or rise) in terrain is steep or gentle look to the spacing between the contour lines. Placed at wide intervals, the lines indicate a gradual slant; at close intervals the drop is rapid. Keeping this in mind will enable you to avoid needless difficult climbs, offering an easier climb by simply altering your course slightly.

Now that you are able to recognize terrain on a topographic map, you are ready to consider combining those skills with the practical use of a compass. Once you are able to do so, the task of reaching any objective within your map's boundaries becomes possible.

To get to your destination, you first must know in which direction to head. The compass, in combination with the map, will give you that direction. First you must understand how the compass functions, and what adjustments must be made between it and your map.

A compass is no more than a magnetic needle which, when

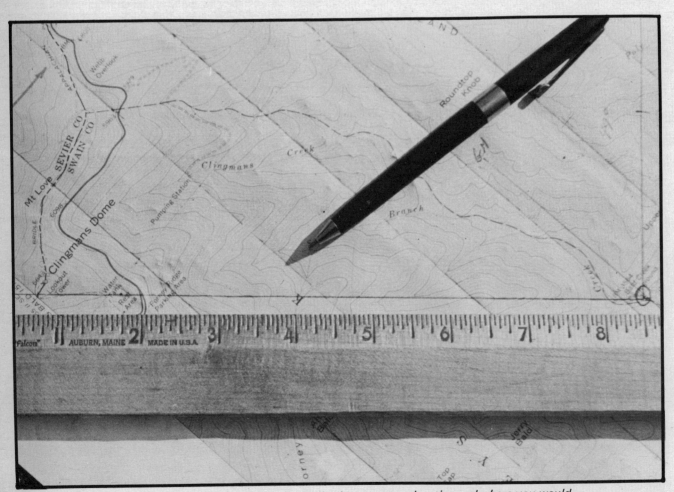

*The first step in getting your bearings is to draw a straight line between your location and where you would like to end up. This forms one base for the reading of your azimuth, although it's not quite all that simple. In getting from one point to another, one must worry about rocks, rills, hills and other impassable terrain features.*

permitted to turn freely, will point to magnetic North. Pivoting at its center, the needle turns in a circle of 360 degrees. Facing directly North, the outer dial of your compass should give a reading of 0 degrees, if set on magnetic North. Often the letter N will be placed at this point, indicating the direction "North." Ninety degrees to your right will be East, 180 degrees becomes due South, and 270 degrees is due West.

To determine in which direction you must go to reach your destination, you must first determine the degree of that destination, termed the azimuth or bearing. By definition, an azimuth is a horizontal angle originating from a fixed point (as true North) through the center of an object clockwise from that point. That fixed point always is considered as North, and that is where you can run into a potential problem. There are three Norths that you can consider: true North, the direction of the geographic North Pole; magnetic North, the direction in which the compass points, toward the magnetic North Pole which is actually located somewhere in Canada; and grid North, the North lines established by the grid, top to bottom, lines on a map. To correlate map and compass you must work with all three Norths, although your concern with true North will be limited to night locations. Your primary concern is with the difference between magnetic North (MN) and grid North (GN).

Since the compass gives you a bearing in relation to magnetic North while map locations are given in relation to grid North, you must be able to recognize the difference between the two, and adjust accordingly. This difference is called the G-M angle, and will be different for every map, dependent on where in relation to the earth that piece of real estate happens to be located.

How do you determine this difference? Actually, the work

*Contour lines on topographical maps indicate elevations. Every fifth line, called an index line, is inked more heavily for quick reference. Contour lines falling close together indicate a steep incline. The contour lines that are widely spaced indicate a more gradual slope. This is of help in determining the easiest route to follow.*

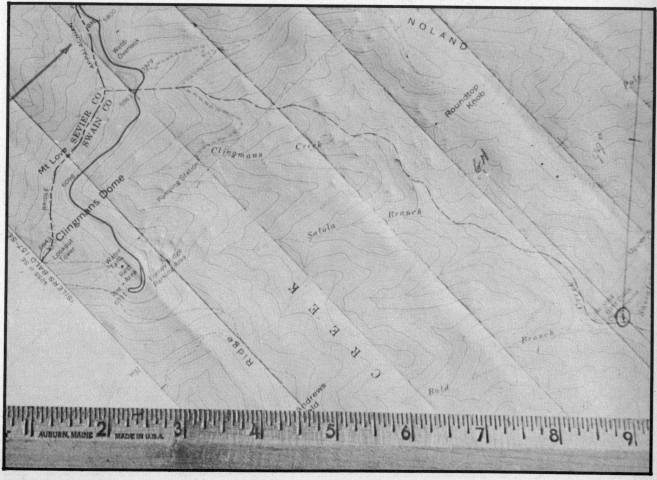

has been done for you. All you need do is look to the legend of your map, where the degree of G-M difference, termed declination, will be given. The diagram looks something like this:

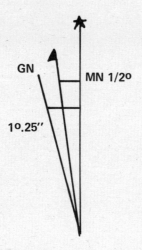

By each North, magnetic and grid, will be given its variation from true North. A star indicates true North, a flag indicates magnetic North, and grid North is indicated by the initials GN. Sometimes this difference may be so small you can ignore it. Other times the difference is so great it must be considered, as failure to do so will place you far from your intended destination.

How do you adjust? You begin by accepting the given degree of difference in the declination diagram as correct. Do not try to measure the angles to prove them out. They were tested long before the map was published, so trust them. In the sample declination diagram you were told that magnetic North lies one-half degree West of true North, while grid North lies 1½ degrees West of it. The total difference between MN and GN is then one degree (1½ - ½). That is the figure you must work with for this particular map, but what do you do with it?

Let's assume, for purposes of illustration, that from your map you have determined where you are and where you would like to be. Using our sample map we will say that you have camped overnight at the Bald Creek Campground. By afternoon, you would like to meet friends at the water tank near Clingman's Dome. On the map, trace a line between the two points. That line forms the base of your conversion. Now measure the angle from that line to a base line drawn north to south along the grid lines. It may help you to draw these grid lines on your map, if you do not already have them on it, before you begin your backpacking journey. With a protractor, if your compass has one included, measure the angle. If not, consider packing a simple protractor; the kind you buy in school supply stores for fifty cents will do. Or you can use the rim of your compass as a protractor, though it probably will offer some inaccuracy. Place the protractor so that 0 is North on the grid line, the 180 degree marking is due South, then read the angle given by your destination line, in the case of our sample map an azimuth of 319 degrees Northwest. This bearing tells you the direction you must take to get to your destination by grid North. To convert to magnetic North so your compass can point the way, add one degree to your angle, the difference between GN and MN.

With your compass, you then will want to proceed at a bearing of 320 degrees Northwest to reach your objective. Proceed in that direction, taking new bearings every 1000 yards or so, until you reach your site. You will also want to check your progress along the way by noting landmarks, such as hilltops, streams, trails you should be crossing as you go. In our sample route, you would cross two such streams.

A rule to keep in mind for converting one azimuth to another: look at the declination diagram and determine which azimuth is larger, either grid or magnetic. If the grid azimuth is larger than the magnetic azimuth, to convert a grid azimuth to a magnetic azimuth you will *subtract* the difference between the two. If the magnetic azimuth is larger, to convert a grid azimuth to a magnetic azimuth you must *add* the difference. Remember, we need to convert our grid azimuth to a magnetic azimuth to use our compass.

We have seen how you can determine your correct course when you know where you are and where you would like to be. But what happens if, as is sometimes the case, you become disoriented and do not know where you are? Can you still use your map and compass to find yourself? You sure can!

To locate your position on your map, begin by orienting

*To locate your position on a map, you first must orient the map by turning it until the North/South grid lines are parallel to magnetic North/South indicated by compass.*

your map; this means turning the map until grid North lines up with magnetic North. Do not worry about the G-M angle. You are only trying to find your current location, not the way to your new position. Once you have North lined up, place something on top of the edges of the map to hold it in that position. Now look around you for a recognizable feature: a stream, trail crossing, etc. Find that same feature on your map. Place a straight edge next to the map feature, then point the other end of the straight edge directly at the actual land feature. Draw a line across your map along this edge.

Next locate a second land feature that is easily recognizable on your map. Using your straight edge repeat the previous steps. Extensions of your lines should cross each other at one point, your present location. This process is called resection. From this point you can determine your proper course by again working with the G-M angles.

## Determining Your Bearings Without A Compass

Although a compass is the best tool for determining direction, should you find yourself in a position where you have no compass available, you can determine your direction by other means. During the day allow the sun to provide direction. Place a stick in the ground, in a level spot at a vertical angle. Note the spot of the tip of the shadow cast by the stick. Place a marker here. Wait thirty minutes or so and again mark the tip of the stick's shadow. Draw a straight line through the two markers and you will have drawn an East/West line. Since the sun rises in the East, the first marker will always be West.

At night, you can determine your direction by using the stars. First find the Big Dipper, drawing your attention to the last two stars in the dipper section, not the handle. These two stars will form a perfect line to the North Star, also called

*A simple method of determining the direction without a compass involves using a stick and the sun. Place the stick vertically in the ground. Then mark with a stone or any small item the tip of the shadow of the stick.*

*Wait a half hour or so and again mark the tip of the stick's shadow. Draw a line connecting these two marks. The line will run East/West with the first mark always indicating West.*

Polaris. The brightest star in the galaxy, it will be located about five times as far as the distance between the Dipper's two stars. Turn to face Polaris and you are facing North. Unless you intend on packing at night, simply orient your map to North, then wait for morning to get your bearings.

The USGS has topographic maps of every state, of all national forests and of many special interest areas within a state. Maps are distributed by region, according to their geographical locations. Maps of areas east of the Mississippi River, including Minnesota, Puerto Rico and the Virgin Islands, can be ordered from: Branch of Distribution, U.S. Geological Survey, 1200 South Eads Street, Arlington, Virginia 22202.

Maps of areas west of the Mississippi River, including

Alaska, Hawaii, Louisiana, Guam and American Samoa can be ordered from: Branch of Distribution, U.S. Geological Survey, Box 25286, Federal Center, Denver, Colorado 80225.

Alaskan residents can order maps of Alaska from: Distribution Section, U.S. Geological Survey, Federal Building, Box 12, 101 Twelfth Avenue, Fairbanks, Alaska 99701.

Prepayment is required. If unsure of the cost of your maps, request a price quote from the USGS branch of distribution in Arlington, Virginia. Indexes, listing areas covered by maps, their name and scale as well as year of survey, are available free of charge by writing to any of the three distribution sections.

# CHAPTER 10

# CROSS-COUNTRY ORIENTEERING

## A Competitive Sport

**N**OW THAT you have mastered the relationships between mind and map you may want to carry your training further — a good deal further — to the realm of orienteering. Here the map becomes more than a guidance tool. A compass is no longer an item you should take with you, but one you must take.

Yours is no longer the role of participant. In orienteering you become a competitor, racing against time and rivals in the quest to be among the first to "find" yourself.

Whether you look upon orienteering with avid enthusiasm or mere interest, a glance into this little known recreational sport, as explained by Ann Forbes-Bradford, can only serve to stimulate those interests.

There was a thrashing noise. Dry leaves crunched, twigs crackled and branches snapped. The hikers looked at each other, bewildered. No large animals were known to inhabit the area. What was that noise? They both turned and gazed into the brush. Seconds later a man galloped out of the vegetation and rushed past them. He had a map in one hand, a compass in the other. Then he disappeared into the foliage again.

The man running through the woods was a competitive cross country orienteer on his way from one checkpoint to the next. He was racing against other competitors to find consecutive markers comprising a given course. The orienteer who completes the course fastest, with the greatest accuracy, is the winner.

Orienteering, determining directions and location using a map and compass, began long ago as a means of finding one's way during cross-country travel. Near the end of the Nineteenth Century, these map and compass skills were adapted for use in competition in Sweden and Norway. Competitions combined route finding with either cross-country running or skiing. In 1900, the term "orienteering" was used for the first time to describe this sport.

The sport was made easier for competitors with the advent of the first simple one-piece protractor compass in the early 1930s. It was developed by the Kjellstrom

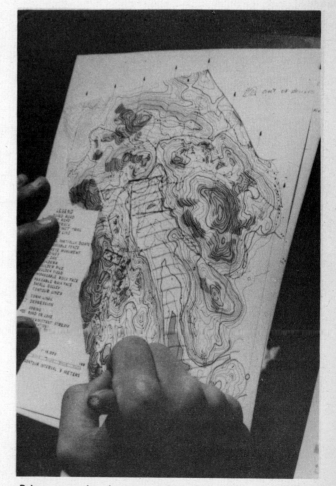

*Prior to running the course, the orienteer should make map notes on the course, indicating areas where vegetation is too thick to traverse. Boundaries are added to the map.*

brothers and Gunnar Tillander and is currently produced in a variety of models. The protractor compass is the type of compass most widely used by orienteers. Special features include a transparent plastic base through which map features can be read, a movable compass housing, orienteering lines painted inside the compass housing, a direction of travel arrow, and distance scales.

The protractor compass can be laid on a map with an edge of the base paralleling the intended route of travel. Thus, possible route obstructions are more readily noticeable. Also, these compasses are easier than others to use on the move while walking, running or even skiing.

Bjorn Kjellstrom, one of the innovators of the protractor compass, brought orienteering to the United States in the mid-1940s. The sport was slow to catch on, but has been increasing in popularity in recent years. In 1971, the United States Orienteering Federation was established.

At the beginning of an orienteering meet, participants check in with a registrar. Usually, several courses have been set for each meet. The orienteer must choose which course he wishes to travel and whether he will go alone or with someone else. The courses differ in total distance covered, number of checkpoints to be found, and difficulty of terrain. Having courses of varying difficulties provides a challenge for everyone and an opportunity for success for the novice.

Not all participants are competing to win a ribbon. Some go in family groups with the slowest member setting the pace. Others take a picnic lunch along to enjoy en route. But the serious competitor races alone, carrying nothing extra with him which might slow him down.

The registrar records which course each participant will traverse and assigns a starting time to each entrant. This procedure provides an efficient means of organizing

*Contestants slated for different courses of varying difficulty sprint toward the starting line, where the master maps are located for the race.*

Orienteer copies control points from master map to his own map. Each of the points is consecutively numbered. Part of the challenge is in copying each point accurately. There is a different master map for each course. Note day pack worn by the orienteer.

contestants to start. The same record also is used to record finishing times, from which elapsed time is figured. A third use of the course records is to be sure each person who begins a course returns. If a contestant does not return within a reasonable time, a search can be initiated to find the lost or injured individual.

The registrar gives each contestant a topographical map of the area within which the courses are set. As explained in the last chapter, a topographical map has contour lines which connect points of equal elevation. An orienteer reads his map by learning how contour lines symbolize different natural features. For example, lines which form Vs usually indicate a re-entrant or gully. U-shaped lines generally signify a spur or hillside. Closed circles denote a hilltop or mountaintop. When contour lines are close together, the terrain is steep. Widely separated lines show nearly flat

areas. Thick, impenetrable brush called "fight" is shaded. Steep cliffs are shown by hash marks. These must be avoided when choosing a route of travel. In addition to contour lines, a topographical map shows water, roads and trails, and other man-made features. Some maps are color coded, others are black and white.

Maps are drawn with true North at the top. Compasses point to magnetic North. True North and magnetic North are not the same. Magnetic North is located 1400 miles south of the North Pole (true North). For most locations, magnetic North does not lie in line with true North, so a correction must be made when using a map and compass together. Depending upon your geographical location, the angle of variation or declination between the two norths will differ. In the eastern United States compass declination varies west of true North. In the western United States it varies east of true North. True North and magnetic North are aligned, meaning there is no declination, along a path from the Atlantic coast near the Georgia-Florida state line northward through Lakes Michigan and Superior.

On most orienteering maps, lines which point to magnetic North are drawn across the face of the maps. These lines are at an angle to the vertical lines of true North. They make compensating for declination (the angle of variation between true North and magnetic North) easy. When the orienteer uses his compass with the map, he needs only to rely upon the magnetic North lines to take his compass readings. The true North lines are ignored.

Each competitor receives a "control card" in addition to his map. This may be a separate card or it may be a space at the bottom of the map paper. The control card consists of a series of boxes which are numbered consecutively. Each box is used to record a clue about the location of a control marker and to receive a punched letter at each marker when the course is run.

Control markers are hidden throughout an orienteering area by course-setters. The same type of marker is used for courses in all difficulties. Sometimes the exact same marker is used for more than one course. Or markers for two different courses may be set very close to each other. The clues and map markings enable each orienteer to find the correct control markers along the particular course he is running.

The control markers that designate each point on the course are three-sided and made of cloth. They are hung from natural features such as low branches. Each of a marker's three panels is approximately one-foot-square and is composed of two triangles, one white, the other red. These are sewn together to form a square. Printed in one corner of the white area are one or two letters which identify the control marker. Identification is important since several courses of varying difficulty are usually set in the same area. It is prudent to check the identifying letters to avoid punching in at the wrong marker.

Attached to each control marker is a punch. The punch is used to verify that the control marker was located. The orienteer uses the punch to pierce a letter onto his control card. Each punch stamps out a different letter which usually does not correspond to the identifying letter or letters on the cloth marker.

Each participant must copy control marker identification letters and location clues, for the course he has entered, onto his control card. The clues use natural features and directions; for example: "east side of the stream," "in the shallow re-entrant," "southwest side of the tree on the boulder pile." Some clues provide more accurate control point location than others. For example, when an area is strewn with rock piles and trees, the last clue is not as helpful as it may appear.

Before an orienteer begins a course, it is wise for him to

*Control markers are hung from tree limbs, other natural features. They must be visible from a distance, but often are camouflaged by surrounding brush and rocks, tough to see if the orienteer is slightly off course.*

learn how to calculate distances. A technique called pacing or pace counting is used to figure the average number of steps an individual takes to cover a given distance. At most meets, two markers are placed on the ground one hundred meters apart. Orienteers can walk, jog or run between the markers, counting every other step they take. After several trials, each individual can calculate the average number of paces he takes within a one hundred-meter distance. During the competition, the orienteer may use pace-counting to determine how far he has traveled from one point to another.

Distances on the map are calculated using the distance scale which is printed on the map. Since not all maps have the same scale, an easy calibration technique is to place a piece of adhesive tape on the edge of the compass baseplate. Then, with a pen, the map scale can be etched onto the tape. The scale attached to the compass is mobile and can be used anywhere on the map. After the meet, the tape is removed and a new piece attached, ready for the next competition.

Orienteer Charles Bradford carefully punches his control card upon reaching one of the course's control points. At conclusion of the race, cards are checked by officials.

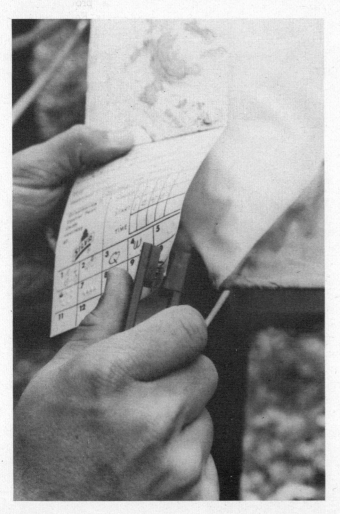

As a means of controlling the race, each punch along the route results in a different letter in competitor's card.

The participant now is ready to start the course. He must watch the clock, waiting for his starting time. The starter will usually give several warnings to each competitor before the final "go."

When an orienteer crouches at the starting table waiting to begin he clutches not only his topographical map, but also his compass. Most orienteers attach a wrist loop to their compass. The wrist loop safeguards against dropping the compass should one loose his grip on it while running.

When starting the course, the orienteer first runs to the master map area. Here he copies the control points in consecutive order from the master map onto his own map.

The starting point where the master map is located is denoted by a triangle. Each control point along the course is a circle. The finish is two concentric circles. Each point is numbered so the orienteer knows in what order to travel. The time it takes to copy the control points from the master map onto the orienteer's map is counted as part of each contestant's total course time. The orienteer must not rush too fast when copying the control points. An error could cost him valuable time later.

After copying the route, the orienteer uses his compass to find the direction toward his first destination. He places his compass on his map tangent to the centers of the triangle and circle number one. To avoid a reciprocal reading, the direction of travel arrow on the compass base plate must point in the direction the orienteer wishes to go, from the start to control point number one.

Then the painted North arrow inside the compass housing is aligned with the magnetic North lines on the map by turning the dial with the degree markings on it, which is

*After punching in, the orienteer determines his bearing to the next control point. He compares visible features of the land with map to determine route to his objective.*

called the housing. When the North arrow is parallel to the magnetic North lines on the map, the heading to the first control marker is read opposite the direction of travel arrow. The heading or bearing is read in degrees; 0 degrees or 360 degrees is North, 90 degrees is East, 180 degrees is South and 270 degrees is West. Leaving the compass

*To obtain a compass bearing from one point to another, the orienteer places the edge of his compass tangent to the circles designating where he is and control point to visit next.*

A day pack such as that manufactured by Camp Trails, the Alpine, can prove invaluable. It hampers one little on the trail, yet allows one to take along the necessities of minimum comfort while competing in orienteering race.

heading untouched, the orienteer places the compass in the palm of his hand directly in front of him. Then he turns his body around until the magnetic needle inside the compass housing lines up over the painted North arrow. When this is accomplished, the orienteer is facing in the direction he wishes to travel to reach the first control point.

The challenge of orienteering is choosing a route of travel from one control point to the next. Facing in the direction of travel to the next point with his map oriented to the land, the orienteer must decide how to get there from where he is standing. A good orienteering course provides at least two alternate routes between control points. The orienteer quickly studies his map to choose the easiest — not always the shortest — route. Perhaps there is a road or trail nearby that goes in the general direction of the next control point. It might be fastest to run down the road a ways and then cut back into the woods instead of running in a straight line through trees and brush all the way. Areas of thick vegetation between the orienteer and his next objective should be noticed and avoided before undue time is lost upon reaching such an area. Other obstacles such as bodies of water or fences must be considered when planning a route of travel.

Precision compass is sometimes the best method of traveling between two points. This means following a straight-line heading all the way to the next control point. If precision compass is not used, the orienteer will travel in more than one direction before reaching the next control point. If this is his choice, he must find an attack point along his route of travel. The attack point is a prominent feature which is used like a checkpoint. The orienteer stops there briefly to take a compass reading to the nearby control point. This gives him a heading to follow straight to the control marker.

Catching features are also useful. A catching feature is located beyond the control point. If the catching feature is reached, the orienteer has passed the control point and must backtrack to find it. The catching feature should also be an easily distinguishable feature.

*In determining next point, compass housing is rotated until the painted North needle inside the housing is parallel to magnetic North lines on the map. Bearing is read across from the direction of the travel arrow.*

Finding each control point is a unique challenge. The orienteer must continuously make quick decisions about what route to take between points. He must also be able to keep track of his location at all times. Reading by thumb is a method of tracking one's progress. The map is folded so the orienteer can run his thumb along his route of travel always pinpointing his exact location on the map.

As the orienteer races through the woods he depends upon both his intelligence and his physical abilities to locate control markers in rapid succession. The beautiful natural surroundings and the challenge of the sport stimulate both the expert and novice.

While competitive orienteering may appear to have little practical application to serious backpacking, it does improve one's familiarity and abilities in the use of map and compass. As outlined in the chapter on maps and their uses, such abilities can save one a great deal of grief in the field. Thus, this type of orienteering can be fun, it can add to your knowledge and — if you want to take a break during your hike — it can be used with other backpackers so that all may improve their capabilities.

*Orienteer holds his compass in his palm, then turns his body until magnetic North needle lines up directly with painted North needle inside the compass housing. This allows one to face in direction of the preset bearing.*

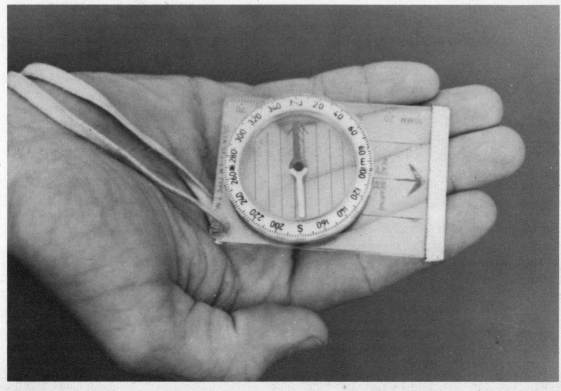

# CHAPTER 11

Rough water, indicated by the whitecaps, usually means rocks not far below the surface. Special canoe designs and handling are required for getting safely through this type of water. Pick areas clear of white water.

# CANOES

## What Better Way To "Take A Break" Than To Pile Yourself And Your Pack Inside A Canoe, And Let The River Do Your Walking.

THE AVERAGE backpacker might never consider the possibilities of combining his backpacking journey with a canoe expedition. Yet the opportunity does exist to do just that, at a gain of immeasurable enjoyment.

It's difficult to view a river without seeing yourself floating leisurely down the middle of it, pack securely stowed, the world seemingly at your beck and call. The canoe greatly expands your opportunities to get away from civilization, taking you to areas you otherwise might never

see. Large enough to carry all of your equipment for an extended stay, the canoe of today is also easy to carry. You can take it almost anywhere, without the concern of an available launch site. And a well made canoe should handle almost all water conditions you will encounter, from swift moving currents to quiet backwaters.

To choose the canoe that will offer you the greatest enjoyment, you must first determine your needs, and the frequency with which you intend on using it. Weigh such factors as how much cargo space you will require, how many people you expect to bring along, and your own physical abilities. As lightweight as today's canoe is, it still must be portaged, and the average fourteen-foot canoe will weigh between fifty and sixty pounds, a weight best shared with a fellow backpacker.

Once you have determined your needs you can then look to design. Your first consideration will probably be of hull materials and styles. For the most part, hull materials generally are restricted to fiberglass, aluminum, Royalex or Kevlar. Which you should buy will be a matter of price and performance. Among the various materials, aluminum has been around the longest, one exception being the old wood or birchbark canoe famed in Indian history.

Today a birchbark canoe is nearly impossible to find; the cost and difficulty of construction are among the reasons, as well as the fact the lack of strength left makers looking for better materials. Birchbark gave way first to canvas and then to cedar and mahogany, and the production of wood canoes has become an art. Skilled craftsmen must begin by cutting the canoe's ribs, then steaming each one into proper shape. They must work carefully, creating a canoe from the inside out. It takes many years of practice and many hours of work to produce the glistening, woodgrained canoe, and because of the time and experience involved, is expensive. For the experienced backpacker/canoeist, the wooden canoe may be ideal. For those of us less experienced, it may prove a lost expense. We would be wise to look instead to the more durable, less aesthetic aluminum canoes.

Late in the 1940s, Grumman introduced the aluminum canoe, made of airplane-type aluminum, with a tensile strength of T-6. Unlike the wooden canoe, these aluminum craft have the distinct advantage of resisting waterlogging. The hull never needs refinishing. Today Grumman canoes are among the finest canoes you can purchase, their 6061 marine aluminum alloy is stretch-formed, heat-treated and age-hardened to near perfection.

Due to mass production, the aluminum canoe is far less expensive than the wooden version, and even more

*Canoes such as this, made of Kevlar, are extremely light, but strong. The material originally was developed by DuPont for use in the aerospace field; it's easily portaged.*

*If the backpacker chooses to break up his trip by doing part of it on water, he can fish for his dinner, but he also has to consider the additional space and weight that paddles, lifejackets, and other equipment entail.*

For effortless canoeing, the Dolphin Princess model has an electric motor for pushing you along the bayou. (Below) Aluminum still is the most popular material for today's canoes, but one should remember to carry a repair kit.

important, when overturned, is self-rescuing in that a person can right the canoe, then empty the water from it. This capability is one of the major features of today's canoe, regardless of the hull material used.

Royalex canoes contain their own unicellular foam core for canoe flotation. The closed-cell foam acts as tiny air sacs to buoy the canoe, making it impossible to sink. Royalex, produced by Uniroyal, is a relatively new hull material, offering a vinyl/ABS/foam/ABS/vinyl structure. As mentioned, a major feature of the material is its foam core, but that is not the only unique feature of Royalex.

Lining either side of the foam is a material known by the designation ABS. A compounded plastic material, ABS gets its name from its three major components: Acrylonitrile, an acrylic-based plastic similar to plexiglass; Butadiene, an organic, rubbery material like that used in tire tread compounds; and Styrene, a common low-grade plastic used for clear plastic cups. Various manufacturers use ABS, altering the percentage ratio of the three compounds, to produce materials of varying degrees of brittleness and flexibility.

According to the folks at Blue Hole Canoe Company,

*If a base camp is set up near a stream, a canoe can be ideal for resupplying the camp or making emergency trips out of the wilderness. The convenience of water transportation for such needs adds to such an outing.*

146

ABS is considered on the high end of available plastics, called an engineering plastic because of its high–strength properties. The telephone casing that you use every day is made from ABS, as is you son's football helmet. There is a drawback to ABS, however, in that it tends to decompose in sunlight. Thus, it must be protected against ultraviolet light by coating its exposed sides. In Royalex hulls that protection is provided by an outer vinyl layer fused to the ABS in processing. The vinyl gives the Royalex both protection and its color.

Crashing against hidden rocks in rivers, the backpacker begins to appreciate another aspect of the Royalex hull, its durability. The foam core, actually another layer of ABS transformed into a cellular layer by processing, absorbs impact and spreads the load, preventing splitting of the hull, leaving more of a dent. Because the hull is more flexible, it is also less rigid to paddle. Where rough waters are the major encounter, it may not be the material of choice; Kevlar may be.

Kevlar, according to Mad River Canoe Company, is a high-strength, high-modulus inorganic fiber produced by Du Pont. Extremely light but strong, the material originally was designed for use in the aerospace field, where strength and light weight were critical. Kevlar canoes provide less weight and easier portage than do the Royalex canoes, but also require more maintenance and care.

Once you have chosen the hull material you require, you must look to hull design. Again, you will make your choice dependent on the type of water you will encounter most often. Canoes may have flat or rounded bottoms, with or without keels. For rough water the flat-bottom design can be a problem. It has a tendency to react heavily to wave action, tipping to the angle of the wave. For rough water travel, you will need a canoe with a round or, even better, a V-shaped hull. Round-bottom hulls allow you to swerve in

In making a portage between waterways, it is the common practice to strap the pack in the interior of canoe, so one should take into account overall weight of load.

In canoeing, the backpacker must think in terms of weight and balance just as he does in rigging his pack. He must stow his pack and associated gear so that the craft is in balance, gear properly distributed with his own weight.

and out of rough water. The V-hull provides its greatest stability when the water is roughest.

Whether or not to include a keel in your canoe is again dependent on the type of waters you intend to encounter. For most waters, you probably will want a shallow keel. It helps hold a straight course in gusty winds, and seems to skid over rocks much better than does the flat-bottom type. Canoes without keels, however, seem to react better to fast waters, turning more deftly.

As a final consideration to hull design you will want to gauge your need of either a single or double-end canoe. The double-end canoe is said to be more versatile than the single-end canoe for most waters. For use with a motor you will need to purchase a single-end, flat stern model. The use of a motor-driven canoe is not outside the practicality of a backpacker, provided he has a companion, or ideally, several companions to share the load. A fourteen-foot Dolphin electric-powered canoe will weigh about ninety pounds, with a carrying capacity of about six hundred pounds, not including the motor.

In shopping for a canoe, you undoubtedly will have in mind a load limit you feel you must adhere to, and well you should. However, bear in mind that there is no actual load limit for a canoe. What there is is an educated estimate of the weight required to dip the hull beneath the water level. The canoe should not sink at this point, however. The degree of freeboard, how much height of the sidewall is left above the water line, will reduce as the weight content is increased. The greater the load, the deeper the canoe will ride in the water, and the "loggier" it will handle.

Among the primary features to seek in a canoe is a high degree of flotation. All good canoes have a self-flotation capability, even when completely swamped, which is why you want to remain with your capsized craft until you can safely reach dry land. If you expect to encounter rough waters you should, however, provide additional flotation. Simple flotation devices you can add include inner tubes, inflatable bags, blocks of foam. Try to keep the carrying weight of these items down, if you can. An inner tube, for instance, will need to be filled at a gas station prior to your trip and will weigh considerably more than a self-inflatable bag or a block of foam. Of the three the self-inflatable bag will require the least packing space as well.

In checking for flotation capabilities look also to bailing

Mad River canoe is made of Kevlar. Because of strength, light weight, it is ideal for rough waters such as the Noatiak River in Alaska, where this photograph was taken. Note manner in which backpacking gear has been stowed.

For those who may prefer the convenience and added speed of a motor, the heavy-duty transom on this boat handles a 5-horsepower outboard engine without great difficulty.

In the Michi-Craft, there is longitudinal widening of the hull above the waterline to increase the stability of the canoe, as well as to add strength and rigidity to design.

abilities. Whether water enters your craft because of rough seas or excessive rainfall, you will want to be able to remove this water with reasonable ease. The design of the gunwale, that lip along the top of the sidewalls, will determine your bailing capabilities. Ideally you will have a gunwale whose design includes a wide outer lip, for fending off water spray, and a narrower inner lip, for ease of emptying.

Next consider the placement and design of the canoe's seats. For best handling, the seat should be placed slightly aft of the center thwart. The seats, themselves, should be comfortable, placed low enough to maintain craft stability, yet high enough to allow free kneeling when desired. You'll find seats made of wood, aluminum, and cane for the most part. Cane is probably the most comfortable, allowing for ventilation beneath you and the opportunity for water to

If a portage is required, one will find it better to have two people: one to carry packs, other to portage.

drain off easily.

The only way to master the technique of paddling is to get into your canoe and paddle it. It isn't difficult, once you understand how the system works, but allow yourself a couple of tries before you take off for the unknown.

Based on the push-pull motion, the pull of the paddle against the water is what moves the canoe. Alternating to the left and right side of the boat (port and starboard) keeps the canoe in a fairly straight course. A series of strokes on the left will turn the craft to the right; strokes on the right move the craft in a counterclockwise direction. For best control and stability in rough waters, it is recommended that you paddle from a kneeling position.

Since a canoe is propelled by paddling, it is best to carry a spare paddle. For backpackers this is probably impractical. The next best solution is a quality paddle, and a roll of duct tape for emergencies. Although you will find paddles made of various types of material, for greatest strength to weight, the paddle of choice seems to be ash.

Although the United States is criss-crossed with thousands of miles of rivers and streams, the time will come when you will need to portage your canoe over land, to carry it. For this reason you will want your canoe to include a yoke. A yoke is a bar spanning the width of the canoe, placed about the center of gravity, designed to include a curved center section that will curve around the

*Flat-bottom canoes are ideal for smooth water, but in rough water, they can react heavily. Also, canoes without keels tend to operate better in fast water, allowing better maneuverability in areas that may have rocks.*

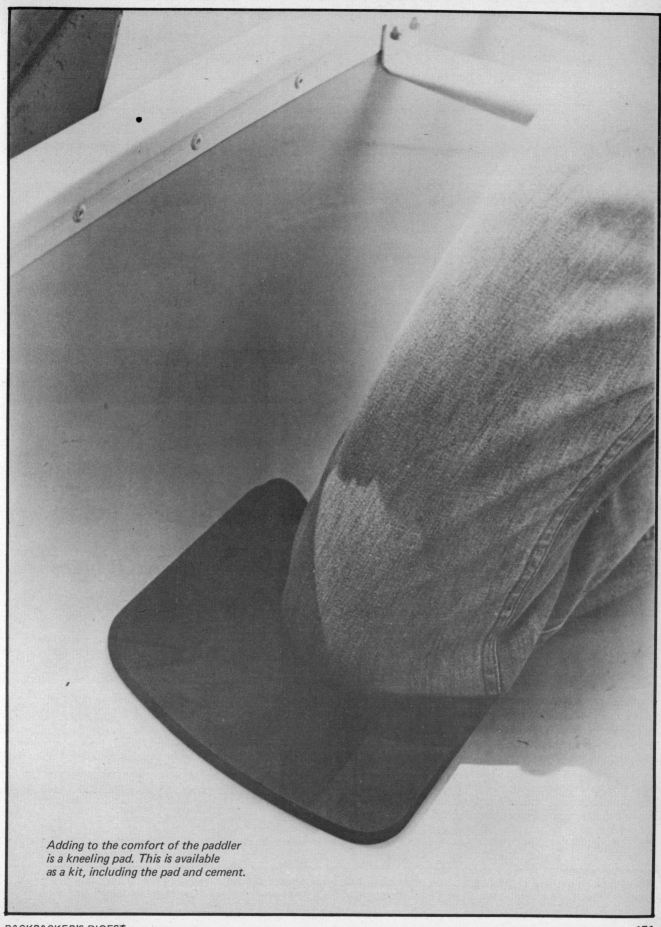

*Adding to the comfort of the paddler
is a kneeling pad. This is available
as a kit, including the pad and cement.*

*While backpackers tend to think of safety in other areas, they sometimes forget the dangers of water. This Extra-Sport PFD (personal flotation device) sells for $36-plus. Again, one must provide room for such in planning trip.*

*One must keep in mind that a canoe does not have the same construction as an ice-breaker. Care must be taken in handling the light craft, if one is not to suffer the serious consequence of having to walk for help or worse.*

neck. The yoke is used to carry the canoe from one body of water to another, and places the load on the shoulders, rather than on the spine, making it much easier to carry. Even easier is sharing the load with a fellow backpacker, each man carrying an end. Backpacks can be placed inside the canoe if secured in place. For single-man portaging, you will need to keep your backpack on your back. Not only does the upside-down position of the portage make carrying the pack inside the canoe impractical, but the pack may offer some padding against the canoe.

In streams too rough to navigate, you might consider lining your craft. Lining, as the term implies, means attaching a length of line to each end of the canoe, then guiding the craft through the rough waters while you are safely standing on dry land. Lining takes a lot of practice, and should be mastered well in advance of your journey if you intend to use it.

Regardless of how well made your canoe happens to be, the chances of never damaging it are remote. There are too many hidden rocks and shoals to expect this. For aluminum canoes, you are likely to encounter dents and dislodged rivets. Carry along replacement rivets and a hammer. Also carry along that roll of duct tape we mentioned earlier. For splicing broken paddles and thwarts it is hard to beat.

Fiberglass canoes may be punctured, requiring an application of fiberglass patching. Repair kits are available

Blue Hole Canoes, a Tennessee manufacturer, has come up with a collapsible canoe that is easily transported and can be put into shape for launching in a matter of minutes. When ready for the water, the canoe weighs only 70 pounds.

154

*The Blue Hole collapsible model has a covering of integral vinyl sheeting inside and out. It's available in six color combos.*

from most marine dealers or from the manufacturers of major brand canoes. Be sure to find out how to repair your craft before you go into the field, when you've plenty of time to understand the procedures.

As with every sport, canoeing has its own language. Depending on who you talk to, some of the terms may change, but there are several which remain unaffected by geography:

*Bow Plate:* Reinforcements at either end of craft, often containing the canoe's identification number.

*Freeboard:* Measure of sidewall left above the water.

*Gunwale:* Frame along top side of canoe, providing strength and shape.

*Inwale:* Width of lip on the inside of the gunwale, held to a minimum for ease of bailing.

*Length:* Dimension from bow to stern.

*Maneuverability:* Ease with which craft changes direction.

*Outwale:* Width of lip on the outside gunwale, providing deflection of spray away from the craft.

*Rocker:* Amount of curve in the hull from bow to stern.

*Speed:* Straight line speed.

*Thwart:* Braces spanning the width of the craft, used to maintain shape, and provide added strength.

*Tracking:* Tendency to travel in a straight line.

*Volume:* Internal space of a canoe.

*Water-line:* Measurement of how deep the canoe is riding in the water.

# CHAPTER 12

*Contributing many times to being lost — or, at least, of feeling lost — is the fact that due to weather, erosion and other factors, the features of the terrain sometimes will not match those that show on your map if it is old.*

# A MATTER OF SURVIVAL

GETTING LOST is the one problem few people expect to happen; at least not to them. And that's too bad, because if they did consider the possibility they would probably take precautions to avoid it and the nation's search and rescue teams could devote all their time to transportation catastrophes. The fact is anyone can get lost, even the most experienced of backpackers. What should you do if you suddenly found yourself alone and confused?

### What Is Lost?

From Webster's dictionary come the words and phrases that describe lost: "unable to find the way; no longer visible; lacking assurance or self-confidence; helpless; ruined, physically or mentally; desperate." All are words that describe imminent danger, unless you face the problem head

## Admitting You Are Lost May Be The First Step Out Of The Wilderness To Finding Your Way

A small mirror is an item that should be carried in your pack. It can be used for signaling if you are lost or if you have an emergency. (Below) The type of mirror that is favored by many is simply a piece of bright flat metal.

on and take responsible, sensible action. You must begin by admitting you are lost. Say it out loud, not because you expect someone to pop out from among the trees and "find" you, but because you cannot handle being lost until you admit to being so. The act of stating you are lost out loud forces you to accept your problem and clears the way for responsible action.

The next step you must take will be to do nothing. That's not a normal action and you will have to force yourself to do it. The normal, often totally subconscious act is to run; to race after what you think to be your previous direction or landmark you know. That's called panic and it only leads to greater problems the majority of the time. It's certainly possible to run blindly into help, but the odds are against you. More probably your flight will take you into greater danger, perhaps hurt you along the way.

What then, do you do when you discover you are lost? Sit down! Right where you are. Make yourself a cup of coffee if you've brought along your supplies; you should at least have a day pack with you. Don't even think about being lost. Concentrate, very hard if you must, on the activities of a local squirrel or an industrious bee. You've admitted you are lost. You needed to do that to clear your mind for constructive thought. But don't dwell on it; that's when panic sets in.

It's a good idea to remain seated for a minimum of an hour. Toward the latter part of that sixty minutes your mind will begin to yield to reason. You'll begin to remember the

*An old familiar technique for calling for aid is to scratch a message in the sand or perhaps in the snow. However, the message being scratched here is not sufficiently large to be noted by an aircraft that is flying high overhead.*

past, the trail you passed an hour ago or the stream not fifteen minutes behind you. Those are landmarks you can find on your map, if you've remembered to bring it along — and you should. It's one of the ten essential items in your emergency pack that you will carry with you no matter how extensive or limited your hike.

If, after the hour has passed, you honestly believe you can find your original position, the place where you did know your location, then try to return to it. But do not waste more than an hour in doing so. Mark your route as you go along so that you can return to your original spot if you do not find your location. A stick carving a line along behind you will give you a trail to follow when you return, and will wash away with the first rain, leaving the land undisturbed.

After a reasonable period of time — say a couple of hours — if you still do not know where you are then you must take steps to shelter and feed yourself. Evaluate your needs. Those needs, in order of importance, are: fresh air, shelter, water, and food. Fresh air should be no problem. Shelter should not be either, if you've included another essential item in your emergency pack: a lightweight tarp. If not, you must make a temporary shelter from your surroundings. It's possible that you will find a cave nearby. If so — once you've made sure no other animal has laid claim to the same shelter — you can consider using this as a temporary shelter. Otherwise you will have to erect something. The shelter that you build need not be elaborate. In fact, the simpler it is to build the better off

you are. You can conserve energy for something else.

To be effective, a shelter must meet certain criteria. It must keep you dry and warm. It should provide sufficient space for you to lie down and rest, or to sit up and eat. It need not be large. In fact, the cozier it is, the easier it will be for you to warm yourself, by body heat if nothing else. A better method, however, is a fire.

### Fires

During routine camping, whether or not to build a fire is often a matter of governing regulations. If the rules say no fires, you don't build an open fire. If there are no rules against it, then the warmth and emotional salve of a campfire is hard to beat. When survival is the consideration, the overwhelming necessity of warmth may negate the governing regulations. Most officials would rather you did not become a national statistic either and will accept a survival fire instead of succumbing to hypothermia.

In making your fire, keep it small and as visible as possible. A campfire, especially in an area where campfires are not permitted, is an excellent way of attracting attention. Use small pieces of broken tree limbs and dry leaves to start your fire. Those waterproof matches in your emergency pack have been stashed there for just this purpose. Coated with melted candle wax or fingernail polish they've remained isolated against past rains, waiting for a time like this to support you.

If, for some reason, you failed to waterproof your matches

*Instead of a small message calling for help, one should find a flat area and use his boot, or if possible, even a shovel to make the plea sufficiently large that it can be seen from a distance or by searchers in overhead planes.*

*Then there is the old saw about moss always growing on the North side of a tree, but if the tree is in constant shade, the moss may grow on any side. However, seeking out heavy growth has a plus, as it usually indicates presence of water.*

*If lost, find a streambed and follow it downward. Such waterways, even if dry, ultimately lead to civilization, as farmers, ranchers and even town builders tend to build in areas where there is sufficient water for their needs.*

it's much easier to sleep when you are warm than when your body is shaking with the cold. It's important that you be able to sleep. Not only will you be able to travel farther the day after a good night's sleep, but your mind will be able to function much clearer. Before you turn in check to be sure that you have plenty of firewood at hand. As the fire dies down and your body begins to cool, you will automatically awaken, only to put a fresh log or so on the fire and return to sleep.

Put your fire near the entrance to your shelter, but not so near as to prevent the circulation of fresh air. Clear the area around the fire for at least ten feet to prevent your campfire from turning into a forest fire. The forest fire will attract attention, but it is doubtful that attention will do you any good, posthumously.

you may still be able to use them. Otherwise you will have to find another method of starting a fire. The old Boy Scout method of rubbing two sticks against each other is said to work, but it takes a lot of time and energy. Better to start your fire while the sun is still up. Use a magnifying glass to concentrate the sun's rays to a small pile of shavings. Once the shavings catch, you can add additional fuel that you have piled nearby.

You'll want to keep your fire burning throughout the night. Not only does a warm fire chase off hypothermia, but

### Water

Once you've taken care of providing yourself with external shelter and warmth you must consider your two internal needs: food and water. Of the two, water is the most important. As mentioned previously, you can survive without food for several weeks, but only for a few days before the effects of dehydration begin to take their toll. Your body normally requires an average of one-half pint of water daily. If need be you can survive on considerably less for an extended period of time. If you have refilled your canteen at

*Matches are essential to everyday backpacking and especially necessary to one who is lost for warmth, cooking, signal needs. Coat your matches with candle wax or buy readymade waterproof matches, store in watertight container.*

every acceptable location, you should have a fairly large supply of water. Most canteens hold a full quart of water, some even more, so you should have several day's emergency supply of water in your canteen. Check your supply and be realistic about your needs. Avoid both the temptation to guzzle water — while you can — and to stringently ration yourself to the point that you begin to suffer from dehydration. (See chapter 14.) Survival time varies with the climate, but you can reasonably expect to survive with little lasting difficulty for a full week on about a half pint of water daily. Under no circumstances should you attempt to go a full day without any water, if you have an option. Such a Viking feat will only hasten the effects of dehydration. Look for other sources of liquids, in the food you eat or that which is growing wild around you.

### Food

While there is little as likely to breed contentment as the satisfied feeling of ingesting a good meal, most of us can manage quite nicely without food, or with a drastic reduction in food intake, for a week or longer. Countless tales have been told of individuals who, whether for political or personal reasons, have fasted for a week or longer with no apparent residual effects. However, when lost is not the time to begin fasting. The mental anguish is not normally worth the full feed bag. What you want to do is go easy on your food supply. Eat frequent short snacks rather than a few full meals. Try to

reduce your intake of proteins, they are said to increase thirst. You'll also want to go easy on the dehydrated foods; not because they cause added thirst, but because they require water to prepare. Save the hot, freeze-dried beef stew for your evening meal, when you've finished erecting your temporary shelter, the fire is cared for, and you've nothing to do but plot your next day's moves.

Look for fresh berries along the way, but be sure that they are edible. If in doubt it is better to avoid them than to risk the possibility of nausea which will only increase the effects of both hunger and thirst.

In your emergency pack you should carry with you

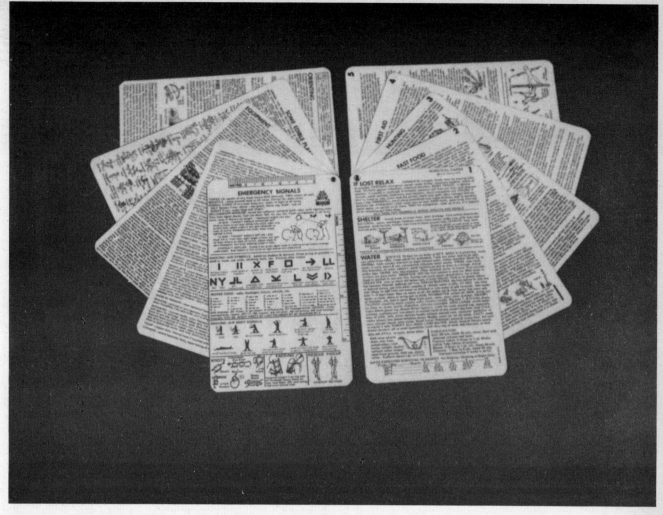

*These five plastic cards supplied by Survival Cards of Bloomington, Indiana, offer vital info on emergency first aid, signals, sources of food and water. They are carried easily and can be a valuable addition to anyone's gear.*

sources of instant energy: candy, boxes of raisins, cereals. Raisins have the added advantage of satisfying, if only temporarily, thirst. Hard candies will also satisfy thirst for a period of time, activating your salivary glands as you suck on them. Gum may ease both hunger and thirst. Any of those items weigh little, so you can carry several rations in your emergency pack.

### Tips For Traveling

While it is usually better to remain in one spot when lost, and let the rescue units come to you, it may become impossible for you to do so. If you feel you must try to find help, try to be logical about your sources. Before leaving camp climb the nearest hill that will afford a view of the terrain around you. Even a tree will do, provided you are agile enough to climb one without falling out. What you are looking for from your lofty window is anything that will lead you to civilization: A trail ahead, a stream, perhaps someone else's campsite. Plan out your route, carefully. Then record it on a piece of paper which you can leave behind for possible rescuers. Once you leave camp stick with your intended route. It will do you little good to leave a message telling of your destination if you fail to follow your route.

In your travels stay away from dense foliage as much as is possible. Remain in the open, where you are highly visible. Wear bright colored clothing, if you have it. Sing, talk to yourself, make noise. You are not trying to sneak up on someone. You *want* to be noticed.

Try to avoid traveling in circles; if you have a compass this will be easy. If not, you might want to consider using landmarks for direction. Select an object ahead of you, then look for another object half that distance that will align with

*It is an ideal situation if your items essential to the problem of survival can be segregated and kept together in a single bag. Such a kit should contain compass, map, flashlight, dry socks, candles, matches, batteries, knife, waterproof matches, a canteen, a whistle for signaling, as well as other items you feel necessary to the terrain.*

you. Keeping the distant object in sight, walk toward the nearer object. Once you reach your objective, look beyond the farther object to one beyond it, then try again. Your second object has now become the nearer and you will walk toward it. In national forests a few miles or less of this type of travel should bring you to a trail, stream or road.

If you come first to a trail or road, stay on it. Do not divert from it if you can avoid it. Camp alongside it. Roads are placed where they are because they are needed and eventually someone else is going to need your road. When they do, you will be found. If you must leave the road to find shelter, try to leave a message. On paved roads, a rock will often function as a piece of chalk to spell out your dilemma. On dirt roads, use rocks or a stick to draw out your message. Searchers or fellow backpackers may see it.

If you come across a stream, follow it downstream. Civilization is normally densest at the bottom of mountains or hills. All streams run downhill, so follow the flow of the water.

## Signals

Eventually you may have the opportunity to signal someone of your location. There are a number of methods available to you. If you have a mirror — there are a variety of metal mirrors available that will slip easily into your emergency pack — you can signal ground or air rescue units by bouncing the sun's rays off it. At night you can use your flashlight, also an emergency pack item. Use the flashlight sparingly, however, and be sure that you have packed spare bulbs and batteries. If you do not have a mirror for signaling, try a belt buckle, knife blade, the metal adornment on your pack or canteen, anything that will reflect light. Either at night or during the day, a fire can be an effective method of signaling for help. Dark smoke usually means trouble. So, also, does a series of three fires in a row. In fact, three of anything can often tip people that you are in need of help. Even three candles, burning a short distance apart, can attract help, especially if placed at the center of a clearing. Candles have many and varied uses and should also be a part of your

*A reflective blanket can serve a double purpose. It can be seen from distances as great as four miles, when the sun is shining on it. It also can be used in survival situations, since it retains 80 percent of the body's heat.*

In an effort to find your home base, if lost, climb the nearest hill that affords a view of the surrounding terrain. (Below) If possible, remain in the open, where it will be much easier for search parties to locate your presence.

*If you decide that you really are lost, don't panic. Instead, sit down and consider your options. Attempt to relax until such time as you decide that you can think clearly and can make rational plans, logical decisions.*

emergency pack. For starting damp wood fires, there's nothing better than the constant flame of a candle and it's amazing the amount of light you can receive from one. You can even heat a small cup of water over a candle, enough to provide you a cup of hot chocolate or hot water for your dehydrated foods.

### Ten Essential Items

Throughout this chapter we have referred to the "ten essential items" of an emergency pack. While authorities will differ slightly on every item to be included in that list of ten, most items are universally agreed upon. In your emergency pack you will want to have: A water supply, waterproof matches, a flashlight with spare bulbs and batteries, candles, a pocket knife, map and compass, spare clothing, food. In addition you will need a basic first-aid kit. If space allows, add to that list a section of nylon cord for erecting temporary shelter, a shrill whistle for attracting attention, and sunglasses for bright sun or snowfall.

### The Buddy System

As a final thought consider the advantages of backpacking with a friend. While it is realized that most backpackers are into backpacking because of the opportunity offered to get away from people and problems, the practice of packing with a friend or two has great advantages. When lost, you have someone to share the burden of finding your way. If you find yourself in physical trouble, unable to continue, there is someone to go on ahead for help. Anxiety, fear and panic are much easier to avoid when shared by two.

Whether packing alone or with friends be sure to let someone back in civilization know where you are headed and when you expect to return. Once in route, do not deviate from that destination. If it becomes necessary to call on officials for help in locating you, these friends will direct the rescue units to the area you have given as your destination. So, if lost, take heart. Rescue will be on the way. For the most part these are men and women who know how to care for people in the field. They have been specially trained and will find you. Just give them the time and be willing to wait. That is, after all, the most difficult part of a rescue; waiting!

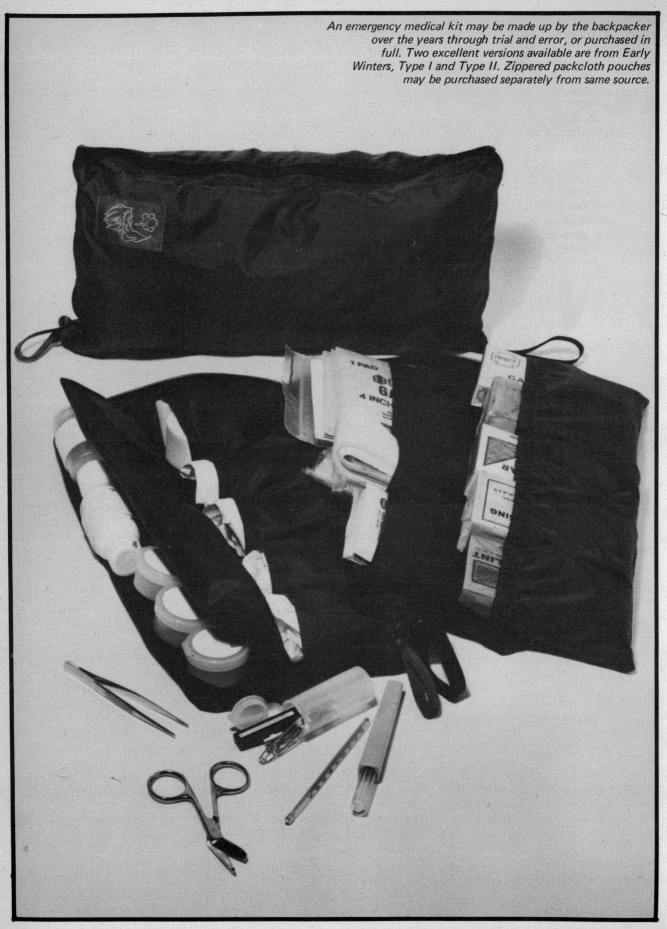

An emergency medical kit may be made up by the backpacker over the years through trial and error, or purchased in full. Two excellent versions available are from Early Winters, Type I and Type II. Zippered packcloth pouches may be purchased separately from same source.

# CHAPTER 13

NOTHING CAN TAKE the fun out of a backpacking journey quicker than an injury. It's extremely difficult to see the beauty of a waterfall through the pain of a broken ankle. Mountains and wild rivers are a basically foreign environment to most of us. That is one of the attractions that draw us to them; the prospect of entering the unknown, roughing it for an abbreviated period of time amid some of nature's finest terrain. But that same majestic mountain that promises adventure and excitement can offer serious injury to the backpacker who temporarily lets down his guard. Here then are some suggestions for making your journey a safe one, and for handling emergencies should they appear.

# ANSWERS FOR DISASTER

## Even Backpackers Suffer Injuries, So Think Ahead As To How To Minimize The Problem

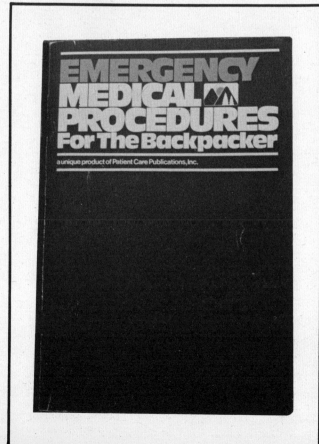

### First Aid Steps Before You Leave Home

In planning your backpacking trip, *plan* on an emergency. If the emergency never arises you'll not likely mind the extra weight you've packed in your first-aid kit. In fact, this is one of the few extra weights you'll find comforting on your journey.

A backpacker's first-aid kit, to be effective, need not be elaborate. The simpler and lighter in weight you keep your kit the more likely you are to avoid leaving it behind on those short day excursions. Accept the fact that a basic first-aid kit is a necessity, not a luxury, of backpacking. *Never* be tempted to leave it behind. All those seemingly reasonable excuses for omitting it from your pack will mean little when disaster strikes. With the variety of products available to you today, you can make that kit as lightweight as you like.

### The Basic Kit

The first item you will need for your first-aid kit is a container to hold all your supplies. It will do no good to carry water soluble supplies, however effective they night be, if you get them wet and destroy them. You can purchase watertight plastic boxes to hold your first-aid gear, or you can improvise with items commonly found at home. Plastic sandwich bags are excellent containers for bandages, tapes, aspirin tablets, etc. Use the thinner, flexible type that will wrap snugly around your items. Design or purchase a pouch to hold these supplies securely in place and you'll find the one item you need much more quickly. One-inch-wide elastic, sewn down to make expandable tubes, usually works well, and costs very little. A one-dollar package will supply all the elastic needed for your kit.

Fragile items, those packed in glass containers or those easily broken, such as thermometers, must be protected. You probably don't need a thermometer on your trip, but if you feel you must carry it, place it inside a toothbrush case, wrapped in a paper towel to prevent it banging against the sides of the container.

You can reduce the weight of your kit by removing most items from their original packing. You do not need the box

*Prior to any outing, the backpacker is wise to take a course in first aid and be familiar with the contents of a good field medical manual, such as at left.*

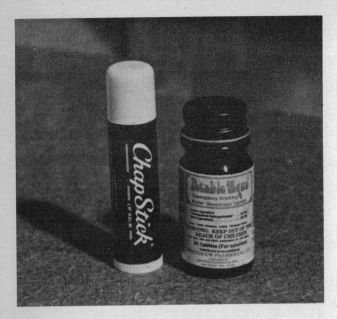

Two basic items for every outing are some sort of lip balm and emergency water purification tablets.

your sterile bandages come in. It only adds weight and increases space requirements. Do not, however, remove the inner wrapping. You want the bandage to remain sterile before use. Place it inside one of your sandwich bags and secure the bag, using tape or a rubber band.

Items such as water purification tablets, aspirin, iodine are often packaged in glass containers. Transfer these items to plastic bottles, being sure to label each bottle correctly and immediately to prevent misapplication on the trail.

Although your first-aid kit may vary in content due to your personal needs, there are a number of items that should be included in every kit:

Band-Aids or equivalent; a half-dozen or so, of several sizes.

Adhesive tape; preferably waterproof, one-inch width.

Two-inch-wide elastic bandage; to handle sprains. The two-inch width can be used on arms, hands or legs with equal ease.

Sterile gauze pads; a couple of sizes. At least three of two different sizes should meet your needs.

One roll of sterile gauze bandage; two-inch size.

A half-dozen pre-moistened towelettes; for cleaning the wound.

Antibiotic ointment; for treatment of cuts and burns. Leave it in its original tube, but place it inside a sandwich bag in case the tube ruptures at altitude.

Contents of homemade first aid kit may weigh as much as six ounces when left in original packaging.

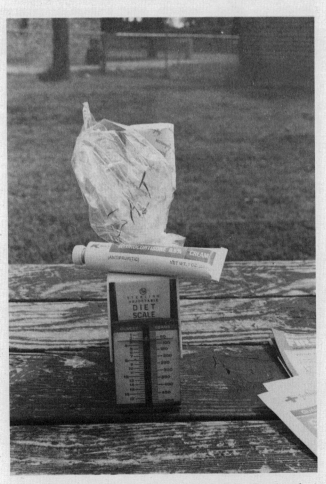

Same items as shown at left with packages removed and left behind. Total pack weight is now only 2½ ounces.

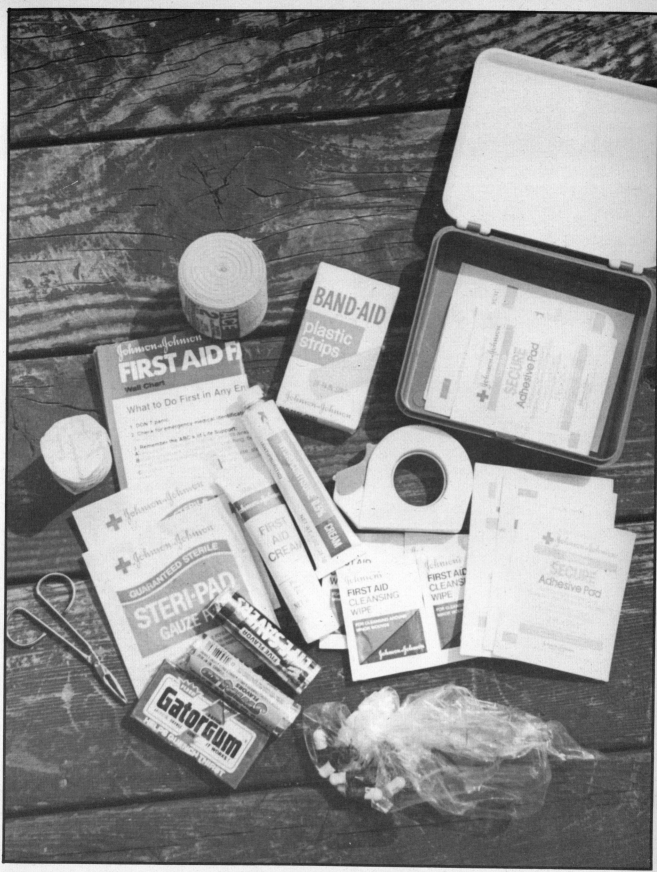

*Basic first aid kit may be made up to suit the climate, conditions the backpacker expects to encounter, all fitting into small plastic container. Included are prescribed medications, elastic bandages, tape, gauze, antiseptic wipes, antiseptic cream, absorbent battle dressings, quick-energy sweets. First aid manual should be included.*

An injured or ill victim on the trail may or may not be conscious. Attempt to rouse the victim with words or action; the person may tell you what's wrong.

An all-purpose topical cream; for treatment of insect bites, poison ivy, poison oak.

Aspirin.

Water purification tablets.

Tweezers and a needle; for removing splinters.

Salt tablets; for use in extremely hot environments.

Snakebite kit; in snake country.

Sunburn preventive ointment.

A first-aid manual.

Small pair of scissors.

Any medications you are required to take on a regular basis. Each backpacker should carry his or her own supplies.

There are a number of additional items you may wish to include in your kit. Items such as moleskin for blisters, a laxative, antacid tablets, a disposable razor blade; all have a legitimate place in your kit. Whatever you bring, be sure that you have labeled it fully.

### Basic First Aid Measures

It does little good to carry along a first-aid kit if no one in your party knows how to use the items, or how to provide basic first aid. The American Red Cross offers first-aid classes in most areas, year around, at a nominal charge. Often there is no charge whatsoever. Many community colleges offer classes in emergency medical treatment. If you can, try to attend one of these classes. If you intend to backpack with children,

teach them the basics of first aid. An 8-year-old is as capable of applying a compress bandage as is a 28-year-old, provided someone has shown him how to do so. Conduct your own first-aid classes, in your kitchen or back yard. Let children practice on each other or an you. Pre-pack practice allows you to teach children slowly, at a pace they can readily follow and more easily retain. A child is capable of applying a splint, dressing a wound, even giving CPR (Cardiopulmonary Resuscitation). Do not underestimate his abilities, there may be a time when you will have to depend on the children.

### A Word About Cardiopulmonary Resuscitation

A person's heart or lung action may stop for a number of reasons, not the least of which is a heart attack. Backpackers, especially adults with any sort of responsibility for children or other adults, should take advantage of training in the techniques of cardiopulmonary resuscitation (CPR). In many places the training is free, presented by your local paramedic or firefighter organization. The training is usually prepared and approved by the American Heart Association, although CPR is applicable to other injuries or ailments. The training is rigid, requires a degree of physical dexterity and is administered by qualified personnel. If you pass the practical application test at the end of the training, you'll receive a pocket or wallet card. When miles from any medical facility, it's nice to know your backpacking partner has a card in his pocket.

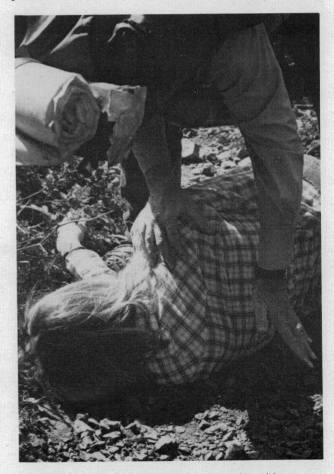

If the victim is choking, lying down, four sharp blows to the upper back may dislodge the obstruction.

Standing, the preferred first-aid for choking is the abdominal thrust. Four upward thrusts with rescuer's hands clasped just above victim's navel are called for.

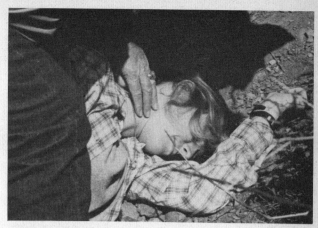

Easiest location to detect pulse is the carotid artery on either side of the victim's neck. Restore breathing first.

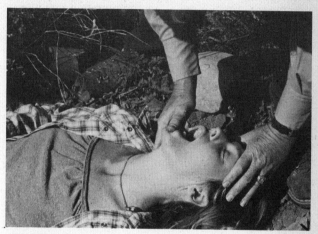

Unconscious, non-breathing victim must have breathing restored at once. Open airway by neck lift, head tilt, or chin lift, head tilt as shown. Try four quick, full breaths. If airway is blocked, keep trying. Seconds count!

The American Heart Association advises that the first signal of a heart attack is an uncomfortable pressure, squeezing, fullness or pain in the center of the chest; perhaps behind the breastbone, which may spread to the shoulder, neck or arms. The pain may not be as severe as we imagine it ought to be. Other signals include sweating, nausea, shortness of breath and a feeling of weakness.

Learn to recognize these signals in yourself and others.

The victim or suspected victim of a heart attack must immediately stop all activity and sit or lie down. If the pain lasts for two minutes or more, take action to save a life; start CPR or call for emergency medical assistance where available.

If the victims' heart has stopped or he has stopped breathing, restarting these functions must take precedence over all other first-aid measures. Stopping bleeding, setting bones, treating for shock, all take secondary importance if cardiopulmonary action is not resumed within minutes.

The CPR training is available for the asking. Ask your local heart association chapter or fire department about it. Classes are offered with regularity in most communities, including updating and annual retesting. Don't leave home without it.

A common cause of injury in the field is a fall. The backpacker may be unconscious, he may have fractured a bone or perhaps fallen on a tree branch and punctured himself. He may even have stopped breathing. The first step you must take in helping him is to determine the extent of his injuries. If he is conscious he will tell you what he thinks is wrong. If not, you must attempt to discover that for yourself. Check for breathing, pulse, bleeding, and breaks, in that order.

For the packer who has stopped breathing, the first four minutes after respiration ceases is the most important. Restore breathing during that time frame and the likelihood of brain damage is remote. Extend that time frame to ten minutes and the chances of not suffering brain damage are extremely remote. Consequently you must act quickly to get to your injured packer and provide aid. Do not, however, become in such a hurry to help that you wind up a victim yourself. You'll do neither of you any good.

The moment you reach the victim, check for injuries. If he is breathing, do not attempt to roll him over onto his back until you are sure he has no back or neck injuries. If, however, he is not breathing, you must place him on his back to begin CPR. Do so as gently as is possible. Check that he has not choked on something; such as a piece of gum or a snack he was eating before he fell. You must remove any foreign matter, with a finger if necessary, before you begin resuscitation.

Currently considered as the preferred method of clearing

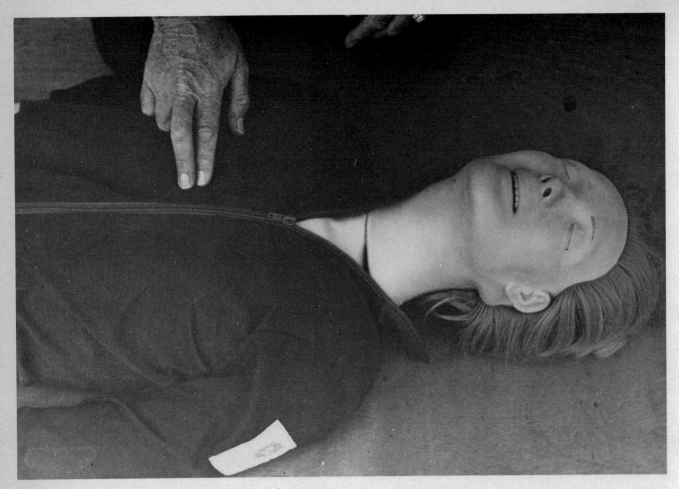

*Care must be taken to correctly locate the sternum before commencing artificial circulation if no pulse can be found. Available training in basic CPR includes practice on realistic dummy, Resus-Anne, under qualified supervision.*

an obstructed airway is the Heimlich maneuver in which you apply either quick upward thrust with the heel of your hand into the upper abdomen or sharp raps on the spine between the shoulder blades. Admittedly such maneuvers may further complicate an abdominal or spinal injury, but you must consider your priorities; that you revive respiration is your *first* priority.

Once the air passage is clear you can begin artificial respiration; the act of introducing fresh air into the victim's respiratory system until normal breathing is resumed. Unless you suspect a neck injury, begin by using one hand to gently lift the back of the victim's neck while pushing the forehead down. Pinch the nostrils closed with the fingers of your top hand, take a deep breath, and with your mouth forming a seal over the victim's mouth, blow air into their lungs. You should be able to see the victim's chest rise with each blow of air. If

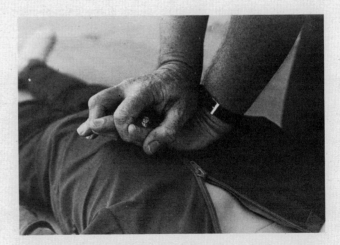

*If no pulse, begin artificial circulation. Hands are clasped as shown; fingers of bottom hand must not press down on sternum or ribs as further injury could result.*

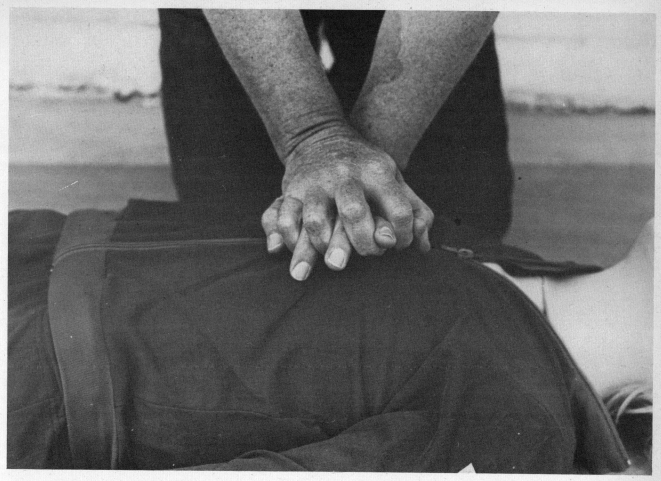

*Arms are straight and locked at elbows as full weight of rescuer's body is brought over victim's chest. If one rescuer, compression rate is prescribed at eighty per minute; fifteen compressions followed by two quick breaths, fifteen compressions, etc. For two rescuers: five compressions, one breath, 60 compressions per minute.*

not, you have yet to clear the airway. Blow an average of twelve bursts per minute of air until the victim is able to breathe on his own.

For children you will follow the same procedure, except that you will place your mouth over both their mouth and nose, and bursts of air will be gentler, at an average of about twenty per minute.

For victims whose hearts have stopped functioning you must simultaneously apply cardiac resuscitation. This procedure is termed cardiopulmonary resuscitation, CPR. Begin by giving artificial respiration as described above. Blow four deep, quick breaths, allowing the victim to expel the air after each breath. Check for a pulse; the easiest location is over the carotid artery at the side of the neck. If there is none, place the heel of your hand over the victim's lower breastbone. Place your second hand over the wrist of the first,

*Correct procedure for artificial breathing has rescuer's mouth completely covering victim's, fingers close off victim's nose. Watch chest for air expansion.*

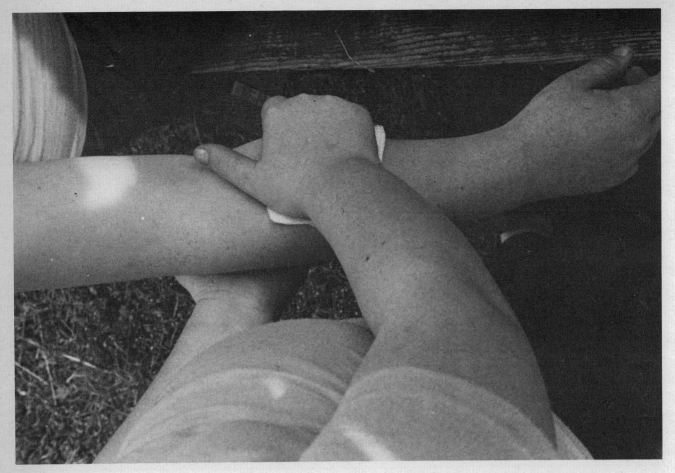

*Most direct method of controlling bleeding is by application of direct pressure. Bandage, cloth handkerchief, shirt or any other handy item may be used as compress. Any wound will result in some shock; watch victim for symptoms.*

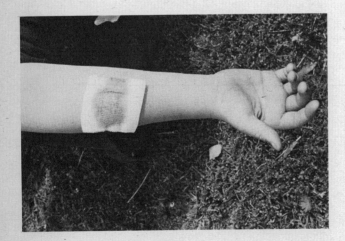

*If bleeding persists through first compress, do not remove from wound. Apply second over first, continue to apply constant pressure until blood flow ceases.*

clasping fingers together. Lean directly over the victim, and with straight-down, straight-arm pressure push the breastbone against the heart. It is the heel of your hands that should be doing the pushing, not the fingers. For children you will use the heel of one hand only.

Continue to compress the breastbone at a rate of about eighty compressions per minute, applying bursts of air about every sixth compression. You should continue CPR until the victim's pulse has returned and breathing is restored, or until help arrives or you are physically unable to continue. Many victims have revived after more than an hour of CPR.

### Control of Bleeding

Once the victim has regained normal breathing patterns you must look to the control of bleeding. Be alert for signs of shock, caused by a large, rapid loss of blood. Try to avoid contaminating the wound. If the wound bleeds readily, the chance of infection will be small, but shock is more probable. If the wound refuses to bleed, there will be less chance of shock, a greater probability of infection.

Of the two concerns, shock and infection, shock is by far the more serious. To control shock you must control bleeding. Remember, it is possible for a backpacker to bleed to death in a short time. Infections will take much longer to cause damage and should place the packer home and within easy reach of medical authorities before symptoms appear.

Your first step, is to stop or at least control bleeding.

First aid for actual or suspected bone fracture is to immobilize break area. Use any handy materials to form splint; sticks, padded with heavy socks may be used.

*In this simulated case of arm fracture, splint sticks should have been broken off shorter as sharp ends are potentially dangerous. Arm is being wrapped, not too tightly, with wide elastic bandage.*

Ninety-five percent of the time you can do so by applying direct pressure to the wound. From your first-aid pack remove a sterile compress, place it over the wound, and hold it in place with the palm of your hand. If you do not have a compress, use an extra piece of clothing, the sleeve of the shirt you are wearing, or even your bare hand will do, at least until you can find something else to use. Resist the temptation to peek at the wound after a few minutes to see how it's doing. What you are attempting to do is to retard the flow of blood until a clot can form. Once you have the compress in place, secure it there with wide strips of tape or gauze, being careful not to tie the compress so tightly that

you cut off circulation to the limb. Watch for coloring and temperature in the limb below the compress. If the compress is too tight the skin beneath it will turn red and cool to your touch. Loosen the compress, even if some bleeding resumes.

If blood flow continues and begins to saturate your first dressing, leave the dressing in place and apply a second dressing over it.

Is it necessary to consider applying a tourniquet? Almost always the answer will be no. The decision to apply a tourniquet indicates that you accept the loss of a limb as necessary in the survival of the victim. It is, in fact, a last alternative.

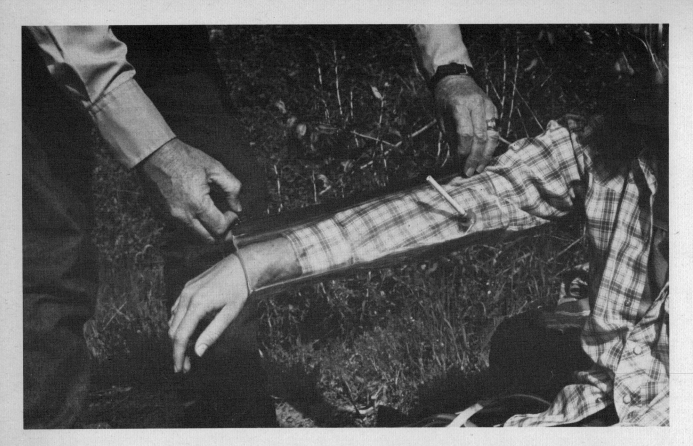

Lightweight, easily packed pneumatic splints are available at many medical supply houses or large drug stores. The backpack leader is well advised to carry a set. Plastic splint is placed over arm, zipped up and inflated as shown.

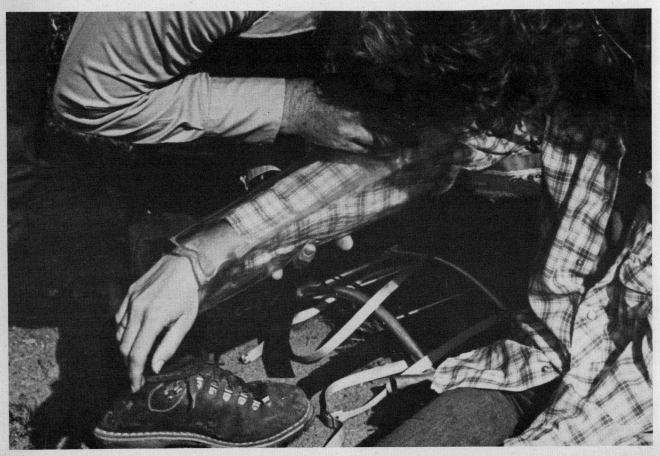

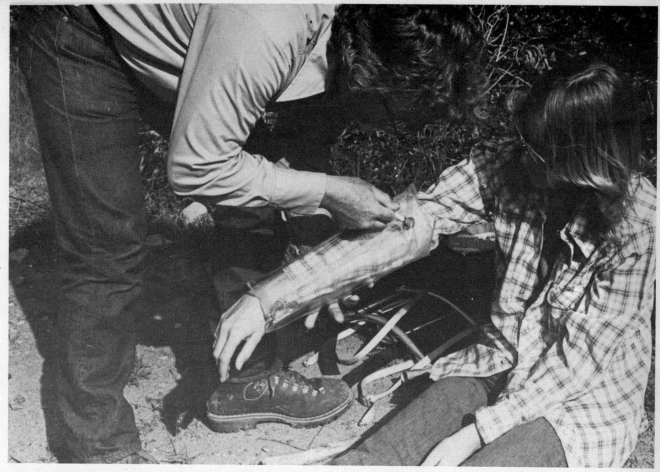

*After plastic splint is inflated, air tube is screwed shut, immobilizing, in this case, the victim's forearm. Broken or dislocated joint should not be reset by other than trained medical personnel. Remember to check for area swelling.*

In the event the wound has been caused by a puncture you probably will have little or no bleeding. What you may have, however, is the foreign object (stick, tree limb, etc.) still embedded in the body. Do not attempt to remove it. Instead, place padding around the object to hold it steady, and seek help.

### Broken Bones

Perhaps the most common of backpacking accidents is the sprained or broken bone, especially of the foot or leg. Whether a break or sprain, movement is going to be severely handicapped. Your task is to protect the injured limb from further damage.

The traditional method of treating both sprains and fractures has been to splint the injured limb. In the field you probably will not have a set of splints with you. You will, instead, have to make do with the nature-supplied splints. Look for reasonably straight tree branches. They may not look as attractive as a professional splint, but are every bit as effective, reducing the movement of a limb and easing accompanying pain. Attach the splint to the injured arm or leg by gauze from your emergency kit. Pad the space between the injured limb and the tree branch with a pair of socks or a folded towel and you'll get even better support with a great increase in comfort.

With a bone fracture there is always a danger of nerve or blood vessel damage. Often the damage is caused by the well meaning first aider who, after applying the splint, fails to check periodically for swelling. Whether broken or sprained you can expect an injured limb to swell. Thus it will be necessary to loosen the ties holding the splint in place after a period of time. Failure to do so can result in an unintentional tourniquet if swelling is of great enough degree.

Never attempt to reset or relocate a dislocated joint. There's a good chance that rather than helping yourself you will only be compounding the damage. Leave relocation to trained medical personnel.

If a sling is needed to support an injury to the arm or shoulder, you have an ample supply of possible slings with you. You don't necessarily call them slings. You're probably more accustomed to referring to them as day or fanny packs, as belts or trousers. The point is any of these items can be fashioned into a reasonably comfortable sling. You might also consider using the victim's shirt or jacket as a sling. Simply slide the wounded arm inside the jacket, buttons holding it secure.

### Burns

Burns are another common problem for backpackers, who camp without benefit of pot holders and heat-resistant pot handles. These burns may be of first, second or third degree.

First-degree burns are a common complaint among

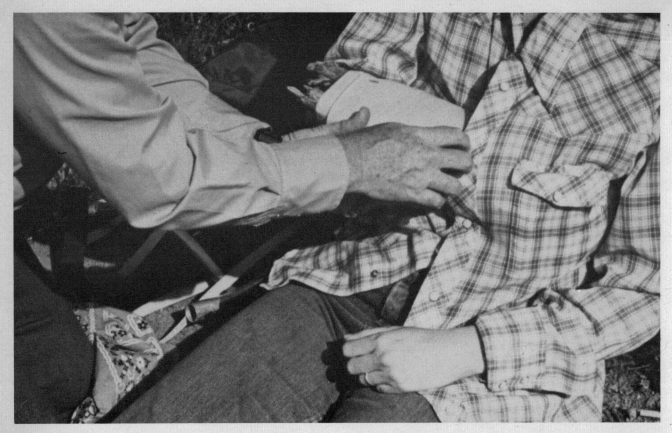

In the absence of any sling, the splinted arm may be placed inside the victim's shirt or jacket to reduce pain, swelling and movement. Victim may now travel.

A dislocated shoulder, sprained muscle or other injury may be partially abrogated by placing the arm in a shirt sling, particularly if not too serious.

campers. Redness of skin with moderate pain and perhaps some degree of swelling are symptoms to expect. Cold, wet compresses applied to the burn area, or immersion in cold water will ease the pain. The skin will normally heal quickly and seldom requires any special treatment other than pain reduction. Most sunburns are classified as first-degree burns.

Second-degree burns may be caused by boiling water or spilled hot coffee or hot chocolate. Signs of a second degree burn include deep reddening of the skin with the probable formation of a fluid-filled blister. Cold, wet compresses are again the recommended method of treatment for the pain. Because the burn involves the loss of skin, you must also be alert to infection. After pain has subsided, dry the area, then apply a sterile dressing. If you have included burn ointment in your first-aid kit, use it. Expect some swelling, which you can ease by elevating the burned area.

Third-degree burns are caused by open flames and, occasionally, by hot grease. Third-degree burns involve all layers of the skin. Nerves and muscles may also be involved. Do not immerse third-degree burns in water or apply cold compresses. Cover the burn with a sterile gauze dressing, lightly applied. Watch for swelling. If nerves are damaged there will probably be little initial pain. Do not let that lead you to false hopes. Third-degree burns are serious and all such burns should be treated by a competent physician as soon as is possible.

### Getting Help

As mentioned in an earlier chapter on survival, no one should backpack alone. As in swimming, the buddy system is best. In fact, a group of four or more is preferred. In the event the injured packer cannot walk out to help, this allows two people to go for help while one stays behind to treat the

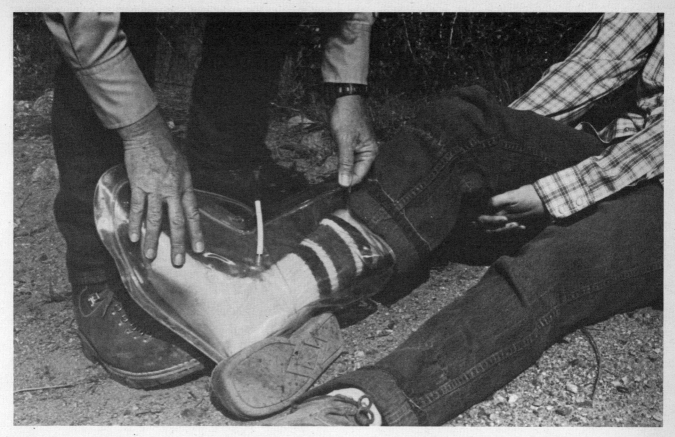

victim. If the victim must be left alone, basic precautions can be taken. Provide the victim with shelter and warm clothing. Make him as comfortable as possible. Be sure that he understands where you are going, that you will be bringing back help, and that he is not to attempt to seek help himself. Leave an ample supply of food and water within reach, kindling for a fire if he is able to maintain one. If there is any possibility the victim might become disoriented or lose consciousness do not leave him. If the injury is severe stay with him. Use emergency signals to summon help.

If it is your responsibility to go for help, be sure to mark your trail clearly. Use rags or branches, anything you can recognize easily. Take a moment before you leave to note your position on a map. Mark the map rather than depend on your memory. When you reach authorities they will need to know a number of things. Be sure you are aware of the exact extent of injuries involved, how they occurred, the name of the victim, when the accident occurred and where. If at all possible try to remain until the rescue units arrive so that you can lead them back to your companion.

Remember that while you are in the wilds you are away from the many conveniences normal to you. There are no phones hanging from every tree. A doctor is not a ten-second dial away. For the most part you must rely on your abilities to constructively plan your actions. Remember, too, that the welfare of every member of your party is dependent on every other member of that party. You must depend on each other.

The chances are you will backpack a hundred times or more and never need anything from your first-aid pack except a bandage or moleskin patch. However, it is wise to plan for an emergency with every backpacking journey you take. If you are disappointed you won't mind. It's a delightfully enjoyable disappointment!

*A break or sprain of the foot, or ankle is perhaps more serious than the upper extremities; the victim cannot walk out to medical aid. Plastic blow-up splint is particularly helpful in this case as immobilization is more difficult for the amateur.*

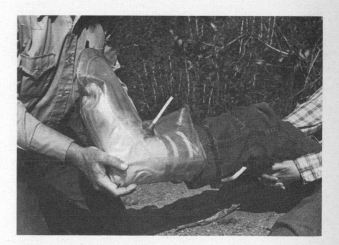

*With the plastic splint inflated, ankle is immobile, remains in correct position to prevent further injury.*

# CHAPTER 14

# HYPOTHERMIA AND HEAT STROKE

## You May Not Realize The Effects Of These Environment-Controlled Illnesses On Your Life

*The Marine Corps' Mountain Warfare School in the Sierra Nevada range near Bridgeport, California, has done much research into hypothermia, coming up with some important thoughts on the cause, the effect and what to do about it.*

**A**S MENTIONED, the human body is a remarkably adaptable system, capable of accepting varying changes in its environment with little difficulty, provided it is given time to do so gradually. You may travel from an elevation of one hundred feet above sea level to 5000 feet, and after a short period of acclimatization you'll probably be able to climb on as if you lived all your life at that elevation. Given the time, you adjust.

It is when you fail to allow for this gradual change, whether deliberately or by accident, that you cross into dangerous, sometimes fatal areas, facing the effects of hypothermia, heat stroke or exhaustion. All are extremely serious illnesses that must be recognized, prevented or effectively treated if a backpacker hopes to survive.

Knowing how these illnesses affect your life and the steps you can take to avoid them could prove the difference between life and death.

### Hypothermia

Hypothermia! The very word should make you sit up and take notice. If it does not, it is probably because you have yet to learn of the devastating effects it produces. You may have

*In cold weather or exposure situations, there is much less likelihood of hypothermia, when others can see what is happening to an individual. With such a diagnosis, it is possible to take steps to raise body temperature at once.*

heard hypothermia referred to in another way; some folks call it "freezing to death."

As sneaky as a one-hundred-proof bottle of vodka, hypothermia gradually grabs hold, easing its way into even the fittest of backpackers. No one is immune to it, for given the right combination of circumstances it can affect anyone, even those who spend most of their time outdoors. It is a life-threatening condition that must be given immediate attention if life is to be sustained.

Simply defined, hypothermia is a drop in internal body temperature to a point that the body can no longer compensate, and eventually ceases to function. As with all exposure conditions it passes through various stages before becoming incapacitating. A surface knowledge of these stages will help you to recognize them and take appropriate action.

The average person, backpackers included, will maintain an internal temperature of about 98.6 degrees Fahrenheit. While we accept variations of a half-degree either way as still within normal range, let that temperature drop a full degree

below the norm and we react. At about ninety-seven degrees we begin shivering, involuntarily and uncontrollably. It is our first warning that hypothermia is approaching.

A further drop in internal temperature and the packer will begin to lose his train of thought, becoming confused, unable to remember even the simplest procedure. His reactions are a good deal like those of a drunk, and numerous cases have been reported of individuals suffering from hypothermia placed in drunk tanks in error.

While our backpacker's internal temperatures may only have dropped about three degrees from norm, at this point he is no longer capable of helping himself and must rely on fellow packers to save him.

At or below ninety-five degrees the packer will stop shivering. This does not mean that he is no longer suffering from cold, but that his body is so exhausted it is no longer able to shiver. Instead his muscles will become rigid. He may begin to lose consciousness or appear only half conscious.

In the final stages of hypothermia, the packer's

As a means of escaping exposure, it is possible to use the deep snows to advantage, digging out a shelter that is sufficiently protective in nature that one can escape the major effects of the cold on, at least, a temporary basis.

*If the backpacker is properly clad for the icy environs in which he may find himself, he usually can escape the problems of hypothermia. The majority of cases come from individuals who venture into cold climes poorly outfitted.*

temperature may drop as low as eighty-five degrees. He will appear as if in death, pupils will be dilated and muscles relax. His heart may stop, requiring CPR to revive. At this point is is imperative that you have professional medical help at hand, as it is doubtful you could aid the packer on your own.

While these are the approximate stages a packer will pass through before succumbing to hypothermic death, you should never encounter the final stages; not if you are alert to the early signals and are prepared to prevent further involvement. Remember that people react differently to levels of cold. What appears to be only chilly to you may be freezing to your companion, literally.

What do you do for a packer you suspect is suffering from hypothermia? At the first sign of uncontrollable shivering, stop! Find shelter. If you are not carrying field shelter with you, look for temporary shelter from a cave, a clump of trees, etc. What you are seeking is an environment that will allow

you to raise the person's internal temperature by raising the external temperature surrounding him. Build a fire, not only to warm the area, but to provide a means of heating drinks. If shivering was caused by wet clothing, see that the packer changes into dry clothes. Warm them over a fire first for even faster response. If caused by insufficient clothing, loan him some of your extra gear. A word of caution, however. Do not remove so much of your own clothing that you also begin to experience your own initial stages of hypothermia. A temporary cure that soon has both of you down will be of no real benefit to either of you.

If you find it impossible to warm your companion with either a fire, warmed clothing, a warm shelter or sleeping bag, you may wish to consider the practice of buddy warming, where you actually climb inside the sleeping bag with him and allow the heat of your body to warm his.

Once the victim has begun to warm, allow him to continue

*Dark glasses are a virtual must in the snow belt, if one is to avoid snowblindness. While not a permanent illness, this can create great problems if one is far from base. A person should never travel alone in such surroundings.*

As an aid in treating heat stroke, be sure that the feet are elevated. In this instance, a backpack has been used to raise the feet and legs, thus lowering the head of the victim. Cool water should be applied to the forehead.

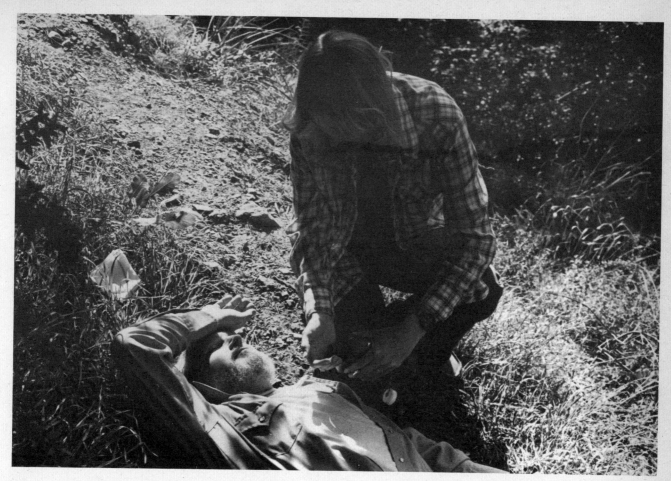

*A person suffering from heat stroke can go into shock, if not treated. Saturating the shirt with water can help.*

on his own. Be sure to watch, however, for signs of recurrence.

Although you have heard that alcohol "warms the innards," and indeed it sometimes feels as if it does, *never* give a hypothermic backpacker alcohol. It does not warm him. What it does do is dilate those blood vessels, further increasing heat loss.

There are steps that you can take to avoid hypothermia entirely. Avoid getting wet or being caught in cold weather without proper clothing. Proper clothing includes a hat and thermal socks, as well as jackets, woolen underwear, etc. You can always remove any clothing you do not need and store it in your pack for when the temperatures begin to dip once again.

Remember that the majority of hypothermia incidents occur not in sub-freezing weather, but around forty-five degrees, a temperature you may not think is particularly cold.

Avoid exhaustion and hunger; they only increase your susceptibility to hypothermia. If you get tired, stop and rest. Be realistic about your capabilities and about those of your companions.

And if you or one of your party does get into trouble, send someone for help immediately. Do not count on your own abilities to overcome the effects of hypothermia. A packer who suffers from it should always be seen by a competent physician, even if he thinks he's fine.

### Frostbite

Frostbite is the freezing or partial freezing of a part of the body, often an extremity or exposed area, such as the face, ears and nose. Do not rely on pain to tell you that frostbite is occurring. Normally you will see patches of white, frozen skin long before you feel the pain. The affected part is more likely to feel numb.

After frostbite your major concern is to warm the affected area, gradually. Resist the temptation to rub. You may cause the frozen skin to slough off, causing more damage than before. Allow the packer's own body heat to rewarm the affected area whenever possible. For frostbitten fingers, place them under the armpits. For frostbitten nose or ears, use your hands, if warm, for reheating. If you have access to lukewarm (not hot) water, you can often reverse the effects of frostbite by placing hands or feet in the warm water. The water must remain lukewarm until the frostbitten fingers or toes turn slightly red.

Do not let a packer walk on frostbitten feet. That will increase the damage done. Get professional help. All persons suffering from frostbite should be seen by a doctor, as often the injury results in lasting complications.

To prevent frostbite from occurring dress for the environment. Carry emergency clothing for use when the temperature dips unexpectedly. Avoid getting wet, from rain or perspiration. Avoid touching metal with bare skin. Watch

*Marines at the mountain warfare training center utilize helicopters, even parachute teams to evacuate hypothermia cases, but the average backpacker is much more on his own in extricating himself from a situation of this nature.*

for signs of frostbite in fellow backpackers and ask that they watch for you.

If backpacking with children keep in mind that they will react more severely to cold exposure than you. Check them frequently and treat any signs of frostbite or hypothermia immediately.

### Sunburn

Just as in the case of hypothermia and frostbite, the body's reactions to extremes of heat can produce serious effects. Your first concern will be for sunburn. Backpackers who pack high altitudes will find the likelihood of suffering sunburn is greatly increased.

Although it is fairly easy to avoid sunburn, a number of packers fail to do so. Most severe burns occur during the first days of a backpacking trip. To avoid them, simply limit the amount of skin you expose to the sun's rays, allowing for brief periods of exposure, increasing the duration as the days go by. Carrying a good sunscreen in your pack is wise. While you would like to return to your office job lean and tanned, it's far better to return somewhat paler than to return traffic-light red and several days early.

### Heat Exhaustion

Heat exhaustion occurs when the body attempts to rid itself of a heat overload by profuse sweating. The packer's clothing will be drenched in perspiration rapidly. He may complain of nausea, weakness and dizziness, a headache or perhaps fainting spells. His skin will feel cold and clammy from the excessive moisture being given off by his body.

Overcoming simple heat exhaustion is normally fairly easy. Simply transport the packer to a shaded area. Have him lie down in a shock position: legs and feet elevated with a pack or sleeping bag. Give him plenty of liquids. You may also give salt tablets, provided you have an ample supply of fresh water available. Salty foods, such as pretzels or potato chips will also help replace lost salt.

Once the packer has recovered you should return to

civilization and a check up by the family physician. You will need to keep a close eye on the victim during the remainder of the time that he is exposed to the heat, since he is apt to be susceptible to relapses.

## Heat Stroke

The more serious of adverse reactions to the heat is termed heat stroke. A packer who is suffering from heat stroke will display some symptoms similar to hypothermia. The illness is every bit as dangerous as is hypothermia.

A heat stroke victim may seem confused or irrational. He may lapse into unconsciousness or begin to convulse. The greatest danger he faces is irreversible brain damage, caused by the excessively high internal body temperature, sometimes rising to above 108 degrees.

Unlike the heat exhaustion packer, there will be *no* perspiration with heat stroke. The skin will, instead, feel extremely hot and dry. It is this lack of perspiration that should signal you of serious danger. It is imperative that you get this packer's temperature down immediately. The longer the temperature remains elevated, the less likely that he will recover. Heat stroke can and does kill.

Were you within the confines of your home you would immediately place a heat stroke victim in a cool bath. It's unlikely you will have a bath tub available to you in the field, however. Instead look for a nearby stream or river. If none is available, remove as much of the packer's clothing as you can, but leave a light, loosely fitting layer that you can saturate with cold water from your's and the canteens of your friends. Be sure to save water for drinking later, however, if you are not positive of the location of fresh supplies. Both you and the affected packer will need it if you are to return safely to civilization.

*If it is an overly warm day, with a burning sun, it becomes important for the backpacker to take rest breaks in a shaded area, drinking lots of water.*

*The importance of plentiful water cannot be understated. In years past, much emphasis has been put on taking salt tablets, but newer thinking suggests that intake of water is much more important than trying to retain it with salt. The canteen should be carried on the pack in such a manner that it is easily available. Refill it at every chance.*

Because the victim is apt to go into shock, you will want to place him in as close an approximation to shock position as you can. Normally this would mean placing him flat on the ground, his feet higher than his head. Obviously you cannot do this if you have him lying in a stream. Keep his feet higher than his head, however. Continue to treat him even after he has regained consciousness, until he feels cool to your touch. Do not leave him. It is essential that this packer receive medical attention as quickly as possible. When possible, someone should be going for help even while the remainder of the backpacking party is tending to the victim.

To avoid suffering from heat stroke yourself, try to limit the physical exertion required in hot weather. Take frequent rest breaks, seeking out shade. Maintain an adequate water supply, and give yourself plenty of time to complete your journey; a record-setting pace does no good for anybody. Be sure that you have marked sources of fresh, drinkable water on your map before you leave home or the trailhead.

There is one final precaution that you should take before leaving home. This should be done regardless of where you intend to backpack, the type of terrain you expect to encounter, or how experienced a backpacker you might be. *Tell someone where you will be going. Then go there.* Do not deviate from your intended route unless there is absolutely no way to avoid it. If you must deviate, return to your original route as quickly as possible. This does not restrict your opportunities of enjoying the freedom of being outdoors. What it does is insure that, in the event an emergency arises and you must be located, rescue units will be looking for you in the area where you are. If you are wise, that is where they will find you, quickly and with the supplies you need to provide your journey with a happy ending.

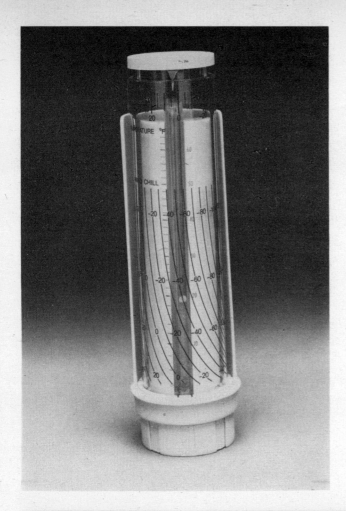

*Left: A wind chill meter such as this manufactured by Taylor Instruments can alert the backpacker to dangers of a lethal wind. (Below) A variety of sunscreens and tanning lotions can help prevent burning by the sun.*

# CHAPTER 15

*Swamps, shallow lakes and sluggish streams comprise the favorite habitat of the cottonmouth moccasin, so-named for the white color of its mouth. This is one species of poison snake that will not flee, so don't challenge it!*

# A MATTER OF POISON

## Plants And Creatures Present A Problem; Here Are The Precautions And The Treatments!

SOME OF THE most dangerous and discomforting aspects of nature come when you least expect them: from beneath a rock, on a tree limb or in succulent-appearing berries. The bright red and yellow bands of the black velvet coral snake may dazzle you with their vividness, but you will be wise to enjoy the rainbow from afar. Wild mushrooms may sound a tempting addition to your evening stew, but unless sure they are non-toxic, you are better off leaving them to the animals. Being able to recognize potentially poisonous plants and animals for the danger that they are is not only nice information to possess, it can be life-saving.

Snakes! The word alone is capable of causing fear in even the seemingly bravest of men. No other creature is as

feared or respected as is this normally timid reptile, which usually will go far out of his way to avoid you if only he has the opportunity. Even the deadly coral snake chooses escape over a confrontation. Unfortunately we do not always give him that chance. Trapped in a corner, he will strike. Fallen upon, he will bite. It is his way of defending himself, of telling you he would prefer that you go away. The fact that you share his feelings will make him no less dangerous to you.

There are four major categories of poisonous snakes in the United States: the coral snake, copperhead, cottonmouth or water moccasin and rattlesnake. Of the four, the coral is believed to be the most lethal.

The most common variety of coral snake is the eastern

194

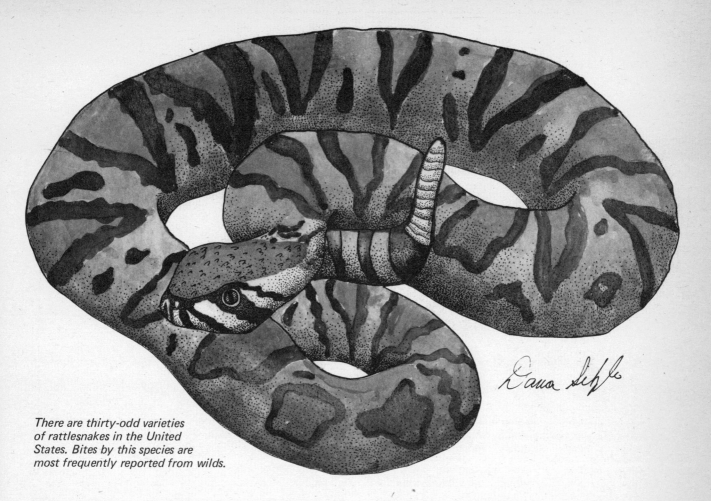

There are thirty-odd varieties
of rattlesnakes in the United
States. Bites by this species are
most frequently reported from wilds.

type, averaging less than thirty-two inches in length. As mentioned, colors are vivid, with wide bands of black and red, separated by narrower bands of yellow, and occasionally by white bands as well. The bands go completely around the snake's body. The coral snake is common to the southern United States, from coastal North Carolina to western Texas. He is a highly toxic snake, but injects a small amount of venom with each bite.

The copperhead seems to be a fighter, inflicting not one but several bites at a time. However there are extremely few cases of death from a copperhead bite, probably because the venom is so weak. The copperhead can be recognized by its pinkish-brown color with dark brown hourglass pattern on the skin, and will average about three feet in length. Copperheads are common to the eastern United States, from Massachusetts to Kansas, and westward into Texas. They prefer wooded, hilly country in the North and West; lowlands in the South. Copperheads can and do inhabit populated areas.

Swamps, shallow lakes and sluggish streams where water lies stagnant or calm are favored homes for the cottonmouth. This species gets its name from the stark white, cotton-appearing inside lining of its mouth, which it readily shows when confronted. The venom of a cottonmouth, although not normally lethal, has a devastating effect on human tissue. Found in southeastern Virginia, throughout the southern lowlands and up the Mississippi Valley to southern Illinois, and west to Kansas and Texas, do not expect the cottonmouth to run when

approached. It is more likely to stay and fight, and should not be challenged.

The most frequent poisonous snake bites come from the rattlesnake, of which there are more than thirty different varieties in the United States. Rattlesnakes are found in all states, and account for more than three-fourths of all reported bites. Because it is so common, all backpackers should know how to avoid contact with the rattlesnake, and what to do if contact is made.

The rattlesnake, like all snakes, is a reptile, which means that he is cold blooded. He depends upon his surrounding temperature for his own body temperature. If it is cold out, he is cold. If it's warm, he's warm.

In the early morning hours, particularly after a cool night, the rattlesnake is apt to seek heat, just as all snakes will do. In the afternoon, when it is hot, he will seek shade. This places him in the same areas we are apt to seek, since humans also seek heat when it is cool and shade when it is hot. Other, non-poisonous snakes do as well. You need to recognize the difference between these non-poisonous snakes and the rattler, because some of them can help protect you from their venomous relative.

The rattlesnake has a broad head, with a narrower neck but thick body; a forked tongue flicks rapidly in and out. This is not a stinger, as some people believe, but actually is part of a sophisticated sense of smell that affords the snake a high sensitivity to odor. All odors are composed of particles. This forked tongue picks up these particles and deposits them in the roof of the mouth where the sense of

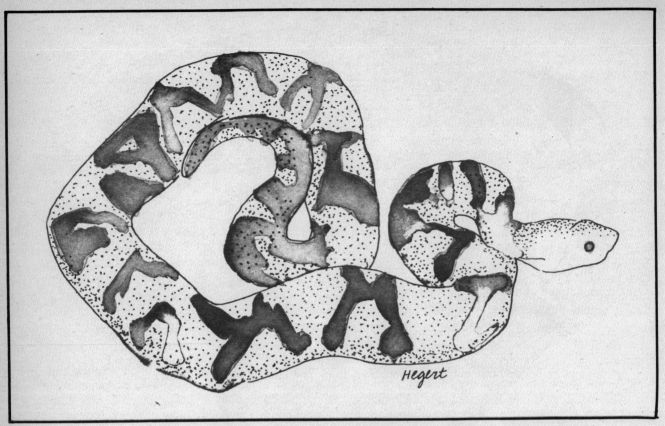

The copperhead has a reputation as a fighter, and often will strike several times without pause. Pinkish-brown in color, it has dark hourglass patterns on its skin. It has been discovered in large numbers in populated areas.

smell originates. The snake thus is able to determine the presence of foodstuff, and to strike.

The rattler's eyes are elongated, mean appearing, as opposed to round eyes. While the lack of elongated eyes will tell you that your "rattler" is nothing more than an imitator, it is unwise to get close enough to see whether the eyes are friendly or not.

All rattlesnakes are part of the viper family. Were you to look at a viper's open mouth from the side, you would see extremely long fangs that retract, when not needed, against the roof of the mouth.

Between the eyes and nostrils on each side of the head are two holes called pits, which serve as heat sensors. They are extremely accurate, and can differentiate between a half a degree or less difference of any object within a foot of them. Because the rattlesnake has the pits and it is a viper, we call it a pit viper.

The rattler, like most snakes, has poor eyesight, but it doesn't need good vision. With its heat sensors, it knows exactly when and where to strike. It does so by biting the foodstuff with its long, hollow fangs — nature's perfect hypodermic needles. A small hole above the point of the fang allows the introduction of venom into the wound instantaneously. The venom is carried by connective tubes, called venom ducts, from the venom sacks into the wound.

How much venom is injected? No one is really sure. It appears the rattler is capable of regulating the amount of venom to correspond to the size of the animal he is biting. Although two backpackers may be bitten by the same snake, the chances are extremely remote that they will each react in the same way to the venom. Some individuals will experience only moderate tissue damage from the poison. Others will have tremendous scar tissue years later as a result of massive tissue destruction. When bitten in the fingers or toes, damage may be so great that amputation is necessary, but few people actually die from a rattlesnake bite. Often a fatality can be traced to an allergic reaction to the venom, or perhaps a cardiac, respiratory or clotting problem. The risk is relative to size. The risk for a child is far greater than for a full-grown adult.

*The coral snake, rarely more than three feet in length, usually has separated bands of black, red and yellow. It is considered extremely dangerous with highly toxic venom, but injects only a small amount of that venom with each bite.*

There is a great deal of difference between destruction of tissue and death. Bitten by a rattler, you can be sure you will experience some degree of discomfort and pain. Your first reaction will be one of burning. The tissue around the bite is being destroyed, actually being digested by the venom. And that destroyed tissue is circulating through your system just as is the venom. You will have swelling, and the swelling will increase because your body has been insulted. There will be pain.

After being bitten by a snake, first, be certain it was a poisonous snake that bit you, and not an imitator. This won't take long in the case of the rattlesnake. There are two ways to tell: by sight and sound. If you hear the rattling sound, you know immediately. There is nothing else that makes that sound, and although you may never have heard it before, you will know the sound for the creature it represents.

Do not, as you have undoubtedly heard people suggest, attempt to bring the snake back with you to the hospital. Many people have been needlessly bitten by snakes while trying to kill them. But do try to be accurate about the type of snake, noting his coloring and size. Try not to exaggerate.

Once certain a poisonous snake has bitten you, move away from it. Snakes are not normally aggressive. Rattlesnakes in particular will make every attempt to get away from you, slithering off in any direction but yours. So if bitten, back off.

Once you are out of the snake's area, find a comfortable position in which to sit. You probably will need to remain there until your companion is able to bring help. A packer should not attempt to pack out a snakebite victim, unless the victim is in dire condition. Even then, the would-be rescuer must be in the best of physical condition.

How much time do you have to effectively get help? That depends largely on the physical condition and size of the individual. If an adult in relatively good condition, thirty minutes duration between the moment of the bite and the beginning of medical attention should be well within acceptable limits. If the victim is a child you will

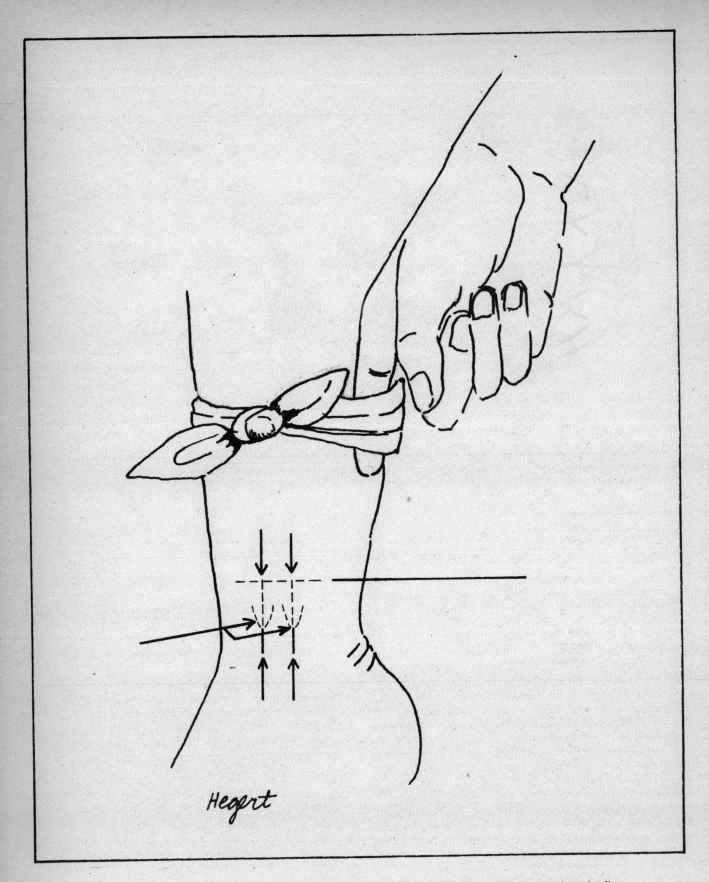

Hegert

If bitten, a piece of cloth should be tied in a constrictive band between the wound and the heart to slow the flow of blood. The band should not be too tight. If there is swelling, it should be loosened. Arrows indicate wound.

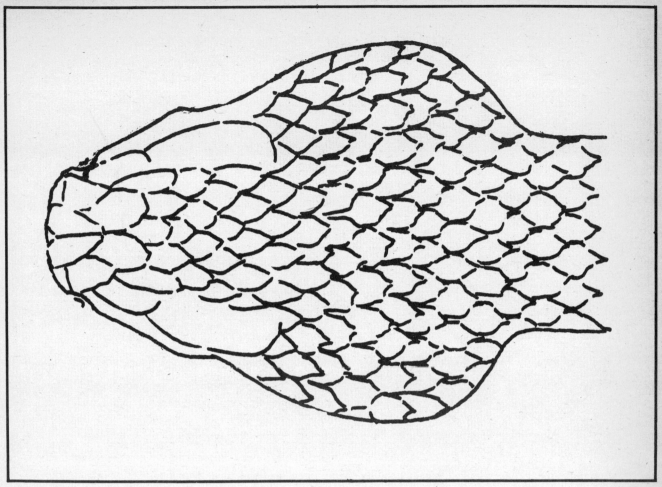

*With the exception of the coral snake, other poisonous species invariably have a flat head that is shaped like an arrowhead. Even if bitten by a nonpoisonous species, care should be taken to treat the wound, cleansing it.*

probably want to carry him out with you. Be sure you are physically capable of doing so; as with any medical emergency, a rescue attempt that leaves both victim and rescuer incapacitated is of no benefit to either person.

If you are backpacking alone, and are bitten by a poisonous snake, you have to get help from somewhere. Head in the direction that will give you the least amount of resistance.

If bitten, there are steps you should complete to give yourself the best chance of survival. Normally you will be wearing some sort of clothing. Use a piece of this clothing — a handkerchief, bandana or a strip of clothing — to tie what is called a constrictive band. This is *not* a tourniquet. It's purpose is to slow down venous blood, not to cut off all blood circulation. The band should be placed between the wound and the heart, and you should be able to slip your little finger under it without too much trouble. Watch for swelling, which will tighten the band, turning it into a tourniquet unless you loosen it periodically.

If you have a knife in your emergency survival pack, simply enlarge the fang puncture holes and withdraw some

of the venom. But, you must do so immediately. If you wait an hour or so after the bite, you are wasting your time. The damage is done.

Snakebite kits can be effective in the treatment of snakebite, provided you are familiar with how to use them. Don't count on reading the directions that come with the kit as you are treating a snakebite victim. The procedures must be accomplished immediately, and do not allow for a leisurely reading of the directions first.

In using a snakebite kit, your first task is to calm the victim. Have him lie quietly, the fang wound kept below the level of his heart, if possible. If the bite is in the hand, remove any jewelry immediately, as swelling soon will make removal nearly impossible. You may or may not need to enlarge the puncture marks before suctioning the venom. Try without cutting initially, applying suction for approximately fifteen minutes. If after that time you do not note swelling or pain, or the swelling is minimal, it's more than likely that the snake was either non-venomous or did not inject a serious amount of venom into the wound. If there is pain, swelling, discoloration or numbness, you

*Snakebite kits are available from various sources, but most of them are used in the same general manner, having a suction device to extract venom from the fang wound. But read the instructions before you go into the field. Do not suck the wound, if you have cuts in your mouth! (Below) The compact Cutter snake kit assembled for packing.*

will need to take further steps. Tie a cloth or belt around the limb, above the wound. Make it secure, but loose enough that a finger can be slipped below. Again, you do not want this cloth to become a tourniquet.

In your kit, you should have an antiseptic for cleaning both the bite area and the small scalpel you will use to enlarge the fang marks. Clean both thoroughly. Using the scalpel, make a linear incision through each fang mark. This incision should be no longer than one-quarter inch, no deeper than one-eighth inch. Caution must be taken that in your effort to aid the victim you do not become overly enthusiastic with the scalpel and wind up cutting important nerves, muscles or blood vessels. Squeeze the suction cup over the incision and release your fingers. Suction will hold the cup in place for several moments. When it releases itself, apply it again. You want the suction to remain as constant as possible, rather than repeated application and removal.

If you have no suction cup, you can use your mouth. Be sure that you have no open wounds inside your mouth, then suction out venom, spit it out, rinse your mouth and try again. Do not be overly concerned with swallowing the venom, it is not a stomach poison.

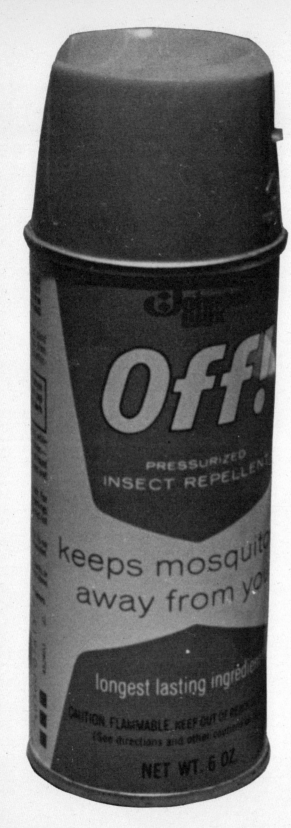

Every ten minutes you will want to remove the cloth, which functions as a lymph constrictor, for a minute or so. Having applied the first constrictor approximately 1½ inches above the bite, you will replace it each time a little higher on the limb.

Constrictors should not be placed on fingers or toes, nor should you attempt to enlarge the fang wounds on these areas. Restrict your treatment to suction only.

Most of the venom should be removed within the first hour. Some authorities suggest that any suction beyond the first thirty minutes is of little benefit, others that regulated treatment during the first twenty-four hours is needed. Hopefully, you will have the victim to a hospital long before the passage of twenty-four hours. Snakebite victims must be seen by a doctor, regardless of how trivial they feel the bite to be.

There are steps one can take to avoid snakebite. Most rattlesnake bites occur accidentally, frequently because the victim cannot see where he is going. He is walking in brush up to his knees or higher and cannot see where he is placing his foot, or he reaches around a rock and startles the sleeping viper. Wear boots in snake country, preferably steel-lined, although that makes for a heavy backpacking boot. Snakes strike at surfaces, so if you are hiking where rattlesnakes are, wear baggy pants.

When you hear a rattlesnake rattle, freeze! Don't move. Make sure you know where the sound is coming from, or you are liable to run in the wrong direction, and step right over it.

To keep mosquitoes away, along with ticks, fleas and a variety of other crawlies, one can buy repellents in a spray can, in liquid rub-on type or as a rub-on stick.

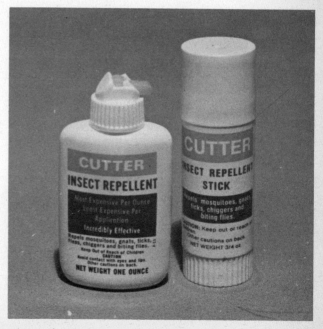

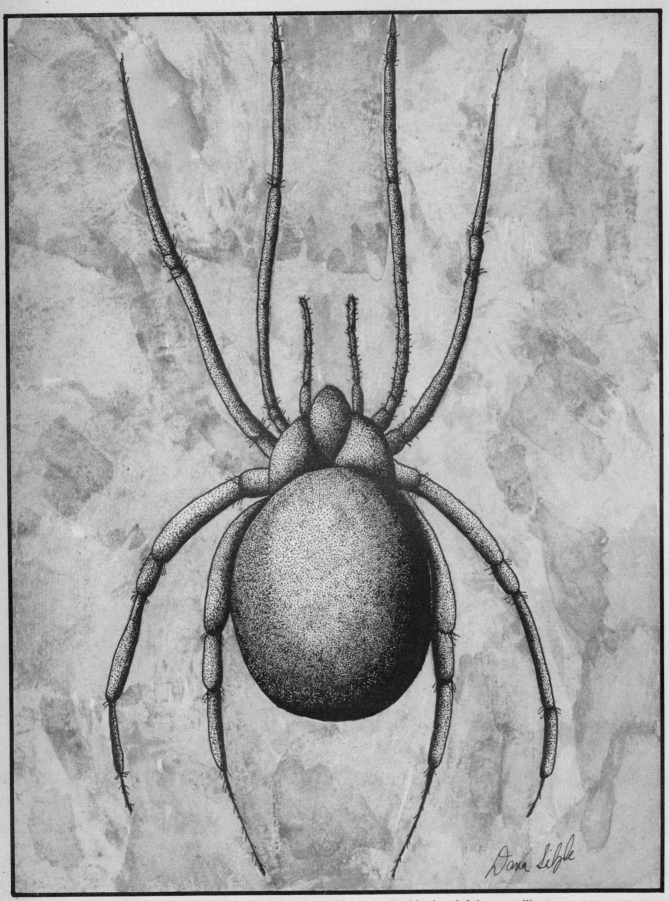

*While rarely fatal, bite of a black widow spider can put a crimp in your trip; bite is painful, causes illness.*

*Tick removal is explained in the text. If bitten, a rash, headache or fever can result, with signs of infection in the affected area. The symptoms usually appear 3 to 10 days later. Medical care should be sought immediately.*

If you hear the rattlesnake rattle, and have not yet been struck, the rattler is trying to tell you something. He's telling you he is frightened, that he feels threatened, perhaps that you have him cornered. He's asking you to leave him alone, and you would be wise to honor his request.

Most people bitten by rattlesnakes do not hear the distinct rattle until after they are bitten. It's as if the snake is saying, "Ah ha, I got you." Remember that the snake does not want to face you. While it's possible he will bite you more than once, given the chance for retreat, he normally will choose that route. Baby rattlers, born alive, are the exception to this rule. Baby rattlers will bite you repeatedly, often having to be knocked off. While the amount of venom they possess is less than that of their elders, it is still as toxic, and after several bites can give a

build-up of serious levels.

You may have heard that snakes will not strike unless coiled. Actually, seldom is the snake coiled before it strikes. They do not have to be coiled. They can strike forward, backward, sideways. They can strike when stretched out straight, and they normally can strike a distance of one-third of their total body length. If you come upon a three-foot rattler, and do not get within one foot of it, you should be able to back safely away. He will not pursue you.

Try to assure that the route your footsteps will take you is visible, that you can see whether a snake is present. If in an area where there are likely to be rattlesnakes, be snake conscious. Teach your children to be snake conscious.

Snakes are not the only creatures of the wild which pose potential problems for the backpacker. The most dangerous may measure a mere half-inch in length, for statistics tell us

*More deaths are caused by stings from ordinary honeybees than snakes, since some persons become more sensitive to the venom with each successive sting. Symptoms can range from swelling to severe pain, nausea, unconsciousness.*

more people die from bee stings than from any other animal poisoning. It's not that the venom of a bee is all that lethal, but that the body seems to build up a sensitivity each time it is stung. The first bite may cause only mild swelling and itching. A subsequent bite may increase the reaction to perhaps itchy eyes, abdominal pains, nausea. A serious reaction may produce wheezing, unconsciousness.

Fortunately, there are no known cases of packers being stung for the first time, and suffering a severe reaction. If you have an allergy to bee stings, you should know it. Before going into the field, ask your doctor for recommended steps and medications to carry in the event of a sting. Be sure someone in your party is aware of your sensitivity and knows how to use any medications you may be carrying with you and where you keep those medications.

Spiders also can cause big problems. The black widow and brown spider (also called *loxoscleles reclusus* or brown recluse) are particularly toxic.

If bitten by a spider, you probably will become aware of it immediately. There will be pain at the time of the bite, followed by nausea and weakness. The site may blister. In the case of the black widow spider, there may be difficulty breathing and muscle rigidity or cramping. Spider antivenom is available throughout the country. Your task is to identify the type of spider, so the proper antivenom can be given, calm the victim while transporting him to help, and perhaps apply a constricting band like that used for snakebites above the bite, to retard the spread of the venom.

For backpackers who pack the Southwest, especially Arizona and its neighboring states, the scorpion can be a serious problem. Again, antivenom is available and you need only to get the victim to medical authorities.

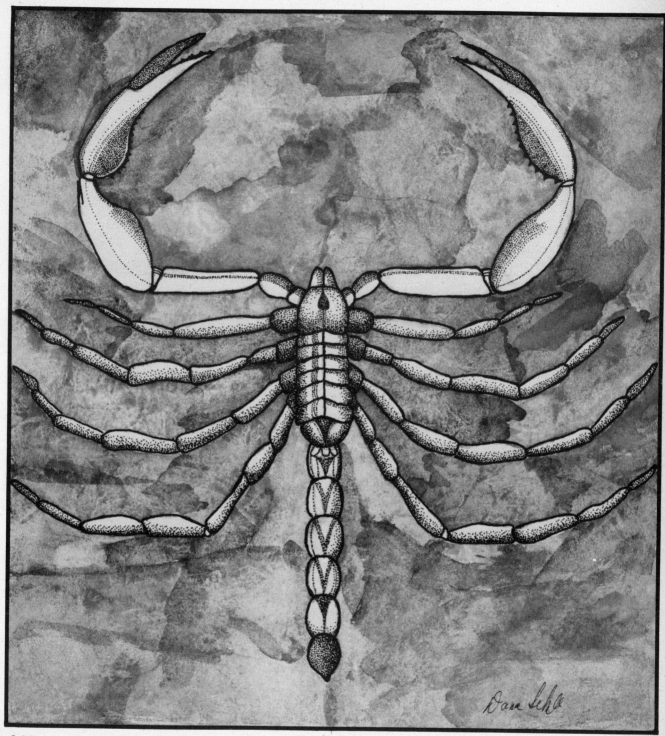

*Seldom more than three inches in length, a lethal species of scorpion is found in Arizona and Southern California. A night creature, it often hides in shoes, sleeping bags and boots. Shake out your footwear before putting it on.*

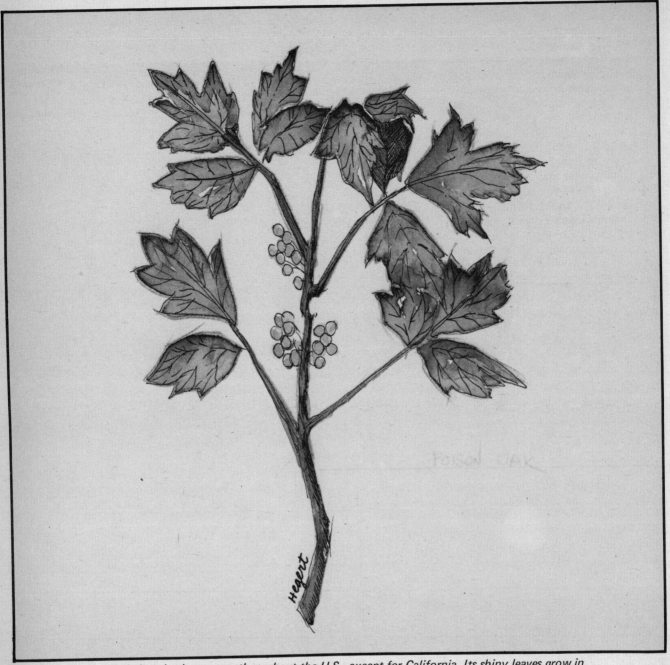

*Poison ivy is a small vine or shrub common throughout the U.S., except for California. Its shiny leaves grow in clusters of three, usually turning red, yellow in the fall. To treat, wash the area with warm water and soap, swab with alcohol. Be sure to wash clothing thoroughly, too. Smoke from burning ivy damages lungs if it is inhaled.*

For those who backpack the Carolinas and Virginia, the tick poses a particular hazard, especially the Rocky Mountain wood tick and common dog tick. These ticks may carry Rocky Mountain spotted fever, a potentially fatal disease. If there is any reason to believe a hiker has been exposed to Rocky Mountain spotted fever, he should be seen immediately by a doctor.

Backpackers hiking in tick areas should make every effort to avoid bites. Check yourselves and each other carefully for signs of infestation. Apply repellents to exposed skin. If you find a tick, remove it carefully. Be sure to remove the entire tick, head included, or infection is likely to follow. Covering the tick with a substance that prevents it from obtaining air through the pores atop its body usually will cause the tick to fall off. Vaseline, lip balm, or grease may work. If it does not fall off after a reasonable period of time, fifteen minutes or so, you will need to remove it with tweezers. If unable to remove it, or you are able to remove only part of it, or if you begin to experience signs of infection, seek medical help immediately.

Animals not normally considered dangerous can be rabid. In national forests, you probably will see signs warning you not to attempt to pet wild animals, because of the chance of rabies. Rabbits, squirrels, porcupines, even skunks can become rabid, so don't take chances. If bitten by a wild animal, try to kill the animal. An examination of the brain tissue will tell doctors whether the animal was rabid. If unable to bring the animal, at least bring yourself to medical authorities. Although the series of shots required to counteract rabies are extremely painful, they are far less painful than the death caused by the disease.

Few backpackers travel the woods for any period of time without encountering at least one variety of plant poisoning. Most common are poison ivy or poison oak. Rarely serious, the infection causes acute itching and discomfort, and can ruin even the best packing journey. The degree of reaction to the infection will vary with the individual. A group of four people may complete a day's packing with three packers experiencing no problems, while the fourth packer squirms and scratches all night long.

If you believe you have contacted poison ivy or poison oak, wash the area immediately and change clothes. The poison can remain in your clothing for weeks, requiring several washings to rid it of residue. A good hydrocortisone cream or ointment will ease the itching and prevent infection.

The best cure for poison ivy and poison oak is to avoid contact. To do this you must be able to recognize the plants. Poison ivy is common throughout the United States; poison oak is a major problem in the West. The leaves of the poison ivy plant are shiny, growing in clusters of three with smooth, spade-shaped leaf design. Green in Summer, they turn to red and yellow during the Fall.

The poison oak plant also has shiny leaves, growing in clusters of three. Leaf design of this plant is leveled, like the shape of a Christmas tree.

Should you come across a clump of poison oak or ivy, go around it. Do not burn branches containing poison ivy or poison oak leaves. Inhaled smoke from burning poisonous plants may enter your lungs, causing serious breathing difficulties.

Being alert to nature's poisons, animal or plant, is a sure way of avoiding a dangerous encounter. Give them the awareness and attention they deserve — for the well being you deserve.

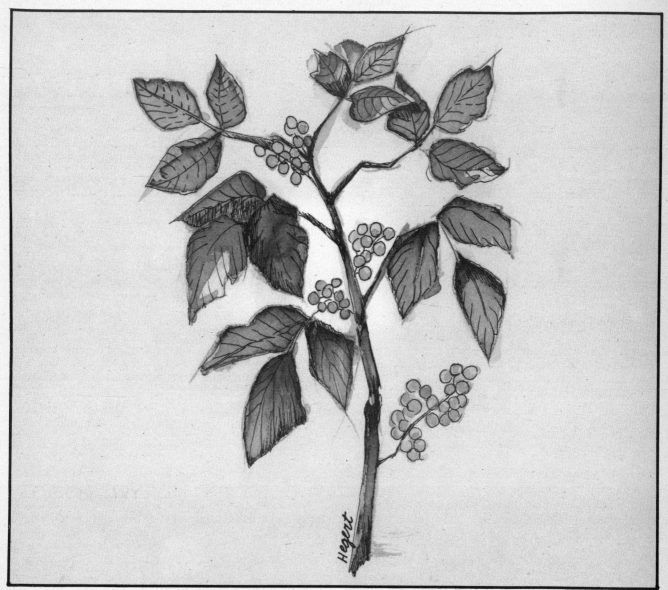

*California has its own problem with poison oak, also found in other surrounding states. It has clusters of yellow berries; undersides of leaves are covered with a hairlike growth. Treatment is the same as that for poison ivy. If smoke is inhaled, treat with antihistamines, seek medical aid. If breathing halts, use artificial respiration.*

WARNING
NO HEAVY TRUCKS
PICKUPS ONLY
3 TON LIMIT

*Even youngsters can join short hikes close at home, and photo records of such events will provide treasured memories later.*

# CHAPTER 16

# SEEING AMERICA

*Nikon's FM is a lightweight model recently added to that maker's line. It accepts the full assortment of interchangeable Nikon lenses.*

# THROUGH A LENS

## Photos Allow The Backpacker To Recall That Once-In-A-Lifetime Journey

**A**S MUCH A PART of backpacking as is the actual hike are the memories that it provides weeks, months, even years later. And what better way to accurately recall these memories than with photographs.

Today few backpackers take to the hills without a camera of some sort. Often as not it is one of the compact, nearly fault-proof Instamatics or, for the more experienced photographer/packer the popular 35mm single lens reflex (SLR) version, many also fully automatic. So compact have these cameras become that tripods, flash attachments and light meters arre no longer needed. A single roll of film may give as many as thirty-six different photographs, allowing the packer to dramatically restrict his supply of film while still returning home with ample photo support.

As shock resistant as today's camera may be, it is not

This Canon Model FTb SLR camera carries a 35-105mm zoom lens that also can be shifted to macro mode for use in making photos at short distances. Thus, one lens offers capability for nearly any photographic requirement.

The 135mm lens, here with sunshade on a Canon Model A-1, is probably the most popular focal length for moderate telephoto effects. It is also an excellent choice for informal portraiture.

*If you can get along with a maximum lens aperture of f3.5, a 50mm macro lens such as this one by Canon offers a high degree of flexibility and versatility. It focuses from infinity down to about four inches, as in the photo below, in which it's set for sharp focus on the box of film.*

impervious to damage. And because it is expensive the backpacker will want to protect it. By all means do so. For Instamatic 110 cameras this may mean only retaining the foam case the camera was sold in, and carrying it in that case when not needed, safely tucked inside your pack or jacket pocket.

For 35mm cameras you will need greater protection and space for packing. There are a number of styles of camera packs now being manufactured, many large enough to hold the camera, spare film and even extra lenses, if you choose to carry them.

For instant access to your camera, consider purchasing a chest strap that allows you to hold it snugly against your chest when not needed. Keep the camera inside a soft case, one with a drop front that allows for immediate use but protects the camera against rocks and tree limbs.

In selecting a camera for backpacking you will need to consider the complexity of use, the camera's adaptability and your own skill in photography. Although you do not need to concern yourself with all of the features a camera may offer, there are some that deserve special notice.

Your first consideration will be of whether or not to purchase an automatic or manually operated camera. Total automation is terrific if you would rather not worry about

*The Olympus Model OM-1 pioneered the reduction in size and weight of conventional, full-frame 35mm SLR cameras and it is an example of an excellent choice in cameras for those who do not wish to compromise the quality of the resulting photographs. At the same time, its weight and bulk are only a bit more than the smallest.*

setting the exposure. On some cameras you do not even have to be concerned with focus. Just point in the general direction and shoot.

For those who like to select their own settings, seeking special effects such as restricted depth of field or silhouettes, the manual setting offers greater flexibility and versatility. If the camera is new to you, however, be sure to click off a practice roll or two of film before your backpacking journey to work out any problems. If you do not know whether or not you would be happier with an automatic or manual camera, consider one that offers both options.

Most cameras today will tell you what their minimum focusing distance might be. This is important to the backpacker who wants to take close-up shots of, for instance, wildflowers. Some cameras will force you to remain no closer than two feet for a focused photograph, others will allow you six inches closer without the need of a telephoto or macro lens.

A self-timer is a nice addition to any camera. To the backpacker it is especially appreciated for it allows him to place himself in the photos. Simply set the self-timer shutter lag to its optimum setting, usually between ten and fifteen seconds, push the shutter release button, then walk around to a pre-determined position in front of the camera. By the time the shutter releases you are firmly in place, smiling and recorded.

Try to keep your camera as simple as possible.

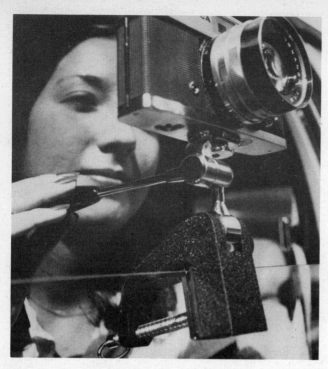

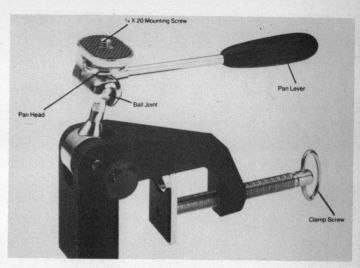

Adjustable mount, from Tasco, can hold cameras, spotting scopes or similar items for steady and vibration-free viewing after attaching to any convenient solid object of suitable dimensions.

Minolta's Mark II 110 zoom couples the compactness and convenience of the 110 film size with the capability of the SLR viewing system, meanwhile providing focal lengths from 25 through 67mm for control of image size.

*In addition to photographic records, it's often helpful to maintain a trip diary in which pertinent details can be recorded. Padded camera bags, as in the photo below, help to keep photo gear organized and protected when backpacking.*

Telephoto lenses and wide-angle lenses are terrific accessories, but on a long backpacking journey they may prove more of a hassle than a help. The average 35mm camera will weigh about three pounds when fitted with a standard, 50mm lens. Adding a telephoto lens will increase that weight by two to three pounds, wide-angle lenses by another pound. Space will also be of consideration. Lenses not in use must be carefully protected, whether packed inside your backpack or within a pack of their own.

While you do not need to carry your film inside its cardboard box, you should leave it inside the plastic canister to protect it from possible light leaks. Loading film outdoors is no problem today. Simply seek the shade of a nearby tree or use the shadow of your body to load. Most camera loading is extremely fast and easy.

There's one precaution that's quite important, when loading the film into 35mm cameras and that is to make certain that the leader of the film strip is fastened to the takeup reel securely. With many 35mm cameras, it is all too easy for the tip of the leader to pull loose from the takeup

The Olympus Model XA is an ultralight full-frame 35mm camera with coupled range-finder and an f2.8 lens of 35mm focal length. Sliding cover eliminates need of a case and matching flash is available for use with it.

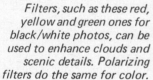

Filters, such as these red, yellow and green ones for black/white photos, can be used to enhance clouds and scenic details. Polarizing filters do the same for color.

Pentax Auto 110 is a compact SLR, with accessory winder, is about the size of a pack of king size cigarettes.

*Konica Model FS-1 has a built-in autowinder and automatic exposure.*

*Konica Model C35 is an automatic-exposure type with coupled rangefinder.*

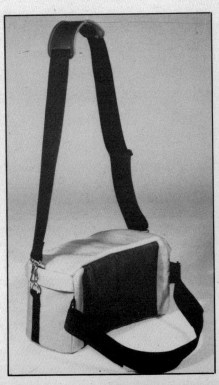

*Two models of camera bags by North Face.*

*The Phoenix camera bag is of waterproof translucent plastic for all-weather protection.*

reel. The direct result is that you go through the motions of taking pictures, but the film remains in its cartridge, unexposed. You discover the depressing state of affairs when your exposure counter indicates you've taken fifty-two pictures and you know the roll of film you put in only had twenty!

There is a positive way to check against such problems, easy to perform with most 35mm cameras. Take up the slack with the rewind knob or crank, gently, until you feel the first small amount of resistance. Then waste a frame of film and operate the film-advance lever or knob, meanwhile watching the rewind knob. As the film advances, you should be able to see the rewind knob make a proportional arc of rotation. That serves as a positive indicator that the film is moving through the camera in the manner desired, and that you won't be robbed of an entire series of photos. Since the photos you shoot on film that didn't move tend to tower in the mind's eye as truly spectacular shots, the simple precaution just described should be regarded as an absolutely mandatory part of the film-loading procedure.

The type of film to carry will depend on your requirements. For true-life renditions nothing beats color slides. They seem to be almost three-dimensional. But many would rather use color negative film for making prints that allow easier viewing. Both have excellent color quality. Do

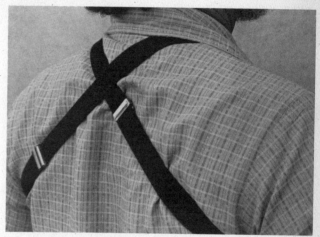

*Rear view of the Kuban Hitch shows the manner in which carrying straps cross.*

*The Kuban Hitch is a uniquely effective system for carrying the camera in readiness, but without the danger of damage if the user leans forward, as would be the case with a conventional carrying strap around the neck.*

Minolta Weathermatic-A uses 110 film and is able to be used underwater to a depth of fifteen feet.

Rollei Model 35TE is a compact, full-frame 35mm camera with pull-out lens barrel.

Rollei's Rolleimat F has coupled rangefinder and integral flash unit for photos at night.

Rollei Model A110 has an integral telescoping cover and accessory flash unit.

*Bushnell's Televar telescope has a 60mm diameter objective lens and eyepieces that rotate to provide a choice of 20X or 40X magnification.*

not overlook the black and white films — they can give some dramatic results, and provide a pleasant change to today's color-oriented world.

To avoid the possibility of forgetting where you were when a particular photograph was taken, develop the habit of carrying a small notebook with you. Special information about a given photograph can be recorded in the book for typing or attaching to the photo when you receive it back from processing.

About the only problems cameras may develop in the field will be a dirty lens or a spent battery. Keep a spare battery in your camera case or inside one of the outer pockets of your backpack. Lens paper is by far superior to your shirt or sleeve for cleaning lenses, and will not scratch the lens as the others are apt to do. It weighs near nothing,

costs about the same and adds no extra space requirements.

For those who are hunting or who are backpacking unfamiliar terrain, a second optic should be included in their packing requirements — a good pair of binoculars or portable spotting scope. For backpacking you will want these optics to be as light in weight as possible while still giving you the view you need.

In selecting a binocular you must concern yourself with the available field of view and magnification. Field of view refers to the span of land you can see through the eyepiece. Normally you will want the field of view to be as wide as possible since it will allow you more quickly to relate that view to your naked eye, which also sees in wide angle.

Magnification is the number of times the view you are seeing has been enlarged as compared to its true size. As an

*Bushnell's Stalker telescope is remarkably light in weight and compact for its power. Accessories are available to adapt cameras to it for use as a photo lens of 1000mm focal length. Eyepiece here is 20X magnification.*

*Right eyepiece of these Bushnell binoculars can be adjusted to compensate for individual vision. Left eyecup is in for use with glasses, right is turned out.*

*Bushnell Custom Compact binoculars have rubber eyecups that can be rolled in for use with glasses or extended for use when spectacles are not worn.*

example, a magnification of 7X means that the object is being viewed through the glasses seven times larger than it actually will be seen through your own eyes.

The binocular you buy will be a compromise between the field of view you want and the magnification you are seeking. Normally the greater the magnification, the smaller or more restricted the field of view.

Because our eyes are not normally of the same strength, we also need a pair of binoculars that allows for individual eye focusing ability. Most good glasses have this adjustable capacity, either through a central or individual focus wheels. If you wear glasses, sunglasses included, you will want binoculars that include fold-down rubber cups for maximum field of view when wearing the glasses.

Unless you use your binoculars frequently you may find that you have some difficulty seeing what you want to see. Frequently the problem will be one of inability to hold the

glasses steady. To steady yours, try bracing your hands against your cheek bones, brow or face. In a sitting position you can support your elbows on your knees for added steadiness. A nearby tree limb may act as a steadying brace for either binoculars or camera.

If you are a nature photographer, and enjoy photographing wildlife close-ups, you might want to consider the advantages of the camera/binocular combination. A 7X binocular is mounted to the front of a 110 camera, and allows you to focus in on your subject, then catch the picture without moving from your position.

Whatever the style of camera or binocular you carry, you'll be glad that you have it along. The ease with which you will be able to pick out your trail and the permanence the photographs will give you make both welcome additions to your pack and to your fun.

*These Zeiss binoculars are of the compact roof prism design, armored with tough rubber. Each eyepiece focuses independently on this model.*

*Lower view of Bushnell Custom Compact 7x26mm shows the two eyecup positions discussed above, the corrective adjustment on one eyepiece and the central focusing wheel. As with most such optics, distance between eyepieces is adjustable.*

Two more roof prisms designs from Zeiss are the 8x20B and 10x25B, both of which fold to extremely compact size, low in weight for the power they offer.

Bushnell's 8x30mm Sportview, above, is a wide-angle, rubber-armored porro-prism model. Below, Bushnell Insta-Focus model zooms from 7X to 12X magnification for added versatility.

Tasco No. 156 8x32mm wide-angle roof-prism binoculars are fully rubberized for protection.

# BACKPACKING

Teri Fivecoat experienced Europe by backpack and train. At right, she relaxes after the climb above Salzburg, Austria.

Below: The windmills of LaMancha on the "plain in Spain" are easily accessible to the Europe backpacker.

## Different Techniques Get You To Different Places On The Continent!

## CHAPTER 17

Below: "Mad King" Ludwig's castle is a sight not to be forgotten in Bavaria, southern West Germany.

TO MAKE your trip to Europe unforgettable, toss your suitcases! For the experience of a lifetime, don a backpack. The "Grand Tour of Europe" can be an affordable reality. Backpacking through Europe is a challenging, exciting alternative to traditional tourism. It is becoming increasingly popular with young and old alike of all countries, who prefer the freedom backpacking offers. The backpacker seems a bit more adventurous by nature, and this willingness to explore opens doors closed to the average tourist.

The way you choose to travel is a reflection of your personality. Ask yourself, "What are my goals?" There is no better learning experience than through travel. Evaluate what you hope to gain from your trip before making commitments.

Personally, I cringe at the thought of organized tours, itineraries, room service, taxis, and the American Plan meal

# EUROPE

*Hiking through the Black Forest of Germany, these backpackers near the end of a 40 km hike from Baden-Baden to Freudenstadt. The Continental hiker will see more of the country than the jet-setter.*

with adjoining bath at every hotel. Luxury tends to be isolating, lacking interaction with the real mainstream of European life.

The tourist pays by sacrificing a real ground level experience of the diversity in landforms, peoples and cultures of Europe. Under the twenty-four-hour guard of a professional tour guide, the average tourist has limited control over his experiences. But harboring thoughts of escape from it all would be a sin after making the tour deposit!

Backpackers can assimilate into European life with ease. The decision to backpack is the decision to pass up bon-bons and that villa on the French Riviera for a pack and a Eurail Train pass.

Unfortunately, I discovered the simplicity of backpacking after I was already overseas. I had chosen to spend my senior year at the University of Southern California with a foreign studies program. I spent four months living with a Spanish family in Madrid, attending classes, and taking off on three-day weekends with friends traveling around Spain. These first excursions taught us valuable lessons, but I would like to have skipped the headaches by being more prepared before my trip.

I left home armed with enough luggage for an entire family instead of one 21-year-old girl. Weighted down with clothes, cosmetics — in heavy glass containers, of course — I could have opened a department store. But surely, I had convinced myself, I would need my stock of "civilized" items which never could be purchased in foreign lands. But after twenty-four hours of solid travel — airplanes, buses and taxis — I was ready to slash my wrists for hoarding so foolishly. Lugging suitcases and travel bags, stumbling in heels, the prepared, well-dressed collegiate traveler was ready to call it all off and head home.

Now, five months later, I'm in a small Swiss hamlet nestled above Lake Geneva. I can see the French Alps from the hill I'm on. I have my thirty-five-pound pack, my journal, and some pastries with me. I can laugh instead of wince when I remember the airport, my cramped arms and hands, those awkward suitcases. I have some comfortable tennis shoes on instead of heels, and in spite of my weighty pack, I feel light; I have everything I need on my back, and my hands are free to pick flowers, take pictures, write, or sketch! If this is what you want out of a trip to Europe — and can prepare beforehand for your travels — you will be ahead of most tourists from the start. The trick is to expect your first travels to be trial-runs. Mine were disastrous!

There was little resemblance to the rosy picture painted in *Europe On $10 A Day*, an invaluable book that was my bible. While enrolled in Madrid, my friends and I took advantage of a four-day school week. When Thursday rolled around, we were packed and on a southbound train. On our first excursions we were overpacked, weighted down, uncomfortable and inexperienced. We paid too much for hostels and were too unknowing to scout for better deals. We didn't order correctly in restaurants and soon realized we would run out of money and be back home at the end of the semester unless we mended our ways. There was so much left to see; we vowed less eating out, more bargain hunting. Planning to go our separate ways in Summer, we set out to purchase backpacks. The minute we changed our style, we suddenly had more adventures, more fun — and more money!

There are steps to be accomplished in the States before your trip. First of all, **don't panic.** You will be bombarded with decisions and advice, packing, plane reservations, passports, medical requirements, purchasing a train pass; the list will seem endless. But be systematic, and start a month — or even two or three — ahead of your departure to avoid hassles. From a travel agent, pick up brochures to familiarize yourself with the geography of Europe. Better still, consult a friend who shares common interests, who already has backpacked Europe. Tips on hostels and camping, map consulting, languages, packing, foods and train travel are invaluable. Knowing what to expect will relieve some of the panic, both at home and abroad.

Here is a list of your first concerns:

*The European backpacker must be flexible. These two were delayed five hours on their Italian train ride and missed the twice-daily boat trip over to Greece.*

*Sudden rainstorms and freezing weather are not unknown in July in the Alps near Zermatt in beautiful Switzerland.*

1. Obtain a passport (allow at least four weeks for them to send it).

2. Go to your doctor, ask what is required for a trip overseas, keep in mind there are different shots required for certain areas (Africa, for example) which vary depending on the presence of a disease. So know (in general) which countries you plan to visit, and the length of your stay.

3. Visit travel agencies. (University travel offices are helpful, too.) Pick up information through brochures on spots of particular interest and beauty. Specify you are backpacking when looking into campgrounds, youth hostels.

4. Inquire at the travel agency about a Eurail Train Pass, which allows unlimited travel in Europe for up to two months, first or second class. If you are a cyclist, remember you are allowed to bring your bike on the trains, too. Allow a few days for your pass to be processed, as the coordinating company is French and your travel agent must correspond with them.

5. Research your airline flight thoroughly. If you dig, you can cut costs. There are all sorts of late-night flights, charters and special deals available. Be diligent and it will pay off. Laker flights from New York or Los Angeles to London are extremely cheap. Another option from East or West Coast is a charter, or advance reservations. Keep in mind that you might want an open-ended flight with an option to return home from any major European city, so that you don't have to backtrack. Also, you might want a flight with an open return date, so you can control the length of your stay.

*Information about the weather, terrain, a book of helpful phrases, maps, and plenty of good bread and sausage are essential items for hitting the road.*

*Above: To take advantage of the photographic opportunities found in Europe, store your pack in a train-station locker or hostel and explore the town. These wildflowers were gathered near Kitzbuhel, Austria, in the Tyrolian Alps.*

## Your Pack

Spend some time shopping for your pack at home. I ended up buying an expensive pack of dubious quality overseas. The purchase was made even more difficult by language differences and ignorance on my part regarding packs. You should require a frame for stability and balance; the weight does not shift to the bottom as much. Find a pack with a second zipper in the middle or bottom to avoid digging and rummaging. Extras like this provide much easier access to clothing and equipment.

Select a pack that sports a good secure anchor for a sleeping bag. Also, buy a small frameless daypack, which you can stash inside the large pack when not in use. Then you can leave your large pack in a train station locker or hostel room or campground, simply taking along food,

*This river near the Swiss-Italian border in the Brenner Pass is swift and icy-cold. The hiker crossing such streams must watch his step to avoid mishaps.*

*Quaint German hamlet is nestled deep within the forest.*

*American Air Force sergeant offers map-reading advice to traveler at isolated base in Germany's Black Forest.*

drink and your valuables in your daypack for shorter jaunts.

Make certain your shoulder straps are padded adequately or you will curse yourself later. A backpacker is constantly removing the pack while traveling — in trains, buses, stores, camps, et al. Even with padding, it can get to be a painful chore. In time, your muscles will adjust to the weight and the wrenching motion when you remove your pack, but expect to be sore at first. Trains and buses are the worst, as taking a pack off, putting it on, in cramped conditions is a killer.

Set your pack in the aisle and sit on it if all else fails. While on foot, relieve painful pressure by switching the weight of your pack to different areas. For example, for aching shoulders, tighten and raise your hip strap around your waist to take pressure off the shoulders. For bruised hips, loosen your hip belt. This switches the weight to your shoulders. To avoid the wrenching motion of hoisting up

your pack and twisting it on, set it on a table or seat first and ease into it. The longer you backpack, the more these awkward weaselings in and out of your pack will become natural.

Sit on the edge of seats, loosening your hip belt to avoid taking off a pack completely on a short bus trip. The action of heaving a heavy pack up on a luggage rack may seem impossible at first, but it soon becomes second nature.

You'll find Europeans exceedingly tolerant and sympathetic to backpackers' woes! I once had a German woman insist she take me home and soak my miserable feet in hot epsom salts. I had just returned from a four-day hike over high, rocky terrain in the Black Forest, foolish enough to attempt it in tennis shoes. Before the end of the hike, the rocks and steep hills had eaten holes in my shoes and my friends had to switch shoes with me as well as listen to me whine until we finally reached a village.

When we arrived, the kind German woman saw my

*Ancient watch tower, right, provides vantage point to view Black Forest, about ten miles from Baden-Baden.*

*Below, hikers soon learn the value of a current trail map as they prepare for 40 km walk through forest. Backpackers must be ready for all weather conditions.*

misery, took me to her home where I enjoyed two days with her delightful family, soaking my feet, being stuffed with unbelievable blueberry cheesecake and German sausage! The moral is, of course, to anticipate this type of misery and pack accordingly. I still wince at my Bavarian experience. The misery is horrible when you abuse your feet and the only cure is to stay off them completely.

## Packing

Get a good pair of sturdy athletic shoes, loafers or Sperry-Topsiders. I wore out three pairs of shoes in four months. Bring both heavy and light socks. Hiking boots are a wise investment if you plan to do any long-distance backpacking over rough terrain. You might be better off buying them in Germany, Switzerland or Austria, if you prefer to wait. The boots are exquisitely crafted, made for the Alps. These countries have excellent equipment for

hiking but you will have to pay for it, and the expensive Northern European countries can shoot your budget.

When packing clothes, you can't lose with jeans. Levis are comfortable, durable and most backpackers live in them. Girls should purchase a versatile denim skirt before leaving. Clothes are ridiculously expensive in Europe, so buy everything at home. The exception is European designer clothes, priced much cheaper abroad. Anything American is priced up, so here's something to keep in mind: If you're broke, sell your Levis! They can go for as much as $50! I had people come up in the street and ask if I would sell them! Also, any T-shirts or sweatshirts with the names of American universities on them are in big fashion demand.

The smartest investment I made before I left home was a bright terrycloth sweatsuit. Sweatsuits can be worn to hike in, sleep in, lounge in, shop in. They are perfect all-purpose travel suits, and the most comfortable thing you can wear. I

*Female travelers in Europe will find the versatile terrycloth sweatsuit invaluable wear. Easy to wash, pack and don, the sweat suit is acceptable by most.*

*Inexpensive, fresh fruit abounds in most European countries. Valencia, Spain, marketplace offers orange of the same name.*

prefer a lightweight style, which can be worn over turtlenecks for cold weather, or the jacket with shorts for hot weather. The bright colors and the stripes are cheery, stand washing well and the terrycloth stuffed easily in my pack without wrinkling. Wrinklefree fabrics are a big asset. Terrycloth and/or khaki shorts are perfect to bring. The longer khaki type of heavy material are durable for hiking, while terrycloth elastic-waistband shorts are great for hot weather. It's a great idea to bring a lightweight raincoat — even in summer, it is rainy in Europe — and a couple of sweaters. I found that I got the most wear out of T-shirts. You will see some things once abroad that you simply *must* have, and you'll need room.

Girls can stash a nice dress or blouse and dressy shoes in a large plastic bag in the bottom of the pack and forget about them until you need them. A useful top is a one-piece bathing suit or Danskin that doubles as a suit and a shirt. Sundresses can be bargains if you look in Greece and Italy. They are gauzy and comfortable. Choose lightweight clothes that pack easily, because chances are you will be returning home with a heavy pack and extra bags crammed with new clothes, souvenirs and gifts. Leave one-third of your pack free for these along with food you will be carrying.

## Food

A bit of advice on the food in Europe: Try everything, as it can be done on a budget. Don't be afraid to ask about the favorite foods in a country. Take note of the "special of the day." Shop in markets for breads and cheeses, sausages and fruits. These staples are cheap, simple to store and can't be beat when you're hungry! The sausage is great fried over a campfire and the bread is excellent all over Europe.

Wine is cheap all over, as is beer. *Cafe con leche* in Spain or Cappuchino in Italy — coffee with hot milk — are great pick-me-ups — or order a hot glass of milk and add instant cocoa or coffee from your pack to personal taste. This is an inexpensive and warming treat when you're tired or cold. And of course, treat yourself to a really nice meal out every once in a while. Stock up on top quality candy bars in Switzerland for long train rides! However, your least expensive and most unique meals will be those preferred by the local people.

## Toilet Articles

Don't go overboard on toilet articles. Pack a roll-on or stick deodorant, plus a bottle of conditioning shampoo. Don't stock up on needless items. You can purchase anything you really need overseas (but usually at a higher cost). You don't need the extra bulk, but do purchase the basic necessities at home where they're cheaper. Pre-soaked astringent pads are great for quick cleanups in camp or when traveling. Bring packets of concentrated detergent and a portable clothesline. Buy plastic bottles and containers.

One item I stress that was a lifesaver — a roll of good old American Baggies! Zip-locs are the best for storing just about anything: food, souvenirs, bottles, soap, toothbrushes. When I got home, I had some dirty clothes in large plastic bags, some wild flowers I gathered in Austria and a bunch of gifts and candy bars from every country in separate bags. They're great for separating shorts from shirts, socks from underwear, wet from dry clothes, dirty from clean. Many European markets also offer light, paper-like plastic bags that work perfectly for this purpose, so save them!

*Touring by train with a Eurail Pass will treat the backpacker to scenes such as this Swiss station.*

## Take The Train

I strongly recommend the purchase of a Eurail youth pass or adult pass, depending on your status. This is how vacationing Europeans travel, and is the most economical. The Eurail Pass, mentioned earlier, allows from four to eight weeks of unlimited travel through Norway, Sweden, Denmark, Germany, Switzerland, Austria, Greece, Italy, France and Spain. By some miracle, the train pass is cheaper to purchase here in the States than it is for Europeans. Most Europeans travel second class, and I found that most young travelers from the States follow this lead. First class is entitled to literas for sleeping, second class is not. Keep in mind that you will be traveling overnight in these compartments, sometimes sleeping sitting up, sharing a compartment with eight people!

*Lush hills above village on the Algarve coast near Lagos, Portugal, offer shelter for campers and a spectacular view of the square.*

*Spanish soldiers host two American backpackers on a stopover between Madrid and Toledo, Spain. Small and light daypacks are ideal for short excursions around larger cities or when off to smaller villages.*

If you have a sleeping bag, you're much more comfortable. Never be without your sleeping bag if you can help it, even in the heat of summer. The summer season brings hordes of travelers and trains get unbearably crowded. These times are bearable only if you have some padding.

In southern Europe, the conditions of trains and stations are poor. The restrooms usually are wet and dirty; always — repeat, *always* — carry your own roll of toilet paper with you! It not only is good for the obvious, but doubles for countless clean-up uses. Carry a small bag for cosmetics and a sponge for quick clean-ups on trains. If the facilities allow, use this opportunity to wash your hair in the sink.

Be prepared for the trains in Italy, Greece and Spain. They are never on time. Depending on them can really mess up your plans and leave you stuck somewhere you don't want to be. Beware when transferring lines late at night when you could be stranded! Also girls, be cautious of men in Italy and Spain. You're easy prey for teasing and it can get out of hand! My girlfriends and I have resorted to kicking and crying. Usually they are so kind, but then there's always a jerk who decides to have some fun at a foreigner's expense, so beware!

The trains in the northern Germanic countries and France are much more modern and relatively clean. Seats replace benches and compartments are roomier. Despite the discomforts found in the southern European trains, there is a charm about them. There always seems to be a guitar playing in a nearby compartment; you can sit between cars on the steps and watch the orange groves and orchards go by and feel the wind in your hair; someone usually will offer you bread and wine. Yes, those trains have atmosphere! Just don't forget the toilet paper!

Wherever you are, try to remember to spend the money of the country you're in before you leave. On trains it's easy to forget and sleep through a border crossing. You are

*Tiny Tyrolian village of Mutters, in the Austrian Alps above Innsbruck, is accessible only by tramline or narrow road, an ideal destination for the backpacker.*

*Roman ruins are tourist-free in early-morning hours.*

then stuck with leftover change. Exchange is tricky, even impossible. Also try to spend your money before you get to the station, as prices are terrible for food, drinks, magazines and books at the depots.

Utilize your train pass to its fullest. Hop off, if you see a charming pueblo or a mountain hamlet. Don't pass up these unique out-of-the-way places. You'll find you'll remember tha little Tyrolian village tucked high in the Alps much better than busy Innsbruck below. I spent five days in a charming little village in Tyrol called Mutters, which I discovered by accident.

Take advantage of trams and commuter trains. This is how to have your most spontaneous adventures! Go out and meet the people who live year-around in these storybook villages! I found in the Tyrolian Alps some of the most beautiful scenery I've ever experienced. Rounded, steep hills and valleys rising to jagged peaks, backdrop steeples in the distance, haystacks and wild flowers!

*Travel in Europe need not be entirely by foot or by train. Venice offers its famous gondolas and canals.*

*Inexpensive libations and a common language are features of popular English piano bar found in southern Spain.*

Hostels in Austria are called *Gasthauser* and can be found for $5 to $10 a night if you need a break from roughing it. Showers are hot in the north. Facilities in the south — pensiones and hostels — tend to be cheaper — $3 to $5 a night — but don't expect a hot shower. As you gain travel experience, learn to ask firmly about the facilities. Better yet, ask to use the bathroom and check the showers yourself. If traveling on a budget, undoubtedly you will only want to spend money to stay where the facilities are usable. You need time to wash clothes, wash up yourself and organize your pack. Breaks like this are a treat, so don't succumb too easily to the charm of a pensione owner before checking the hot water!

The people who operate and own these hostels all over Europe will warm your heart! They usually are older couples or families, eager to accommodate and help with directions. They love to hear of your adventures, and are of great help if you are having language difficulties. When people are so kind, it can be sad to say goodbye. I've been tired and had thick Austrian quilts piled on me when I cried from homesickness. I've had a Spanish grandmother take me in and feed me in Mallorca on Easter Sunday; and an old man in an Italian pensione did my washing for me.

Not only will you meet Europeans in the pensions and hostels, but you will find traveling companions from other countries. Many, I split up with and visited later in my trip, thus having friends and places to stay within Sweden, Denmark and Switzerland. You will be amazed at the ease with which friends are made. Backpacking is a natural for this, since most backpackers are of the same character.

*A quiet Venitian waterway beckons the backpacker seeking solitude.*

Even if traveling alone, you probably won't be that way long!

While traveling alone at the end of my trip in southern Spain, I stopped to visit a jolly English family my friends and I knew from the school year. We had visited them on weekends at their boisterous English piano bar. I ended up staying a week as a guest in their apartment. For rowdy times, you shouldn't miss these unique offbeat little pubs and cafes. Everyone you meet seems to have a fascinating story to tell!

A word of caution: Be trusting, for Europeans are friendly and eager to help you, but don't be foolish. Trains are the most likely places for thefts to occur. Try to keep your pack under your head while sleeping, if there's room in the compartment. Next best is to keep your pack on the luggage rack near the window, away from the door and outside corridor. Many people are relieved of their cameras and packs in this way, so keep your possessions away from the door.

Pickpockets are common on Italian trains. The safest way to guard your passport, Eurail pass and money is to wear a thin purse around your neck with a long strap. This can be tucked inside your sweatshirt, worn at all times without hindrance. Men like the waist-belt version, but both are effective in avoiding theft.

Another common mistake is to place cameras and wallets in the small outside zipper compartments of

*The necessities of life may be provided by only a few drachmas a day, plus a swimsuit on the beach such as this at Corfu, Greece.*

*An uncooperative donkey blocks this Greek hiking trail.*

backpacks. This is asking for trouble, since all a pickpocket has to do is unzip and lift. In a crowd he usually will go unnoticed. Watch for this on crowded buses, in subways and in train-station crowds.

When staying in hostels, don't go out and leave valuables around. The locks usually are old and not too effective. Slide your pack under a bed or store it in a closet out of easy reach, in case of a break-in.

When covering a lot of ground, don't push yourself! You will find that the tram stations and cities have become merely places to chalk off on your map. Hectic, hurried travel can ruin your attitude, your pleasure. If you catch yourself wincing in a museum, frantically sightseeing in large cities and racing the clock to hop trains, stop and take a break. I found I was exhausted after zig-zagging through Munich, Paris and Rome. These long train rides and such fast-paced extensive touring can squelch your enthusiasm for travel.

If you purchase a Eurail pass, you will receive a map of Europe with every available train line. The map is detailed and should become a near-sacred possession. Study your map and ask questions about points of exceptional beauty or charm. Listen to other backpackers' stories and favorite places. Don't stick to the large cities or you will find travel a chore instead of an enjoyable experience.

I found it wise to start with the northern Europe circuit, for you're eager to see everything in the first few weeks, with plenty of energy. Work your way to the south, you will need a couple weeks relaxation by then. Southern Europe, i.e., Spain, the south coast of France, Italy and Greece, and the Mediterranean islands of Mallorca and Ibiza offer a haven for tired backpackers. Relax on the beaches in the sun, then you are ready to hit the classy southern sites in Rome, Nice and Madrid.

My favorite spot was the Greek island of Corfu, off the coast of northern Greece and Yugoslavia. The island is gorgeous, with tangled olive trees and old Greek villages in the mountains to send you back in time. The coast has the clearest light blue waters and the brightly colored fish such as found in the Caribbean. There are rugged mountains with windblown grasses, yellow flowers, and grapevines all over the place. Goats and donkeys roam the steep hillsides and gypsies camp in the olive groves. This charming island also has to be one of the cheapest paradises on earth! Gypsies and peasants sell homemade wine for thirty-five cents a bottle and Retsina, a unique Greek wine, is sold for practically nothing.

Understandably, Corfu is a favorite of European vacationers. Here we find British, Australian and Swedish travelers backpacking in flocks. This rowdy bunch settles on the beaches and under the thatched roofs of outdoor cafes all summer for the Greek food, dancing and sun. There are many campgrounds and hostels can be found for $2 to $6 a night! You can dine on Greek Moussaka eggplant casserole, Greek salads, Feta cheese and delicious loaves of bread for almost nothing.

I strongly recommend that you wrap up your trip by relaxing here in the sun. Corfu is reached by boat from Venice or Brindisi, Italy, the trip costing under $20, lasting about twelve hours. I heard of this island through other backpackers, who raved of its beauty and the inexpensive way of life. Hopefully, islands like Greece's Corfu, Mallorca and Ibiza of Spain will not be developed too soon. Catch their charm while they are still relatively unspoiled.

Whatever route you follow through Europe, go with the willingness to learn from your encounters, and maintain an open mind. The unique and unexpected experiences in store are worth a hundred tour packages! Backpacking Europe, whether alone or with friends, can be the experience of a lifetime. Each day is a new adventure, for your pack allows you the freedom of spontaneity.

So stock up on camera film, Levis — and toilet paper! — then go by foot, bicycle, moped and train. There isn't much to it when you're prepared — and there is no greater satisfaction or fulfillment than knowing you did it your way. — *Teri Fivecoat*

*The French Riviera and Monaco are not known to be cheap for the tourist. However, staying in hostels and eating mostly bread, cheese and apples permits the European backpacker to enjoy the best.*

Backpackers pause for breath in the environs of the Finger of Fate in the famed Sawtooth Range, a favored area.

# CHAPTER 18

# SEEING AMERICA WITH A PACK

## Our Many National Forests Offer Nearly 98,000 Miles Of Hideable Land

IN RESPONSE TO the country's growing demand for backpacking lands, the National Forest Service now provides more than 97,000 miles of trails, streams and woodland for recreational backpacking as well as other outdoor recreational sports. Most of these trails offer the safety of well-maintained and well patrolled land, a bonus for novice and experienced backpacker alike, and yet there are still remote stretches of comparatively untouched land where the true adventurer can "get away from it all."

Regional offices of the Forest Service have been set up to assist backpackers seeking information and maps concerning specific national forests. Maps are available at a current cost of fifty cents each. The best way to obtain information is to write directly to the forest itself, or write to the regional offices. Addresses of regional offices are as follows:

**Northern Region:** Federal Building, Missoula, Montana 59801

**Rocky Mountain Region:** 11177 West 8th Avenue, Box 25127, Lakewood, Colorado 80225

**Southwestern Region:** 517 Gold Avenue, SW, Albuquerque, New Mexico 87102

**Intermountain Region:** Federal Building, 324 25th Street, Ogden, Utah 84401

**Pacific Southwest Region:** 630 Sansome Street, San Francisco, California 94111

**Pacific Northwest Region:** 319 SW Pine Street, P.O. Box 3623, Portland, Oregon 97208

**Southern Region:** 1720 Peachtree Road, NW, Atlanta, Georgia 30309

**Eastern Region:** 633 West Wisconsin Avenue, Milwaukee, Wisconsin 53203

**Alaska Region:** Federal Office Building, Box 1628, Juneau, Alaska 99801

To aid you in selecting your next backpacking site, the following guide to national forests has been provided by the Forest Service. Before your departure be certain to write to the nearest regional forester for up-to-date directories of sites and maps.

## ALABAMA

**William B. Bankhead National Forest** (181,000 acres).
Montgomery, Ala. Highways: US 31, 78, 278; Alabama 5, 74, 195. Attractions: Limestone gorges, Lewis Smith Reservoir, two natural bridges, wildlife refuge and management area. Deer, turkey, and squirrel hunting. Bass and bream fishing in Brushy Lake. Facilities: 3 camp and picnic sites, 4 picnic only; 2 swimming sites. Nearby towns: Cullman, Decatur, Haleyville, Jasper, and Russellville.

**Conecuh National Forest** (85,000 acres).
Montgomery, Ala. Highways: US 29; Alabama 137. Attractions: Large, clear ponds. Bass and bream fishing. Deer, turkey, and small-game hunting. Facilities: 1 camp and picnic site, 2 picnic only; 2 swimming sites. Nearby town: Andalusia.

**Talladega National Forest** (360,000 acres).
Montgomery Ala. Highways: US 78, 231; Alabama 5, 6. Attractions: South Sandy Wildlife Management Area; Skyway Motorway; Mount Cheaha, 2407 feet, highest point in Alabama; Lake Chinnabee. Deer, turkey, duck and squirrel hunting, bass, bream and perch fishing; swimming at Cheaha State Park. Facilities: 5 camp and picnic sites, 11 picnic only; 3 swimming sites. Resort, hotel, and cabins at Cheaha State Park. Nearby towns: Anniston, Centerville, Heflin, Marion, Selma, Sylacauga, Talladega, and Tuscaloosa.

**Tuskegee National Forest** (11,000 acres).
Montgomery, Ala. Highways: US 29, 80; Alabama 81. Attractions: Pine plantation of advanced size. Bream fishing in streams. Facilities: 1 camp and picnic site, 1 picnic only. Nearby towns: Auburn and Tuskegee.

## ALASKA

**Chugach National Forest** (4,723,000 acres).
Anchorage, Alaska. Highway to Anchorage, Seward, and Kenai. Ferry service to Valdez and Cordova from Whittier, and Seward to Kodiak. Rail services from Anchorage and Portage to Seward and Whittier. Extensive charter and commercial air travel. Attractions: Fiords and glaciers, lakes and rivers. Unexcelled scenery. Salmon spawning runs, salmon, crab, and clam canneries. Kenai Mountains with access by road system throughout the Kenai Peninsula. Trout and saltwater fishing. Hunting for moose, sheep, mountain goats, Alaskan brown bear and elk, also for waterfowl and grouse. Facilities: 39 camp and picnic sites; 9 picnic only; 2 winter sports areas. Nearby towns: Anchorage, Cordova, Kodiak, Seward, Valdez, and Whittier.

**Tongass National Forest** (16,001,000 acres).
North Division — Juneau, Alaska. Alaska Highway to Haines, with road and ferry to Juneau, June 1-Nov. 1; also direct plane service to Juneau. Attractions: Rugged Alaska coast; hundreds of islands, fiords, snowcapped mountains above the sea; totems; territorial museum and Indian villages. Salmon canneries. Gateway to Canadian hinterland and Yukon, "Trail of '98" gold miners. Glaciers; "Ice Cap" back of Juneau; fiords of Tracy Arm. Admiralty Island. Trout fishing, also saltwater fishing for salmon and halibut. Hunting for Alaska brown and grizzly bear, mountain goat, and deer. Boating on lakes and inland waterways. Scenic wilderness trails; mountain climbing. Facilities: 95 camp and picnic sites, 14 picnic only; 1 swimming site; 2 winter sports areas. Hotel accommodations in all southeastern Alaska towns such as Juneau, Petersburg, Sitka, and Skagway; all of these are served by plane.

**Tongass National Forest**
South Division — Ketchikan, Alaska. Direct plane service to Ketchikan. Attractions: Fiords of Walker Cove and Rudyerd Bay of the Behm Canal, and Portland Canal. Trout fishing; saltwater fishing for salmon and halibut. Alaska brown, black, and grizzly bear, goat, and deer hunting. Totems. Indian villages. Salmon canneries; pulpmill. Boating on inland waterways. Facilities: 10 camp and picnic sites, 1 picnic only; 3 swimming sites; 1 winter sports area. Hotel accommodations in all southeastern Alaska towns, such as Ketchikan and Wrangell; all these served by plane.

## ARIZONA

**Apache National Forest** (1,808,800 acres — partly in New Mexico).
Springerville, Ariz. Highways: US 60, 180, 666. Attractions: Scenic Coronado Trail and other drives through spruce and mountain-meadow country. Prehistoric Blue River cliff dwellings, Big Lake, Crescent Lake, Luna Lake, Blue Range Primitive Area; Mount Baldy Primitive Area. Lake and stream trout fishing. Big-game hunting: elk, deer, bear, antelope; also turkey hunting. Horseback riding; pack trips, hiking. Facilities: 30 camp and picnic

sites, 4 picnic only; boats without motors for rent on Big and Luna Lakes. Resorts and motels. Nearby towns: Alpine, Greer, and Springerville, Ariz.; Luna and Reserve, N. Mex.

**Coconino National Forest** (1,814,000 acres).
Flagstaff, Ariz. Highways: US 66, 89, 89A. Attractions: Graceful San Francisco Peaks, 12,611 feet, highest in Arizona; Oak Creek Canyon and the Red Rock country near Sedona offer exceptional scenic and photographic opportunities; Sycamore Canyon Wilderness Area and Mogollon Rim. Scenic drives: Lake Mary-Long Valley Road; Mogollon Rim Road; Baker Butte Fire Lookout offering vast view of Arizona timber. Numerous national monuments nearby plus Lowell Astronomical Observatory, Museum of Northern Arizona, Flagstaff; Meteor Crater near Painted Desert. Hunting deer, antelope, turkey, elk, mountain lion; lake and stream fishing; horseback riding; boating on Lake Mary. Facilities: 16 camp and picnic sites, 15 picnic only; Arizona Snow Bowl Winter Sports Area. Resort-hotels, dude ranches. Nearby towns: Camp Verde, Clarkdale, Cottonwood, Flagstaff, Sedona, and Winslow.

**Coronado National Forest** (1,791,000 acres — partly in New Mexico).
Tucson, Ariz. Highways: US 80, 84, 89, 666; Arizona 82, 86. Attractions: rugged mountains rising abruptly from surrounding deserts; cactus to fir trees, swimming to skiing in an hour's time — 40 miles apart. Santa Catalina Mountains Recreation Area with Rose Canyon Lake, Sabino Canyon, and Mount Lemmon Snow Bowl, southernmost winter sports area in the Continental U.S. Chiricahua Mountains with Chiricahua Wilderness and several small trout lakes. Pinaleno Mountains Recreation Area with Mount Graham, 10,713 feet, Riggs Flat Lake. Pena Blanca Lake, 52 acres of bass fishing 4 miles from the international boundary with Mexico. Galiuro Wilderness. Nearby are Arizona-Sonora Desert Museum, Colossal Cave State Park, Tucson Mountain Park. Hunting for deer, javelina, mountain lion, quail, and dove. Scenic drives: Pack-trip and hiking trails in the rugged ranges of southern Arizona (caution: carry adequate water). Dude ranch and winter resort country. Facilities: 22 camp and picnic sites; 27 picnic only. Nearby towns: Benson, Bisbee, Mexican border towns of Douglas and Nogales, Fort Huachuca, Patagonia, Safford, San Simon, Tombstone, Tucson, and Wilcox.

**Kaibab National Forest** (1,720,000 acres).
Williams, Ariz. Highways: US 66, 89, 64, 67. Attractions: Grand Canyon National Game Preserve with the famous North Kaibab deer herd, a wild buffalo herd and the only habitat of the Kaibab squirrel. Indian village in Havasu Canyon. Other points of interest are beautiful North Kaibab high country; pine, spruce, and aspen forests with open meadows; East Rim, North Canyon, Bill Williams Mountain, Whitehorse Lake, Cataract Lake, and Sycamore Canyon Wilderness. Hunting of deer, elk, antelope, bear, mountain lion, turkey, and limited buffalo. Scenic drives, fishing, riding, pack trips. Photographic opportunities; wildlife and vivid geologic formations. Facilities: 8 camp and picnic sites, 1 picnic only. Motels, resorts, guest ranches. Hunting camps with groceries open in season. Nearby towns: Ashfork, Cottonwood, Flagstaff, Fredonia, Grand Canyon, and Williams, Ariz.; Kanab, Utah.

**Prescott National Forest** (1,249,000 acres).
Prescott, Ariz. Highways: US 89. Attractions: Ideal year-round climate. Rugged back country, many roads primitive. Granite Basin Lake near Granite Mountain, Hassayampa Lake. Limited trout fishing. Sycamore Canyon and Pine Mountain Wildernesses. Jerome, Nation's largest ghost town. Deer, antelope, dove, and quail hunting; many horse trails; scenic drives. Facilities: 18 camp and picnic sites, 1 picnic only. Resorts, motels, dude ranches. Nearby towns: Clarkdale, Cottonwood, Jerome, Mayer, and Prescott.

**Sitgreaves National Forest** (811,000 acres).
Holbrook, Ariz. Highways: US 66; Arizona 77, 173. Attractions: Scenic Mogollon Rim Drive; pueblo ruins, Woods Canyon Lake. Hunting of deer, turkey, antelope, and bear. Saddle and pack trips. Facilities: Public golf and swimming at White Mountain Country Club; 8 camp and picnic sites, 3 picnic only; numerous resorts, hotels, summer homes, guest ranches. Nearby towns: Holbrook, Lakeside, Pinetop, Show Low, Snowflake and Winslow.

**Tonto National Forest** (2,885,000 acres).
Phoenix, Ariz. Highways: US 60, 77, 80, 89. Attractions: Semidesert to pine-fir forests, elevations 1500 to 7300 feet. The lakes in the low country from an all-year haven in the desert; the cool pine forest along the Mogollon Rim are very popular in summer. Famous Mazatzal and Superstition Wildernesses, Pine Mountain Wilderness; Sierra Ancha Wild Area. Thirty-thousand acres of manmade lakes including Roosevelt, Apache, Canyon, and Saguaro Lakes on the Salt River; Bartlett and Horseshoe Lakes on

the Verde River. Popular for boating, swimming, skindiving, water skiing, bass fishing. Public boat ramps at most lakes. Boats and tackle also for rent. Limited trout fishing in high country. Hunting for deer, elk, bear, javelina, turkey and mountain lion. Saddle and pack trips. Scenic drive: Apache Trail, Beeline Highway, Mogollon Rim drive. Facilities: 42 camp and picnic sites, 13 picnic only. No lifeguards. Swim with care. Resorts, dude ranches. Nearby towns: Globe, Mesa, Miami, Payson, Phoenix, Pine, Superior, and Young.

## ARKANSAS

**Ouachita National Forest** (1,570,000 acres — partly in Oklahoma). Hot Springs, Ark. Highways: US 59, 70, 71, 270, 271; Arkansas 7, 10, 21, 27. Attractions: Ouachita, Kiamichi, and Winding Stair Mountains; 8 major and numerous smaller artificial lakes in or near the National Forest. Caddo Gap, where DeSoto fought Indians; lands explored by La Salle and DeTonti, accounting for the many French names. Bass fishing; deer, quail, and squirrel hunting; scenic drives, hiking, and swimming. Facilities: 21 camp and picnic sites, 23 picnic only; 14 swimming sites. Hotels, resorts, and cabin camps. Nearby towns: Booneville, Hot Springs, and Mena, Ark., Heavener and Poteau, Okla.

**Ozark National Forest** (1,103,000 acres).
Russellville, Ark. Highways: US 64, 71; Arkansas 7, 22, 23. Attractions: Inviting summer climate, oak forest, rock cliffs, and pools, scenic drives. Three recreational lakes; Mount Magazine. Stream and lake fishing, deer and small-game hunting, 2 large reservoirs near the National Forest. Facilities: 24 camp and picnic sites, 21 picnic only; 9 swimming sites. Mount Magazine Lodge and cabins. White Rock Mountain cabins, others nearby. Nearby towns: Clarksville, Fayetteville, Ft. Smith, Harrison, Ozark, Paris, and Russellville.

## CALIFORNIA

**Angeles National Forest** (650,000 acres).
Pasadena, Calif. Highways: US 6, 66, 99; California 2, 39. Attractions: Steep, rugged mountains adjoining Los Angeles metropolitan area; Old Baldy, 10,000 feet. Chiefly a chaparral forest that serves as a watershed for the Los Angeles area and as an easily reached mountain playground for the area's inhabitants. San Gabriel Wilderness. Scenic drives with wonderful views, especially of the city lights at night. Riding and hiking trails, skiing season, fishing and hunting, some swimming and boating. Facilities: 98 camp and picnic sites, 33 picnic only. (Because of extreme fire danger in southern California, no open campfires are permitted in this National Forest.) Boating and swimming; winter sports areas with ski lifts and other facilities. Resorts, cabins, pack and riding stables. Hotels and motels in Los Angeles and foothill towns.

**Calaveras Big Tree National Forest** (350 acres — see Stanislaus).

**Cleveland National Forest** (395,000 acres).
San Diego, Calif. Highways: US 101, 395, 80; California 78, 79, 71, 74. Attractions: Primarily a watershed forest with an unusually mild climate, between the desert and the sea. Agua Tibia Primitive Area. The world's largest telescope at Palomar Observatory on Mount Palomar. Camping; warm water fishing and duck hunting on the impounded lakes of the water systems. Hunting of dove is very popular with a necessarily short season; pigeon and quail hunting. The Mexico-to-Oregon Trail starts here. Facilities: 57 camp and picnic sites, 11 picnic only. (Because of extreme fire danger in southern California, no open campfires are permitted in this National Forest.) Dude ranches, resorts, motels. Nearby towns: El Centro, Los Angeles, Oceanside, and San Diego.

**Eldorado National Forest** (653,000 acres).
Placerville, Calif. Highways: US 50; California 88. Attractions: Rugged mountains in the Sierra Nevada. Hundreds of mountain lakes; including south shore of spectacular Lake Tahoe, 23 miles long, 13 miles wide, elevation 6225 feet. California Gold Rush country, famous Mother Lode mining communities including site of Sutter's Mill. Mokelumne Wilderness and Desolation Valley Primitive Area. Lake and stream fishing, deer and bear hunting. Scenic drives: Highway 50 to Lake Tahoe, Carson Pass Highway 88 (route of Fremont expedition of 1844); Georgetown to Wentworth Springs. Riding trails, wilderness trips. Facilities: 47 camp and picnic sites, 26 picnic only. Boating, swimming, winter sports. Resorts, motels, and dude ranches. Nearby towns: Placerville and Sacramento, Calif., Carson City and Reno, Nev.

**Inyo National Forest** (1,836,000 acres — partly in Nevada).
Bishop, Calif. Highways: US 395, 6; California 168. Attractions: John Muir Wilderness, Mt. Dana-Minarets Wilderness, Hoover Wilderness. Palisade Glacier, southernmost glacier in the United States. Ancient Bristlecone Pine Forest Botanical Area with many 4000-year-old trees — the oldest living things on earth. Many wild granite peaks 12,000 to more than 14,000 feet in elevation. Mount Whitney, 14,495 feet, highest point in continental United States, and its closest approach road. Lake and stream fishing, deer hunting, wilderness trips. Dozens of natural lakes, some accessible by paved road up to 9700 feet in elevation. Mammoth and Reversed Creek recreation areas. Facilities: 17 camp and picnic sites. Boating, swimming, winter sports. Resorts, motels. Nearby towns: Bigpine, Bishop, Independence, Leevining, and Lone Pine.

**Klamath National Forest** (1,699,000 acres — partly in Oregon).
Yreka, Calif. Highways: US 99; California 96, 97. Attractions: Big timber forest. Klamath River and tributaries, famous for salmon and steelhead. Marble Mountain Wilderness and Salmon-Trinity Alps Primitive Areas. High mountain lakes and streams. Great scenic beauty in a wild setting. Steelhead and salmon fishing; deer hunting. Hiking, riding, pack trips. Facilities: 28 camp and picnic sites, 4 picnic only. Motels, resorts, dude ranches. Nearby towns: Eureka, Mount Shasta, and Yreka, Calif.; Medford, Oreg.

**Lassen National Forest** (1,048,000 acres).
Susanville, Calif. Highways: US 395; California 36, 89. Attractions: Caribou and Thousand Lakes Wildernesses. Many lakes; southern end of Cascade Wonderland; volcanic lava flow tubes, hot springs, mud pots. Indian pictographs and hieroglyphics, old emigrant trails. Lake and stream fishing for rainbow, Lochleven, and steelhead trout; deer and bear hunting; riding and hiking trails. Facilities: 44 camp and picnic sites, 9 picnic only. Boating, swimming, winter sports. Privately owned resorts, hotels, cabins. Nearby towns: Chester, Chico, Mill Creek, Red Bluff, and Redding.

**Los Padres National Forest** (1,724,000 acres).
Santa Barbara, Calif. Highways: US 101, 99, 399; California 1, 166, 150, 178. Attractions: Undeveloped, rugged country, varying from lonely coast to semidesert, from brush to oak country to pine timber; elevations from near sea level to almost 9000 feet; home of the rare California condor. Ventana Primitive Area and San Rafael Wilderness; snowcapped peaks in winter. Quail and pigeon hunting, some deer and wild boar hunting, trout fishing; scenic drives; oceanside camping, wilderness trips. Facilities: 325 camp and picnic sites, 22 picnic only. (Because of extreme fire danger in Southern California, no open campfires are permitted in this National Forest.) Swimming and winter sports areas including Kern County Ski Lodge. Hotels, cabins, and a few dude ranches. Nearby towns: Atascadero, Carmel, King City, Monterey, Ojai, Paso Robles, Taft, San Luis Obispo, Santa Barbara, Santa Maria, and Ventura.

**Mendocino National Forest** (873,000 acres).
Willows, Calif. Highways: US 99W, 101; California 20. Attractions: Coast Range of California about 100 miles north of San Francisco. Peaks up to 8600 feet. Beautiful lake country. Yolla-Bolly-Middle Eel Wilderness. Columbian black-tailed deer. Hunting, fishing, saddle and pack trips. Facilities: 325 camp and picnic sites, 22 picnic only. Dude ranches, motels. Nearby towns: Corning, Laytonville, Sacramento, Ukiah, Willits, and Willows.

**Modoc National Forest** (1,694,000 acres).
Alturas, Calif. Highways: US 299, 395; California 139. Attractions: remote northeast corner of California. Scenic rides, wilderness trips on trails such as the summit trail through South Warner Wilderness. Glass Mountain lava flows, scene of Modoc Indian wars. Winter range of interstate deer herd, Clear Lake Reservoir migratory bird refuge. Stream and lake fishing; mule deer and waterfowl hunting. Facilities: 20 camp and picnic sites; 4 picnic only. Swimming, winter sports. Hotels, cabins; hunters' camps during deer season. Nearby towns: Adin, Alturas, Canby, Cedarville, and Tulelake.

**Plumas National Forest** (1,154,000 acres).
Quincy, Calif. Highways: US 40A, 395; California 89, 24. Attractions: Beautiful Feather River country; Feather Falls, one of the highest and most picturesque waterfalls in the United States. Historic gold mining areas of La Porte, Johnsville, and Rich Bar; extensive hydroelectric developments. Limestone caves; large beautiful mountain valleys, such as Indian, American, Mohawk, and Sierra Valleys. Lake and stream fishing; hunting of mule and black-tailed deer, bear, duck, geese, quail, and dove. Scenic drives include Feather River Canyon, Bucks Lake, Bald Rock Canyon, Quincy-La Port, and Lakes Basin Recreational Areas, and Little Last Chance Creek. Pacific Crest Trail. Facilities: 9 camp and picnic sites, 2 picnic only. Boating, winter sports. Resorts, hotels, and cabins. Nearby towns: Chico, Greenville, Marysville, Oroville, Quincy, Sacramento, and Sierraville.

**San Bernardino National Forest** (621,000 acres).
San Bernardino, Calif. Highways: US 60, 70, 99, 66, 395; California 2, 18, 74. Attractions: Highest mountains in southern California: San Gorgonio, 11,485 feet; 6 others more than 10,000 feet. San Jacinto, San Gorgonio, and Cucamonga Wildernesses. Historic landmarks: Big Bear and Arrowhead Lakes; Mt. San Jacinto. Lake and stream fishing, deer hunting. Life zones from desert to alpine within a few miles. Camping and pack trips, winter sports. Facilities: 11 camp and picnic sites, 2 picnic only. Swimming and winter sports. (Because of extreme fire danger in southern California, no open campfires are permitted in this National Forest.) Resorts, hotels, motels, cabins at Arrowhead, Big Bear Lakes, Idyllwild. Nearby towns: Banning, Indio, Palm Springs, Riverside, and San Bernardino.

**Sequoia National Forest** (1,116,000 acres).
Porterville, Calif. Highways: US 395; California 190. Attractions: Giant sequoia bigtrees, Hume Lake, Boydens Cave, Dome Land Wilderness, High Sierra Primitive Area, Mineral King Game Refuge. High mountain lakes and stream fishing, home of the golden trout. Big-game hunting, mule deer and bear. Scenic drives: Kern River Canyon, Kings River Canyon. Wilderness hiking and riding trails. Facilities: 10 camp and picnic sites. Swimming, boating, winter sports. Motels, resorts, lodges. Nearby towns: Bakersfield, Fresno, Porterville, and Visalia.

**Shasta-Trinity National Forest** (2,073,000 acres; two National Forests).
Redding, Calif. Highways: US 99, 299; California 44, 96, 89. Attractions: Beautiful Mount Shasta, 14,162 feet with eternal snow, 5 living glaciers. Whiskeytown-Shasta Trinity Recreation Area. Shasta and Trinity Lakes with outstanding boating. Lava beds, Glass Mountain, and Castle Crags. Salmon-Trinity Alps Primitive Area and Yolla Bolly-Middle Eel Wilderness. Lake and stream fishing; home of Dolly Varden trout. Waterfowl, upland birds, deer, bear, small game hunting. Limestone caves, lava caves, and chimneys. Riding trails in the wilderness. Skiing. Scenic drives. Facilities: 102 camp and picnic sites, 14 picnic only. Swimming, boating, winter sports. Resorts, hotels, motels, guest ranches. Nearby towns: Callahan, Dunsmur, McCloud, Mount Shasta, Redding, Weaverville, and Weed.

**Sierra National Forest** (1,294,000 acres).
Fresno, Calif. Highways: US 99; California 168, 180, 41. Attractions: Huntington Lake, Florence Lake, Shaver Lake, Dinkey Creek, and Bass Lake Recreation Areas. Nelder and McKinley Groves of Big Trees (giant sequoia), Central Sierra section of the John Muir Trail. John Muir and Minarets Wildernesses. Rainbow Falls in the Reds Meadow area. Lake and stream fishing; deer, bear, and quail hunting. Boating, mountain climbing, pack and saddle trips, winter sports. Facilities: 111 camp and picnic sites, 20 picnic only. Swimming, boating, winter sports. Hotels, resorts, dude ranches. Nearby towns: Fresno and North Fork.

**Six Rivers National Forest** (966,000 acres).
Eureka, Calif. Highways: US 101, 299; California 36, 96. Attractions: Giant coast redwood and fir forests stretching 135 miles south from the Oregon line. Klamath, Smith, Eel, and Mad Rivers. Mild, cool climate yearlong in redwoods; rugged back country. Trout fishing, spring and summer; steelhead and salmon fishing fall and winter in 6 rivers; deer and bear hunting; riding trails, scenic drives. Facilities: 28 camp and picnic sites, 2 picnic only. Resorts, hotels, cabins. Nearby towns: Arcata, Crescent City, Eureka, Fortuna, Klamath, Orick and Orleans.

**Stanislaus National Forest** (907,000 acres — includes Calaveras Big Tree National Forest).
Sonora, Calif. Highways: US 99, 395; California 4, 108, 120. Attractions: Nearest high mountain country to San Francisco Bay region and portion of San Joaquin Valley; elevations 1100 to 11,575 feet. Deep canyons cut by Merced, Tuolumne, Stanislaus, and Mokelumne Rivers; fine timber stands; Emigrant Basin Primitive Area. Gold Rush country with many a tall tale. Routes of pioneers, Sonora and Ebbets Passes. Fishing in lakes and 715 miles of streams; hunting for deer and bear. Scenic drives, saddle and pack trips, winter sports. Facilities: 67 camp and picnic sites, 10 picnic only. Swimming, boating, packer stations. Nearby towns: Angels Camp, Columbia, Groveland, Jamestown, San Andreas, and Sonora.

**Tahoe National Forest** (698,000 acres).
Nevada City, Calif. Highways: US 40; California 20, 49, 89. Attractions: Squaw Valley, site of 1960 Winter Olympics. Outstanding conditions and facilities for winter sports; adjacent valleys being developed. Lakes and streams, including northwest shore of beautiful Lake Tahoe. Historic Donner Pass Emigrant Trail; Gold Rush country. Lake and stream fishing, hunting for deer and bear. Riding and hiking trails, scenic drives through historic gold

mining towns. Facilities: 70 camp and picnic sites, 11 picnic only. Swimming, boating, winter sports. Summer resorts, cabins, hotels. Nearby towns: Downieville, Grass Valley, Nevada City, Sierra City, Sierraville, and Truckee, Calif.; Carson City and Reno, Nev.

## COLORADO

**Arapaho National Forest** (1,004,000 acres).
Golden, Colo. Highways: US 6, 40. Attractions: highest auto road in U.S. to the crest of Mount Evans, 14,260 feet. Gold, silver mining; ghost towns. Gore Range-Eagle Nest Primitive Area. Moffat Tunnel, 6.2 miles long under Continental Divide. Lake and stream fishing. Big-game hunting for elk, deer, and bear; small-game hunting. Scenic high mountain routes; Loveland and Berthoud Passes, Peak-to-Peak Highway. Riding trails, wilderness trips. Facilities: 38 camp and picnic sites, 29 picnic only; 7 winter sports areas. Resorts, hotels, cabin camps, dude ranches. Nearby towns: Denver, Dillon, Golden, Granby, Grand Lake, Hot Sulphur Springs, Idaho Springs, and Kremmling.

**Grand Mesa-Uncompahgre National Forests** (1,291,000 acres; two National Forests).
Delta, Colo. Highways: US 50, 550, 6. Attractions: Grand Mesa Plateau, 10,500 feet; 250 lakes and reservoirs; cliffs, canyons, waterfalls, wild flowers. Uncompahgre Plateau. Uncompahgre and Wilson Mountains Primitive Areas; Ouray and Telluride Scenic Areas. Lake and stream fishing. Deer, elk, bear, duck hunting. Scenic drives, saddle trips. Facilities: 30 camp and picnic sites, 8 picnic only; 1 winter sports area. Motels, resorts in and near the National Forest. Nearby towns: Delta, Grand Junction, Montrose, Norwood, Ouray, and Telluride.

**Gunnison National Forest** (1,663,000 acres).
Gunnison, Colo. Highways: US 50; Colorado 135, 149. Attractions: Trout fishing streams, many high lakes. Twenty-seven mountain peaks more than 12,000 feet; Ruby Range. Taylor Park Reservoir and valley; ghost towns. West Elk Wilderness. Trout fishing. Hunting of elk, deer, mountain sheep, and bear. Saddle trips, wilderness trips. Facilities: 45 camp and picnic sites; 1 winter sports area. Commercial hotels, resorts, motels in and near the National Forest. Nearby towns: Gunnison, Lake City, Montrose, and Salida.

**Pike National Forest** (1,105,000 acres).
Colorado Springs, Colo. Highways: US 24, 85, 87, 285. Attractions: Pikes Peak with highway to summit, historic Cripple Creek and Alma gold camps, scenic Rampart Range Road. Devil's Head Forest Fire Lookout, Monument Forest Nursery, Platte and Arkansas River watersheds. Abyss Lake and Lost Creek Scenic Area. Hunting and fishing; scenic drives. Mountain sheep and other wildlife. Facilities: 46 camp and picnic sites, 46 more picnic only; 3 winter sports areas. Commercial hotels, resorts, motels in and near the National Forest. Nearby towns: Colorado Springs, Cripple Creek, and Denver.

**Rio Grande National Forest** (1,800,000 acres).
Monte Vista, Colo. Highways: US 160, 285. Attractions: Mountain lakes and trout streams, Wolf Creek Pass, rugged high country. Upper Rio Grande Primitive Area and La Garita Wilderness. Fishing; deer, elk, and duck hunting. Saddle and pack trips, scenic drives. Facilities: 40 camp and picnic sites, 15 picnic only; 1 winter sports area. Motels in and near the National Forest. Nearby towns: Alamosa, Antonito, Creede, Monte Vista, and Saguache.

**Roosevelt National Forest** (776,000 acres).
Fort Collins, Colo. Highways: US 34, 287; Colorado 14, 160. Attractions: Arapaho, Isabelle, and South St. Vrain Glaciers; rugged Continental Divide with many alpine lakes; Poudre, Big Thompson, St. Vrain, and Boulder Canyons. Rawah Wilderness. Boating; fishing; hunting for deer, elk, mountain sheep, bear, mountain lion, grouse and duck. Saddle and pack trips, scenic drives. Facilities: 27 camp and picnic sites, 32 picnic only; 1 winter sports area. Motels and dude ranches in and near the National Forest. Nearby towns: Boulder, Denver, Estes Park, Fort Collins, Longmont and Loveland.

**Routt National Forest** (1,125,000 acres).
Steamboat Springs, Colo. Highways: US 40; Colorado 84, 131. Attractions: Continental Divide with perpetual ice and snow, trout streams and alpine lakes. Mount Zirkel Wilderness, Big Creek Lakes Recreation Area. Fishing; deer, elk, grouse, and duck hunting. Saddle and pack trips; scenic drives. Facilities: 26 camp and picnic sites, 8 picnic only; 1 winter sports area. Commercial cabins, motels in and near the National Forest. Nearby towns: Craig, Kremmling, Steamboat Springs, Walden, and Yampa.

**San Isabel National Forest** (1,106,000 acres).
Pueblo, Colo. Highways: US 24, 50, 85, 87; Colorado 69, 165. Attractions: Highest average elevation of any National Forest; Sangre de Cristo Range; 12 peaks more than 14,000 feet; Mount

Elbert, second highest in the United States. More than 40 timberline lakes. Snow Angel on Mount Shavano; molybdenum mines; Lake Isabel Recreation Area. Fishing; hunting for deer, elk, bear, mountain goat, grouse, and duck. Scenic drives, saddle and pack trips. Facilities: 19 camp and picnic sites, 14 picnic only; 2 winter sports areas. Motels and dude ranches in and near the National Forest. Nearby towns: Canon City, Leadville, Pueblo, Salida, and Walsenburg.

**San Juan National Forest** (1,866,000 acres).
Durango, Colo. Highways: US 160, 550; Colorado 145. Attractions: Alpine lakes; Mount Wilson, 14,250 feet; canyons, waterfalls, cataracts, peculiar geologic formations. Archeological ruins, historic mines. San Juan Primitive Area; Wilson Mountains Primitive Area. Fishing; hunting for deer, elk, bear, mountain lion, grouse and duck. Scenic drives; saddle and pack trips. Facilities: 38 camp and picnic sites, 10 picnic only; 2 winter sports areas. Motels and dude ranches in and near the National Forest. Nearby towns: Cortez, Durango, Pagosa Springs, and Silverton, Colo.; Farmington, N. Mex.

**White River National Forest** (1,960,000 acres).
Glenwood Springs, Colo. Highways: US 24, 6; Colorado 82, 132. Attractions: Spectacular Glenwood Canyon, Hanging Lake, Bridal Veil Falls, mineral hot springs, caves, alpine lakes. Source of marble for Lincoln Memorial and Tomb of the Unknown Soldier. Flat Tops Primitive Area; Gore Range-Eagle Nest Primitive Area; Maroon Bells-Snowmass Wilderness. Fishing; elk, deer and bear hunting. Saddle and pack trails; scenic drives. Facilities: 45 camp and picnic sites, 4 picnic only; 6 winter sports areas. Motels and dude ranches in and near the National Forest. Nearby towns: Aspen, Craig, Eagle, Glenwood Springs, Gypsum, Leadville, Meeker, and Rifle.

## FLORIDA

**Apalachicola National Forest** (557,000 acres).
Tallahassee, Fla. Highways: US 98, 319; Florida 20, 65, 369. Attractions: Pine-hardwood forests, Coastal Plain type. Natural sinks, bottomland and hardwood swamps along large rivers with trees typically found far to the north. Old Fort Gadsen, old river landings. Three rivers and their tributaries with many miles of fishing waters — bass, bream, perch. Quail, deer, and bear hunting. Numerous lakes, sinks, and ponds provide boating and swimming. Facilities: 27 camp and picnic sites, 33 picnic only; 16 swimming sites. Hotels not far away. Nearby towns: Apalachicola, Bountstown, Bristol, and Tallahassee.

**Ocala National Forest** (366,000 acres).
Tallahassee, Fla. Highways: US 17, 301; Florida 19, 40, 42, 314. Attractions: Juniper Springs and Alexander Springs; large clear-flowing streams through subtropical wilderness; botanical lore, palms, hardwoods, and pine. Hundreds of clear lakes. The Big Scrub, characterized by vast stands of sand pine, is unique. Wildlife management area, annual deer and bear hunts. Silver Springs is nearby. Numerous lakes, streams, and ponds with fishing and camping sites. Facilities: 7 camp and picnic sites, 16 picnic sites; 4 swimming sites. Hunting camps; commercial accommodations near the forest. Nearby towns: Deland, Eustis, Leesburg, Mount Dora, Ocala, and Palatka.

**Osceola National Forest** (157,000 acres).
Tallahassee, Fla. Highways: I-10; US 41, 90, 441; Florida 100. Attractions: Flat country, dotted with numerous ponds, sinks, and cypress swamps. State game breeding ground. Bass, perch, and bream fishing; deer, turkey, quail, and dove hunting. Swimming and boating at Ocean Pond. Facilities: 2 camp and picnic sites, 5 picnic only; 2 swimming sites, opportunities for aquatic sports. Nearby towns: Jacksonville and Lake City.

## GEORGIA

**Chattahoochee National Forest** (720,000 acres).
Gainesville, Ga. Highways: US 19, 23, 27, 41, 76, 123, 129, 441; Georgia 5, 60, 75. Attractions: Visitor Center in Brasstown Bald, at 4784 feet, highest point in Georgia; Blue Ridge Mountains; lakes; Tallulah Gorge; waterfalls; southern end of Appalachian Trail. Deer and small-game hunting, archery hunting for deer; trout and bass fishing. Swimming, boating, hiking. Facilities: 25 camp and picnic sites, 23 picnic only; 6 swimming sites. Nearby towns: Atlanta, Blue Ridge, Clarksville, Clayton, Dahlonega, Dalton, and Toccoa, Ga.; Chattanooga, Tenn.

**Oconee National Forest** (104,000 acres).
Gainesville, Ga. Highways: US 278, 129; Georgia 15, 44, 77. Attractions: Heavily forested Piedmont hills, archeological remains, Rock Eagle Lake, effigy of EAGLE, Mammoth 4-H Center, Piedmont Wildlife Refuge; deer and small-game hunting, bass and bream fishing. Facilities: 2 camp and picnic sites, 4 picnic only; 1 swimming site. Nearby towns: Eatonton, Greensboro, and Madison.

## IDAHO

**Boise National Forest** (2,639,000 acres).
Boise, Idaho. Highways: US 20, 30, 95; Idaho 15, 16, 17, 21, 52, 68. Attractions: Rugged back country including portions of Sawtooth Primitive Area. Abandoned mines and ghost towns. Scenes of early Indian camps and massacres. Virgin stands of ponderosa pine. Arrowrock, Anderson Ranch, Cascade, Deadwood, and Lucky Peak Reservoirs; other lakes. Includes headwaters of Boise, Payette, and Salmon Rivers. Lake and stream fishing for trout and salmon. Hunting for bear, elk, and deer. Spectacular scenic drives in Payette and Boise River Canyons, along Boise Ridge and edge of Sawtooth Primitive Area. Facilities: 116 camp sites, 5 picnic sites, 1 swimming site; Bogus Basin Winter Sports Area. Resorts, motels, dude ranches with horses, boats, and other facilities. Nearby towns: Boise, Cascade, Emmett, Horseshoe Bend, Idaho City, and Mountain Home.

**Caribou National Forest** (978,000 acres — partly in Utah and Wyoming).
Pocatello, Idaho. Highways: US 91, 191, 30N. Attractions: High country: towering mountain ranges divided by beautiful valleys. Historic markers and trails, natural soda springs, rushing streams and waterfalls. Stream fishing; game bird, deer, and bear hunting. Scenic drives: Mink Creek to Scout Mountain, Skyline Road, Snake River-McCoy Road along south bank of South Fork of Snake River, Georgetown Canyon-Diamond Creek and Snowslide-Crow Creek Roads. Numerous riding trails into wilderness country. Facilities: 21 camp sites, 6 picnic sites; 1 winter sports area. Resorts and motels. Nearby towns: Idaho Falls, Malad City, Montpelier, Pocatello, Soda Springs, and Swan Valley, Idaho, Afton, Wyo.

**Challis National Forest** (2,448,000 acres).
Challis, Idaho. Highways: US 20, 93, 92A. Attractions: Lost River Range with Mount Borah, 12,655 feet, highest peak in Idaho. Lemhi, Lost River, and White Cloud Peaks; Salmon River and White Knob Mountain Ranges, headwaters of the Salmon River. Majestic Sawtooth Primitive Area and Stanley Basin; Middle Fork of the Salmon River in the Idaho Primitive Area. Stream and lake trout, salmon fishing. Hunting for deer, elk, mountain goat, mountain sheep, antelope, and bear. Stanley Basin scenic drive, riding and hiking trails, wilderness boating and pack trips. Facilities: 52 camp sites, 7 picnic sites. Resorts, hotels, cabins, and dude ranches; commercial packers and guides. Nearby towns: Challis, Mackay, Salmon, and Stanley.

**Clearwater National Forest** (1,678,000 acres).
Orofino, Idaho. Highways: Idaho 9, 11. Attractions: Famous Lolo Trail, Selway-Bitterroot Wilderness. Spring log drive on the Middle Fork and North Fork, Clearwater River; large stands of virgin white pine. Large timber operations. Trout and salmon fishing in back country. Hunting for elk, deer, bear. Lolo Pass Visitor Station. Scenic drives; North Fork and Lewis & Clark Highway. Facilities: 23 camp and picnic sites, 4 picnic only. Motels, cabins, pack trip outfitters available. Nearby towns: Kooskia, Lewiston, Orofino, and Pierce, Idaho; Lolo, Hot Springs, and Missoula, Mont.

**Coeur d'Alene National Forest** (725,000 acres).
Coeur d'Alene, Idaho. Highways: US 10, 10A, 95A. Attractions: Lovely Coeur d'Alene Lake, 30 miles long and with 104 miles of shoreline. Cataldo Mission, built in 1846. Coeur d'Alene River; fishing; hunting for elk, deer. Rich Coeur d'Alene mining district (zinc, lead, silver); several large sawmills. Facilities: 9 camp and picnic sites, 5 picnic only; Lookout Pass Winter Sports Area. Resort hotels and cabins. Nearby towns: Coeur d'Alene, Kellogg, Spirit Lake, and Wallace, Idaho; Spokane, Wash.

**Kaniksu National Forest** (1,622,000 acres — partly in Montana and Washington).
Sandpoint, Idaho. Highways: US 95, 195, 10A, 2; Washington 6. Attractions: Rugged back country, Selkirk Mountain Range. Massive Pend Oreille Lake (Loop Drive, 107 miles); Priest Lake. Kullyspell House, Clark Fork River; Roosevelt Ancient Grove of Cedars; Chimney Rock; Cabinet Mountains Wilderness. Lake and stream fishing; big game hunting. Scenic drives, boating. Facilities: 26 camp and picnic sites, 11 picnic only; 3 swimming sites, Schweitzer Basin Winter Ski Area. Resorts, hotels, lodges, cabins. Nearby towns: Bonners Ferry, Clark Fork, Priest River, and Sandpoint.

**Nezperce National Forest** (2,198,000 acres).
Grangeville, Idaho. Highways: US 95; Idaho 9, 13, 14. Attractions: Selway-Bitterroot Wilderness. Salmon River Breaks Primitive Area.

Seven Devils Range between Salmon and Snake Rivers, Hells Canyon on the Snake River, Red River Hot Springs. Hells Canyon-Seven Devils Scenic Area. Historic Elk City. Wilderness big-game hunting, elk, deer, and bear; lake and stream fishing. Hiking and horse trails; wilderness pack trips. Scenic drives: Lochsa River, Salmon River, Selway River. Facilities: 36 camp and picnic sites, 6 picnic only. Resorts, hotels, cabins, pack trip outfitters. Nearby towns: Grangeville, Kamiah, Kooskia, and Riggins.

**Payette National Forest** (2,308,000 acres).
McCall, Idaho. Highways: US 95; Idaho 15. Attractions: Idaho Primitive Area. Hells Canyon of Snake River, 5500 to 7900 feet deep, deepest gorge in the U.S.; Payette Lakes Recreational Area, Seven Devils Mountains. Fishing for trout and salmon, 154 fishing lakes, 1530 miles of fishing streams. Big-game hunting for deer, elk, mountain goat, bighorn sheep, and bear. Scenic drives, wilderness trips. Facilities: 26 camp sites; Payette Lake Winter Sports Area. Dude ranches. Nearby towns: Cascade, Council, McCall, New Meadows, and Weiser.

**Salmon National Forest** (1,768,000 acres).
Salmon, Idaho. Highways: US 93; Idaho 28. Attractions: Idaho Primitive Area, Big Horn Crags, historic Lewis and Clark Trail, Salmon River Canyon. Fishing; big-game hunting, including deer, elk, bighorn sheep, mountain goat, bear, cougar, and antelope. Salmon River and Panther Creek forest roads; boat trips on "River of No Return" and Middlefork. Facilities: 20 camp sites, 2 picnic only. Dude ranches. Nearby towns: Leadore and Salmon.

**St. Joe National Forest** (864,000 acres).
St. Maries, Idaho. Highways: US 95A; Idaho 7, 8, 43. Attractions: Rugged Bitterroot Range of Idaho-Montana divide; St. Joe River drainage; St. Maries River Valley; canyon areas of Little North Fork of Clearwater River, Clearwater-St. Joe divide, Palouse River area; virgin stands of white pine. Large timber operations. Big-game hunting, elk, deer, bear, and mountain goat; lake and stream fishing. Scenic drives along St. Joe River from source to mouth in Coeur d'Alene Lake. Facilities: 22 camp and picnic sites, 3 picnic only; 1 swimming site and North-South Winter Sports Area. Dude ranch nearby. Cabins on St. Joe River. Nearby towns: Avery, Clarkia, Moscow, Potlatch, and St. Maries.

**Sawtooth National Forest** (1,804,000 acres — partly in Utah).
Twin Falls, Idaho. Highways: US 30N, 30S, 93. Attractions: Panoramic views of Snake River Valley. Sawtooth National Recreation Area, Sawtooth Primitive Area. Colorful mountains, lakes, developed hot springs. Sun Valley with its four-season opportunities for outdoor sports. "Silent City of Rocks," fantastic formations worn by wind and water. Fishing; swimming; big-game and grouse hunting in season; saddle and pack trips, scenic drives. Facilities: 64 camp sites, 14 picnic only; 1 swimming site; 8 winter sports areas including Magic Mountain, Mount Harrison, Soldier Creek, and Sun Valley. Numerous dude ranches, camps, and motels. Nearby towns: Burley, Gooding, Sun Valley, and Twin Falls.

**Targhee National Forest** (1,666,000 acres — partly in Wyoming).
St. Anthony, Idaho. Highways: US 20, 26, 89, 91, 191; Idaho 22, 28, 31, 32, 47. Attractions: Island Park Reservoir; Grand Canyon of the Snake River; Teton and Snake Ranges, Big Falls; North Fork of Snake River; Cave Falls, Falls River; Palisades Dam. Lake and stream fishing; hunting for bear, deer, elk, and moose. Many riding and hiking trails into remote mountain country. Scenic drives. Facilities: 26 campsites, 3 picnic only; Bear Gulch, Moose Creek, and Pine Basin Winter Sports Areas. Resorts, motels, dude ranches, boating facilities, pack outfits for hunting parties, fishing camps. Nearby towns: Ashton, Driggs, Dubois, Idaho Falls, Rexburg, Rigby, St. Anthony and Victor, Idaho; Afton and Jackson, Wyo.

## ILLINOIS

**Shawnee National Forest** (241,000 acres).
Harrisburg, Ill. Highways: US 45, 51; Illinois 1, 3, 34, 127, 144, 145, 146, 151. Attractions: Prehistoric stone forts and Indian mounds; interesting rock formations. Much of the Illinois shore of the Ohio River and some of the Mississippi; their confluence nearby at Cairo, Ill. Stream and river fishing; hunting for quail, migratory waterfowl, squirrel, rabbit, fox, and raccoon. Artificial lakes in and adjacent to the National Forest provide fishing, boating, and swimming. Facilities: 14 camp and picnic sites, 32 picnic only; 2 swimming sites. Hotels and cabins. Nearby towns: Anna, Cairo, Carbondale, Harrisburg, Marion, Metropolis, and Murphysboro, Ill.; Paducah, Ky.; St. Louis Mo.

## INDIANA

**Hoosier National Forest** (152,000 acres).
Bedford, Ind. Highways: US 50, 150; Indiana 37, 46, 62, 64. Attractions: Pioneer Mothers Memorial Forest containing Nation's outstanding specimen of black walnut. Final outlet of Lost River; Ten O'Clock Indian Boundary Line crosses the forest. Old trail of migrating buffalo between Western Plains and French Lick. Squirrel, fox, and quail hunting; fishing in the East Fork of the White River, Salt Creek, and the Ohio. Los and Patoka Rivers for catfish, bass, and bluegill. Scenic drives among spring flowers (dogwood and redbud) and fall coloring. Facilities: 13 camp and picnic sites, 24 picnic only; 1 swimming site. Hotels and motels. Nearby towns: Bedford, Bloomington, Evansville, Jasper, Paoli, and Tell City.

## KENTUCKY

**Daniel Boone National Forest** (487,000 acres).
Winchester, Ky. Highways: US 25, 27, 60, 421, and 460. Attractions: Western rim of Cumberland Plateau, sandstone cliffs 100 feet high, Red River Gorge, natural rock arches, numerous limestone caves and mineral springs. Cumberland Falls and Natural Bridge State Parks within the National Forest. Bass and pike fishing in larger streams. Lake Cumberland created by Wolf Creek Dam provides 250 miles of National Forest shoreline. About 500 miles of fishing streams. Hunting for squirrel, deer, cottontails, and upland game birds. Facilities: 27 camp and picnic sites, 30 picnic only. Swimming at Cumberland Falls and Natural Bridge State Parks; also hotels and cabins. Motels and cottages at the boat docks on Lake Cumberland at confluence of Laurel and Rockcastle Rivers. Nearby towns: Boonesboro, Corbin, Lexington.

## LOUISIANA

**Kisatchie National Forest** (595,000 acres).
Alexandria, La. Highways: US 71, 165, 167, 84; Louisiana 19, 21, 28. Attractions: Colonial homes; Natchitoches, oldest town in Louisiana on Old San Antonio Trail; Stuart Forest Service Nursery, a pine seed extractory and superior seed orchard. Extensive plantations of longleaf, loblolly, and slash pines. Many bayous and lakes screened with Spanish moss. Fishing in lakes and 41 bayous; hunting for deer, quail, and migratory birds; boating, camping, and scenic drives. Facilities: 9 camp and picnic sites, 12 picnic only; 4 swimming sites. Hotels. Nearby towns: Alexandria, Leesville, Minden, and Winnfield.

## MAINE

**White Mountain National Forest** (see New Hampshire).

## MICHIGAN

**Huron National Forest** (420,000 acres).
Cadillac, Mich. Highways: US 23, 27; Michigan 33, 65, 72, 144, 171. Attractions: Lumberman's Monument. A National Forest easily reached from heavily populated southern Michigan, northern Ohio, Indiana, and Illinois. Trout fishing in the Au Sable River and smaller streams; deer, small-game, and bird hunting. At eastern edge, Lake Huron with excellent beaches. Facilities: 13 camp and picnic sites, 6 picnic only; 2 swimming sites; Au Sable and Silver Valley Winter Sports Areas. Many resorts, hotels, and cabins. Nearby towns: Grayling, Harrisville, Mio, Oscoda, and Tawas City.

**Manistee National Forest** (481,000 acres).
Cadillac, Mich. Highways: US 10, 31, 131; Michigan 20, 37, 46, 55, 63, 82. Attractions: Another National Forest less than a day's drive from Chicago, South Bend, Detroit, Toledo, and Cleveland. Lake and stream fishing for trout, bass, northern and walleyed pike, perch; deer and small-game hunting. Good skiing on northern part of the National Forest. Many of the lakes, including Lake Michigan, have fine beaches for swimming. Canoeing. Chittenden Forest Service Nursery at Wellston. Facilities: 17 camp and picnic sites, 17 picnic only; 1 swimming site; Caberfae and Manistee Winter Sports Areas. Many resorts, hotels, and cabins. Nearby towns: Big Rapids, Cadillac, Ludington, Manistee, Muskegon, and Reed City.

**Ottawa National Forest** (910,000 acres).
Ironwood, Mich. Highways: US 2, 45; Michigan 28, 35, 64, 73. Attractions: Sylvania Recreation Area. Numerous accessible lakes and streams; Bond, Agate, Sturgeon, Conglomerate, Gorge, Sandstone, and Rainbow Falls. Victoria Dam, James Toumey Forest Service Nursery, State Fish Hatchery, forest plantations, Porcupine Mt. State Park. Lake and stream fishing, deep-water trolling in Lake Superior, deer and bear hunting. Several winter sports areas nearby. Many scenic drives. Facilities: 25 camp and picnic sites, 19 picnic only; 7 swimming sites. Numerous hotels and cabins. Nearby towns: Bessemer, Iron River, Ironwood, Ontonagon, Trout Creek, Wakefield, and Watersmeet, Mich.; Duluth, Minn.

**Hiawatha National Forest** (855,000 acres — two separate sections).
Escanaba, Mich. Highways: US 2, 41; Michigan 28, 94, 48, 123.

*The Shoshone National Forest offers some of the nation's most beautiful scenery. This Wyoming forest now is managed for multiple resources, while scenic values are preserved. In the background are Pilot and Index Peaks.*

Attractions: Lakes Huron, Michigan, and Superior; some shoreline in the National Forest. Many small lakes among mixed evergreen and hardwood forests. Pictured Rocks on Lake Superior; Mackinac Island country; scenic drives; waterfalls. Lake and stream fishing for trout, bass, northern and walleyed pike, perch; smelt dipping; deer, black bear, ruffled and sharptailed grouse hunting. Canoeing. Facilities: 24 camp and picnic sites, 15 picnic only; 3 swimming sites; Gladstone Winter Sports Area. Resorts, hotels, many cabins. Nearby well-equipped State parks. Nearby towns: Escanaba, Gladstone, Manistique, Munising, Rapid River, Saint Ignace, Sault Sainte Marie, and Trout Lake.

## MINNESOTA

**Chippewa National Forest** (650,000 acres).
Cass Lake, Minn. Highways: US 2, 71, 371; Minnesota 6, 34, 38, 46. Attractions: Headwaters of the Mississippi River; Leech Lake, Lake Winnibigoshish, Cass Lake, and hundreds of smaller lakes; stands of virgin red pine. Home and present headquarters of the Chippewa Indians. Lake fishing for walleyes, northern pike, and pan fish; waterfowl and upland game bird hunting; big-game hunting for deer and black bear. Hundreds of miles of good roads and scenic drives; swimming, boating, and water sports. Winter sports include skiing, tobogganing, snowshoeing, and ice fishing. Facilities: 25 camp and picnic sites, 21 picnic only; 4 swimming sites; Shingobee Winter Sports Area. 300 resorts in and adjacent to the National Forest. Hotels, cabins. Nearby towns: Bemidji, Blackduck, Cass Lake, Deer River, Grand Rapids, Remer, and Walker.

**Superior National Forest** (2,143,000 acres).
Duluth, Minn. Highways: US 53, 61; Minnesota 1, 35, 73, 169. Attractions: 5000 lakes, rugged shorelines, picturesque islands, sand beaches, more than a million acres of virgin forest. Boundary Waters Canoe Area, part of the National Forest Wilderness System. Finest canoe country in the United States here in the land of the French voyageurs, along their historic water route to the Northwest. Unusual canoe routes in wilderness country. Adjacent Quetico Provincial Park in Canada also maintains a canoe-wilderness character over a large area. Lake and stream fishing, deer hunting. Two ski areas nearby. Scenic drives: Honeymoon and Ely Buyck Roads, Gunflint and Sawbill Trails. Facilities: 185 canoe camp sites, 63 camp and picnic sites, 24 picnic only. Resorts, hotels, cabins outside the wilderness area. Nearby towns: Duluth, Ely, Grand Marais, International Falls, Two Harbors, and Virginia, Minn.; Port Arthur and Winnipeg, Canada.

## MISSISSIPPI

**Bienville National Forest** (177,000 acres).
Jackson, Miss. Highways: US 80; Mississippi 35. Attractions: Coastal Plain second-growth pine and hardwood forest; numerous forest management demonstration areas. Eighty acres of virgin loblolly pine surrounding Bienville Ranger Station. Quail hunting; fishing. Facilities: 3 camp and picnic sites, 3 picnic only; 1 swimming site. Nearby towns: Jackson and Meridian.

**Delta National Forest** (59,000 acres).
Jackson, Miss. Highways: US 61; Mississippi 16, 14, 3. Attractions: Hunting and fishing. Greentree Reservoir (2000 acres) popular for waterfowl hunting in the fall. Red Gum Natural Area is an example of a natural bottomland hardwood stand. Facilities: 2 picnic sites. Nearby towns: Rolling Fork, Vicksburg.

**DeSoto National Forest** (500,000 acres).
Jackson, Miss. Highways: US 11, 49, 90; Mississippi 26. Attractions: Site of South Mississippi Gun and Dog Club field trials. Quail hunting, fishing, boating. Ashe Forest Service Nursery. Facilities: 3 camp and picnic sites, 11 picnic only; 1 swimming site. Gulf Coast resorts. Nearby towns: Biloxi, Gulfport, Hattiesburg, Laurel, and Wiggins.

**Holly Springs National Forest** (145,000 acres).
Jackson, Miss. Highways: US 72, 78; Mississippi 7, 15. Attractions: Intensive erosion control projects. Annual bird-dog field trials at Holly Springs. Quail and small-game hunting. Facilities: 2 camp and picnic sites, 3 picnic only; 1 swimming site. Nearby towns: Holly Springs, New Albany, and Oxford.

**Homochitto National Forest** (192,000 acres).
Jackson, Miss. Highways: US 61, 84; Mississippi 33. Attractions: One of the finest natural timber growing sites in the United States;

Parklike ponderosa pine forest, many beaver colonies. Fort Watson and Camp Maury, frontier-day army posts; scenes of early-day range wars. Steins Pillar, geological landmark. Trout fishing, elk and deer hunting, scenic drives. Facilities: 27 camp and picnic sites, 3 picnic only; 4 boating sites. Motels, cabins. Nearby towns: Bend, Burns, and Prineville.

**Rogue River National Forest** (621,000 acres — partly in California). Medford, Oreg. Highways: US 99, 199; Oregon 62, 66. Attractions: Beautiful Rogue River, lakes, trout streams, and waterfalls; extensive sugar pine and Douglas-fir forests; mammoth sugar pine roadside specimen. Table Rock, site of bloody war with Rogue River Indians. Rainbow and steelhead trout fishing; deer hunting. Oregon Skyline trail extends through National Forest from Crater Lake almost to California line. Scenic drives, saddle and pack trips, skiing. Facilities: 45 camp and picnic sites, 7 picnic only; 1 swimming site; Union Creek and Mt. Ashland Sports Areas. Resorts, motels, cabins. Nearby towns: Ashland, Grants Pass, Klamath Falls, and Medford.

**Siskiyou National Forest** (1,083,000 acres — partly in California). Grants Pass, Oreg. Highways: US 99, 101, 199. Attractions: Beautiful Oregon coast, famous salmon fishing in lower Rogue River Gorge; early-day gold camps. Home of rare species, including Port-Orford-cedar, "Oregon myrtle," rock rhododendron, Brewer weeping spruce, and Saddler oak. Profuse growth of wild lilac, rhododendron, azaleas, and pitcher plants. Kalmiopsis Wilderness. Cutthroat and steelhead trout and salmon fishing. Deer, bear, and cougar hunting. Boat trips up the pristine Rogue River, saddle and pack trips, scenic drives. Facilities: 26 camp and picnic sites, 2 picnic only. Resorts, outfitters, and cabins in and near the National Forest. Nearby towns: Brookings, Gold Beach, Grants Pass, Port Orford, and Powers.

**Siuslaw National Forest** (620,000 acres). Corvallis, Oreg. Highways: US 20, 99, 101; Oregon 18, 34, 36, 38. Attractions: Heavy stands of Sitka spruce, western hemlock, cedar, and Douglas-fir; pitcher plants, rhododendron, azaleas. Bordered by Pacific Ocean; 34 miles of public beach, shoreline, and sand dunes. Cape Perpetua Recreation Area and Visitor Center. Oregon Dunes National Recreation Area. Marys Peak, highest in the Coast Range, with road to camp sites near summit. Ocean, lake, and stream fishing; deer, bear, cougar, and migratory bird hunting. Swimming, boating, clam digging, SCUBA diving, scenic drives. Facilities: 31 camp and picnic sites; 8 picnic only; 6 boating sites. Resorts, motels. Nearby towns: Corvallis, Eugene, Florence, Mapleton, Reedsport, Tillamook, and Waldport.

**Umatilla National Forest** (1,390,000 acres — partly in Washington). Pendleton, Oreg. Highways: US 30, 395, 12; Oregon 11. Attractions: Skyline trip along summit of Blue Mountains on the Kendall-Skyline Forest Road. Spectacular views of Touchet and Wenaha River Canyons. Wenaha Backcountry area. Extensive stands of ponderosa pine. Oregon Trail route; hot sulfur springs. Stream fishing for steelhead and rainbow trout; elk, deer, pheasant, and numerous forest management demonstration areas. Picturesque eroded loess country near Natchez. Fishing, swimming. Facilities: 3 picnic sites and 1 swimming site. Nearby towns: Brookhaven, Gloster, Meadville, and Natchez.

**Tombigbee National Forest** (65,000 acres). Jackson, Miss. Highways: US 82; Mississippi 8, 15, Natchez Trace Parkway. Attractions: Upper Coastal Plain pine and hardwood forests. Indian mounds, Davis and Choctaw Lakes, Natchez Trace Parkway. Deer and quail hunting, fihsing, boating. Facilities: 3 camp and picnic sites, 3 picnic only; 1 swimming site. Nearby towns: Ackerman, Houston, Kosciusko, and Tupelo.

## MISSOURI

**Clark National Forest** (791,000 acres). Rolla, Mo. Highways: US 60, 61, 66, 67; Missouri 8, 17, 21, 32, 49, 72. Attractions: Clear fast-flowing streams, Ozark Mountains covered with oak and pine forests, spring bloom of redbud and dogwood and brilliant fall coloring. Smallmouth bass and other fishing; squirrel, coon, and fox hunting. Black and St. Francis Rivers and other provide hundreds of miles of streams for float trips. Riverbank campsites in places. Several lakes. Facilities: 14 camp and picnic sites, 21 picnic only. Nearby towns: Fredericktown, Ironton, Piedmont, Poplar Bluff, Potosi, St. Louis, and Salem.

**Mark Twain National Forest** (622,000 acres). Springfield, Mo. Highways: US 60, 63, 66, 160; Missouri 5, 14, 19, 39, 76, 87, 95, 125, 148, 173. Attractions: Ozark Mountains,

numerous caves, rock cairns, and Big Springs. Current and Eleven Point Rivers; hundreds of miles of streams for "John-boat" float trips. Fishing for pan fish, bass, and walleye; deer, quail, and small-game hunting. Fall color tours. Several State parks. Facilities: 19 picnic and 15 campsites; 6 swimming sites. Resorts and hotels. Nearby towns: Branson, Doniphan, Springfield, Van Buren, West Plains, and Willow Springs.

## MONTANA

**Beaverhead National Forest** (2,112,000 acres). Dillon, Mont. Highways: US 91; Montana 41, 34, 43, 287. Attractions: Anaconda-Pintlar Wilderness Area, Big Hole Battlefield Monument, Sacajawea Memorial Area, Bannack, the first capital of Montana. Gravelly Range self-guided auto tours. Tobacco Root, Madison, Gravelly, Snowcrest, and Continental Divide Ranges; Madison, Ruby, Beaverhead and Big Hole Rivers; alpine lakes. Fishing; hunting for deer, elk, moose, antelope, and bear. Hot springs, scenic drives, wilderness trips. Facilities: 36 camp and picnic sites, 5 picnic only; Rainy Mountain Winter Sports Area. Resorts, hotels, cabins and dude ranches in and near the National Forest. Nearby towns: Dillon, Ennis, Jackson, Lima, Sheridan, Virginia City and Wisdom.

**Bitterroot National Forest** (1,576,000 acres — partly in Idaho). Hamilton, Mont. Highways: US 93; Montana 43, 38. Attractions: Bitterroot Valley and spectacular Bitterroot Mountains, scores of mountain lakes and hot springs. Ancient Indian hieroglyphics, Saint Mary's Mission and Fort Owen. Selway-Bitterroot Wilderness; Anaconda-Pintlar Wilderness. Lake and stream fishing; hunting for elk, deer, and mountain goat. Lost Trail Pass Visitor Station. Bitterroot Valley scenic drives, riding trails, wilderness trips. Facilities: 30 camp and picnic sites; Lost Trail Winter Sports Area. Resorts, hotels, cabins, and dude ranches. Nearby towns: Corvallis, Hamilton, Missoula, and Stevensville.

**Custer National Forest** (1,186,000 acres — partly in South Dakota). Billings, Mont. Highways: US 10, 12, 85; Montana 8, 7; South Dakota 8. Attractions: Spectacular Beartooth Highway; snow-clad peaks and alpine plateaus; Granite Peak (12,799 feet), highest point in Montana; hundreds of lakes; Woodbine Falls, 900 feet high; glaciers and ice caverns. Rich fossil beds, Indian hieroglyphics, and burial grounds. Beartooth Primitive Area. Trout fishing, big-game hunting, saddle and pack trips. Facilities: 32 camp and picnic sites, 11 picnic only; Red Lodge Winter Sports Area. Resorts, hotels, cabins, and dude ranches. Nearby towns: Absarokee, Ashland, Billings, Columbus, Hardin, Laurel, and Red Lodge.

**Deerlodge National Forest** (1,181,000 acres). Butte, Mont. Highways: US 10, 10A, 91; Montana 38, 41. Attractions: Anaconda-Pintlar Wilderness, Tobacco Root Mountains, Mount Powell and Flint Creek Range, numerous alpine lakes. Lake and stream fishing; big-game hunting, bear, deer, elk, and special moose seasons. Riding trails, wilderness trips. Facilities: 25 camp and picnic sites, 12 picnic only; Wraith Hill Winter Sports Area. Resorts, hotels, cabins and dude ranches. Nearby towns: Anaconda, Boulder, Butte, Deer Lodge, Phillipsburg, and Whitehall.

**Flathead National Forest** (2,346,000 acres). Kalispell, Mont. Highways: US 2, 93; Montana 35, 40. Attractions: Spectacular geological formations, including massive Chinese Wall and jagged Mission Mountains; hanging valleys; glaciers and scores of glacial lakes. Hungry Horse Dam Visitor Center and lake. Mission Mountains Primitive Area; Bob Marshall Wilderness. Fishing; big-game hunting, elk, deer, moose, bear, mountain sheep, and goats. Boating; canoeing; riding; scenic drives around Flathead Lake; wilderness trips. Facilities: 35 camp and picnic sites, 13 picnic only; 2 swimming sites; Big Mountain Winter Sports Area. Resorts, hotels, cabins, and dude ranches. Nearby towns: Belton, Bigfork, Columbia Falls, Coram, Kalispell, and Whitefish.

**Gallatin National Forest** (1,711,000 acres). Bozeman, Mont. Highways: US 191, 20, 10, 89; Montana 19, 287. Attractions: Fertile Gallatin Valley; Crazy Mountains; snow-clad peaks; 11 outstanding waterfalls; more than 200 lakes and thousands of miles of trout streams. Madison River Canyon earthquake area and Visitor Center. Spanish Peaks, Beartooth, and Absaroka Primitive Areas. Lake and stream fishing; hunting bear, moose, elk, and deer. Scenic drives: Gallatin Canyon, Boulder Canyon, Yankee Jim Canyon; trail riding and wilderness trips. Facilities: 41 camp and picnic sites, 19 picnic only. Bridger Bowl and Lionhead Winter Sports Areas. Resorts, hotels, cabins, and dude ranches. Nearby towns: Big Timber, Bozeman, Gardiner, Livingston, and West Yellowstone.

*A day hiker pauses in the Cabinet Mountains Wilderness of Montana to inspect the rushing falls in Leigh Creek.*

USDA Forest Service Photo

*California's famed John Muir Trail is open to horsemen as well as to backpackers and hikers. This scene was photographed at Seldon Pass overlooking Marie Lake. The trail has experienced growing popularity in recent years.*

**Helena National Forest** (969,000 acres).
Helena, Mont. Highways: US 12, 91; Montana 20. Attractions: Continental Divide; Big Belt and Elkhorn Mountain Ranges. Boat trip up through Gates of the Mountains Wilderness on Missouri River; old Fort Logan original blockhouse; ghost towns: Diamond City, Marysville, Crow Creek Falls. Lake and stream fishing; hunting deer and elk. Scenic drives. Trout and Beaver Creek Canyons. Hiking and horse trails, wilderness trips. Facilities: 11 camp and picnic sites, 7 picnic only; Grass Mountain Winter Sports Area. Resorts, hotels, cabins, and dude ranches. Nearby towns: Helena, Lincoln, Townsend, Boulder, and White Sulphur Springs.

**Kootenai National Forest** (1,820,000 acres — partly in Idaho).
Libby, Mont. Highways: US 2, 93; Montana 37. Attractions: Cabinet Mountains Wilderness; Yaak River, Kootenai Canyon, and Fisher River. Libby Dam and lake. Lake and stream fishing; hunting black bear and deer. Ten Lakes and Northwest Peaks Scenic Area. Scenic drives: Yaak River, Kootenai Canyon, Fisher River; riding trails. Facilities: 20 camp and picnic sites, 6 picnic only; Turner Mountain Winter Sports Area. Hotels, cabins, and dude ranches. Nearby towns: Eureka, Libby, and Troy.

**Lewis and Clark National Forest** (1,835,000 acres).
Great Falls, Mont. Highways: US 12, 87, 89, 91; Montana 21, 287. Attractions: Bob Marshall Wilderness. Chinese Wall and Continental Divide, scenic limestone canyons and rolling mountains with many open parks. Stream and lake fishing; hunting for deer, elk, antelope, grizzly, and black bear. Wilderness trips; riding trails; numerous scenic drives: Kings Hill, Judith River, Crystal Lake, Sun River, and Teton River. Facilities: 21 camp and picnic sites, 3 picnic only; Kings Hill Winter Sports Area. Many resorts, cabins, and dude ranches. Nearby towns: Augusta, Choteau, Great Falls, Harlowton, Lewistown, and White Sulphur Springs.

**Lolo National Forest** (2,087,000 acres).
Missoula, Mont. Highways: US 10, 10A, 93; Montana 20; Idaho 9. Attractions: Selway-Bitterroot Wilderness; Rattlesnake, Bitterroot, and Swan Ranges. Clark Fork and Blackfoot Rivers. Stream and lake fishing; hunting for native grouse, elk, deer, and bear. Wilderness pack trips; scenic drives; Lochsa River, Seeley Lake, Buffalo Park, Rock Creek. Mountain saddle trails, foot trails to a hundred lakes and peaks. Facilities: 27 camp and picnic sites, 9 picnic only; 1 swimming site; Snow Bowl Winter Sports Area. Resorts, dude ranches. Nearby towns: Alberton, Drummond, Ovando, Plains, St. Regis, Superior, Thompson Falls, and Missoula (Forest Service Regional Office — also Aerial Fire Depot and Smokejumper Headquarters).

**NEBRASKA**

**Nebraska National Forest** (255,000 acres).
Lincoln, Nebr. Highways: US 20, 83; Nebraska 2. Attractions: Bessey Nursery; extensive forest plantations on sand hills; entire forest in game refuge; mule deer; nesting ground for great blue heron, grouse, and prairie chicken. Fishing. Facilities: 3 camp and picnic sites, 3 picnic only; 1 swimming site. Hotel accommodations at Broken Bow, Valentine, and Halsey.

**NEVADA**

**Humboldt National Forest** (2,514,000 acres).
Elko, Nev. Highways: US 40, 93, 95; Nevada 43, 46. Attractions: Jarbridge Wilderness; Wildhorse Reservoir; Owyhee River Canyon; Humboldt, Independence, Ruby, and Santa Rosa Mountains. Spectacular canyons, colorful cliffs, old historic mining camps. Fishing in streams and Wildhorse Reservoir; deer hunting, saddle and

pack trips. Facilities: 20 camp sites, 6 picnic only, Ward Mountain Winter Sports Area. Resort and dude ranch at Wildhorse Reservoir; hotels. Nearby towns: Ely, Elko, Mountain City, Wells and Winnemucca.

**Toiyabe National Forest** (3,133,000 acres — partly in California).

Reno, Nev. Highways: US 395, 6, 50, 95; California 4, 108; Nevada 8A, 52, 39, 31, 28, 27, 22. Attractions: Lake Tahoe; Nevada Beach Forest Camp; historic ghost towns; rugged High Sierra country. Many beautiful lakes and streams. Notable trout fishing. Hoover Wilderness. Big-game hunting, saddle and pack trips. Scenic drives: Mt. Rose, Lake Tahoe, Ebbetts, and Sonora Passes; wilderness trips. Facilities: 40 camp sites, 5 picnic only; 1 swimming site; Lee Canyon, and Reno Ski Bowl Winter Sports Areas. Motels, resorts, dude ranches. Nearby towns: Austin, Carson City, Minden, Reno, and Tonopah.

## NEW HAMPSHIRE

**White Mountain National Forest** ((727,000 acres — partly in Maine). Laconia, N.H. Highways: US 2, 3, and 302; N.H. 16. Attractions: Very popular mountains and forest including a major part of the White Mountains. Mount Washington 6288 feet, highest point in New England; Presidential Range; Great Gulf Wilderness; Glen Ellis Falls; Tuckerman Ravine; the Dolly Copp Recreation Area. Some 650 miles of streams, 39 lakes and ponds, provide brook trout fishing. Deer, bear, and small-game hunting. Scenic drives through famous notches and over mountain highways. Outstanding skiing with spring skiing often lasting into June. Rock climbing; 1000 miles of foot trails; swimming. Facilities: 72 camp and picnic sites, 17 picnic only; 26 shelters and high-country cabins for hikers; 1 swimming area; Wildcat, Tuckermans Ravine, Waterville Valley Winter Sports Areas. Cabins, motels, hotels. Nearby towns: Berlin, Conway, Gorham, Lancaster, Littleton, Pinkham Notch.

## NEW MEXICO

**Carson National Forest** (1,440,000 acres).
Taos, N. Mex. Highways: US 64, 285, 84; New Mexico 3, 75, 38. Attractions: Massive timbered Sangre de Cristo Mountains and other ranges flanking the upper Rio Grande Valley. Wheeler Peak, 13,151 feet, highest in New Mexico. Pecos Wilderness; Wheeler Peak Wilderness; alpine lakes and timberline country. Trout streams, 12,000-13,000-foot peaks. High green valleys with Spanish-speaking village. Scenic drives, Taos-Questa-Red River-Eagle Nest Loop. Tres Piedras-Lagunitas lake country. Santa Barbara Canyon near Penasco. Taos: Home and burial place of Kit Carson; well-known art colony; Taos Indian Pueblo. Near Abiquiu, Ghost Ranch Museum. Facilities: 40 camp and picnic sites, 4 picnic only. Fine skiing at Red River, Taos Ski Valley (Hondo Canyon), and Sipapu. Nearby towns: Chama, Cimarron, Espanola, Farmington, Taos and Tierra Amarilla, N. Mex.; Alamosa and Pagosa Springs, Colo.

**Cibola National Forest** (1,595,000 acres).
Albuquerque, N. Mex. Highways: US 85, 66, 60. Attractions: Magdalena, Manzano, Sandia, San Mateo, and Zuni Mountain Ranges. Mount Taylor, 11,389 feet, Sandia Crest, 10,700 feet, accessible by car and aerial tramway. Deer and antelope hunting; bighorn sheep often visible at Sandia Crest in summer. Nearby are Pueblo Indian villages, prehistoric ruins, ancient "sky city" of Acoma. Fishing at Bluewater and McGaffey Lakes. Scenic drives. Facilities: 16 camp and picnic sites, 15 picnic only; Sandia Peak Ski Area in Sandia Mountains. Motels, hotels, dude ranches. Nearby towns: Albuquerque, Belen, Bernalillo, Gallup, Grants, Magdalena, Mountainair, Socorro.

**Gila National Forest** (2,702,000 acres).
Silver City, N. Mex. Highways: US 60, 70, 80, 85, 260; New Mexico 61, 25, 78. Attractions: Semidesert to alpine country, most of it very remote and undeveloped. Elevation 4500 to 10,700 feet. Pack trips into the Gila Wilderness and Black Range Primitive Area. Mogollon Rim; many prehistoric ruins. Lake fishing in Wall Lake, Lake Roberts, and Bear Canyon Reservoir. Stream fishing in the three forks of the Gila, other streams; most of it "packing in" to little-used streams. Abundant game; uncrowded big-game hunting; black bear, mule deer, white-tailed deer, antelope, elk, mountain lion; turkey. Scenic drives: Outer Loop, Inner Loop; ghost town of Mogollon. Riding and hiking trails. Facilities: 13 camp and picnic sites, 3 picnic only. Some motels, resorts, dude ranches. Nearby towns: Deming, Las Cruces, Lordsburg, Reserve, Silver City, and Truth or Consequences, N. Mex.; Springerville, Ariz.

**Lincoln National Forest** (1,093,000 acres).
Alamogordo, N. Mex. Highways: US 54, 70, 380; New Mexico 24, 37, 48. Attractions: Sierra Blanca, 12,000 feet (summit is in

Mescalero Apache Indian Reservation) with beautiful scenery, hiking trails. White Mountain Wilderness. Sacramento, Capitan and Guadalupe Mountain Ranges with extensive ponderosa pine and fir stands. Resort cities of Cloudcroft, Ruidoso. Fishing, big-game hunting. Limited winter sports; scenic drives; saddle and pack trips. Golfing at Ruidoso (7000 ft.) and at Cloudcroft (9000 ft.). Facilities: 12 camp and picnic sites, 5 picnic only; 1 winter sports area. Resorts, hotels, dude ranches, organization camps. Nearby towns: Alamogordo, Artesia, Capitan ("Birthplace of Smokey Bear"), Carlsbad, and Roswell, N. Mex.; El Paso, Tex.

**Santa Fe National Forest** (1,477,000 acres).
Santa Fe, N. Mex. Highways: US 285, 85, 64, 84; New Mexico 4, 126, 96, 63. Attractions: Southern Sangre de Cristo Range including 13,000-foot Truchas Peaks; across Rio Grande to the west, Jemez and San Pedro Ranges, 10,000-12,000 feet. Headwaters Pecos, Jemez, and Gallinas Rivers; mountain streams and lakes; Pecos Wilderness; San Pedro Parks Wilderness. Wilderness pack trips, saddle trails. A dozen living Indian Pueblos nearby, great vistas, ancient ruins, Spanish missions, cliff dwellings. Turkey, elk, deer, and bear hunting. Facilities: 29 camp and picnic sites, 13 picnic only. Winter sports at Santa Fe Basin; scenic double chair lift to 11,600 feet, operates summer by appointment (inquire Santa Fe). Resorts, hotels, guest ranches on Pecos River up as far as Cowles, and Jemez River near Jemez Springs. Nearby Towns: Albuquerque, Bernalillo, Cuba, Espanola, Las Vegas, Pecos, and Santa Fe.

## NORTH CAROLINA

**Croatan National Forest** (152,000 acres).
Asheville, N.C. Highways: US 17, 70; N.C. 24, 58. Attractions: Historic New Bern, founded 1710; Civil War breastworks. Five large lakes; pine and swamp hardwoods, 3 miles from Atlantic Ocean, Neuse River Estuary. Deer, bear, turkey, quail, and migratory bird hunting; fishing, boating, swimming. Facilities: 2 camp and picnic sites, 2 picnic only; 2 swimming sites. Resorts and motels nearby. Nearby towns: Goldsboro, Morehead City, New Bern, and Wilmington.

**Nantahala National Forest** (452,000 acres).
Asheville, N.C. Highways: US 19, 23, 64, 129; N.C. 28, 107. Attractions: Fontana, Hiwassee, Santeelah, Nantahala, Cheoha, Glenville, and Apalachia Lakes; Fontana Dam, 8 resorts, Cullasaja, White Water River, Bridal Veil, Toxaway, and Dry Falls, Joyce Kilmer Memorial Forest; 60 miles of Appalachian Trail. Annual big-game hunts: European wild boar, deer; also turkey and bird hunting. Southern Appalachian Mountains, famous for azaleas and rhododendrons. Lake and stream fishing for bass and trout. Hiking, swimming, and boating. Scenic drives. Facilities: 19 camp and picnic sites, 10 picnic only; 1 swimming site. Nearby towns: Bryson City, Franklin, Hayesville, Highlands, Murphy, and Robbinsville.

**Pisgah National Forest** (482,000 acres).
Asheville, N.C. Highways: US 19, 23, 25, 64, 70, 211, 276, 321, and Blue Ridge Parkway. Attractions: Mount Mitchell, 6684 feet, highest point east of the Mississippi; Shining Rock Wilderness; Linville Falls and Gorge. Annual hunts for deer, bear; also small-game hunting. Craggy Gardens and Roan Mountain, famous for purple rhododendron; Cradle of American Forestry Visitor Center; Appalachian Trail. Trout, bass, and perch fishing. Hiking, horseback riding, swimming. Scenic roads and trails. Facilities: 6 camp and picnic sites, 9 picnic only; 4 swimming sites. Resorts and cabins available nearby. Nearby towns: Brevard, Burnsville, Canton, Hot Springs, Lenoir, Marion, and Waynesville.

**Uwharrie National Forest** (44,000 acres).
Asheville, N.C. Highways: US 220, 64, 52; N.C. 49, 109, 27. Attractions: Regulated hunting on the Uwharrie wildlife management area. Fishing in the Uwharrie River and Badin Lake. One camp and picnic site. Nearby towns: Asheboro, Troy, Albemarle.

## OHIO

**Wayne National Forest** (141,000 acres).
Ironton and Athens, Ohio (ranger stations). Highways: US 21, 23, 33, 35, 50, 52; Ohio 75, 141, 124, 7, 37. Attractions: Particularly beautiful fall coloring of hardwoods. Nearby are historic Marietta, Gallipolis, Blennerhasset's Island, and Amesville "Coonskin Library." Old charcoal furnaces. Small-game hunting, fishing on numerous streams and lakes. Horseback riding, auto tours, scenic lookout points. Facilities: 1 camp and picnic site, 3 picnic only; 1 swimming site. Overnight accommodations at numerous motels, tourist homes, and hotels along the main highways and at the larger towns. Nearby towns: Athens, Ironton, Jackson, Marietta. Forest Supervisor's office: Bedford, Ind.

## OKLAHOMA

**Ouchita National Forest** (see Arkansas).

## OREGON

**Deschutes National Forest** (1,588,000 acres).
Bend, Oreg. Highways: US 126, 97, 26, 20. Attractions: Beautiful southern Cascade Range. Snowclad peaks, ice caves, waterfalls, and over 300 lakes; lava caves. Deschutes River; Newberry Crater; scenic Cascades Lake Highway; Bend Forest Service Nursery; historic Willamette Military Road; Mount Jefferson Primitive Area and Three Sisters, Mount Washington, and Diamond Peak Wildernesses. Sections of Oregon Skyline Trail from Mount Jefferson to Mount Thielsen. Cast Forest and Lava Butte Geological Areas in ponderosa pine setting. Rainbow trout fishing, deer hunting. Scenic drives, saddle and pack trips, skiing. Facilities: 119 camp and picnic sites, 21 picnic only; 4 swimming sites; 1 winter sports area; 42 boating sites. Dude ranches, motels, and resorts. Nearby towns: Bend, Crescent, Redmond, and Sisters.

**Fremont National Forest** (1,209,000 acres).
Lakeview, Oreg. Highways: US 395; Oregon 66, 31. Attractions: Indian paintings and writings. Protected herds of antelope; Oregon Desert; Gearhart Mountain Wilderness. Drier inland forests. Deer and bird hunting, winter sports. Abert geologic fault east of Lake Abert, second largest vertical fault in the world. Facilities: 33 camp and picnic sites, 3 picnic only; 1 winter sports area; 3 boating sites. Motels. Nearby towns: Bly, Chemult, Klamath Falls, Lakeview, Paisley, and Silver Lake.

**Malheur National Forest** (1,452,000 acres).
John Day, Oreg. Highways: US 26, 395. Attractions: Mountains, fishing streams, archers' hunting reserve, fossil beds of prehistoric plants and animals, extensive stands of ponderosa pine. Strawberry Mountain Wilderness. Steelhead and rainbow trout fishing; elk and deer hunting. Cabin of Joaquin Miller. Scenic drives, saddle and pack trips. Facilities: 36 camp and picnic sites, 2 picnic only; 1 winter sports area. Motels, cabins in and near the National Forest. Nearby towns: Burns, Dayville, John Day, and Prairie City.

**Mount Hood National Forest** (1,118,000 acres).
Portland, Oreg. Highways: US 30, 99E, 26. Attractions: Beautiful Mount Hood with Timberline Lodge; Multnomah Falls; glaciers, lakes, hot springs, and flower-filled alpine meadows. Mount Hood Wilderness and Mount Jefferson Primitive Area. Mount Hood Loop and Columbia Gorge scenic drives; Oregon Trail route. North end of Oregon Skyline Trail, a segment of the Pacific Crest Trail system. Stream and lake fishing, swimming, saddle and pack trips, huckleberry picking, winter sports. Facilities: 107 camp and picnic sites, 24 picnic only; 6 winter sports areas. Timberline Lodge, Multnomah Falls Lodge, and other resorts in and near the National Forest. Nearby towns: Gresham, Hood River, Maupin, Oregon City, and Portland.

**Ochoco National Forest** (846,000 acres).
Prineville, Oreg. Highways: US 26, 126, 97, 20. Attractions: other bird hunting. Saddle and pack trips, scenic drives, skiing. Facilities: 54 camp and picnic sites, 16 picnic only; 3 boating sites. Tollgate-Spout Springs Winter Sports Area. Hotels, resorts, dude ranches. Nearby towns: La Grande and Pendleton, Oreg.; Clarkston, Pomeroy, Waitsburg, and Walla Walla, Wash.

**Umpqua National Forest** (984,000 acres).
Roseburg, Oreg. Highways: US 99; Oregon 138. Attractions: Spectacular North Umpqua Cataracts, Steamboat and Watson Falls, Umpqua River; a "little Matterhorn," Mount Thielsen, rising above beautiful Diamond Lake. Unique stands of incense-cedar. Steelhead and rainbow trout fishing; deer, bear, cougar hunting. Oregon Skyline Trail from Windigo Pass to Crater Lake. Scenic drives, saddle and pack trips, skiing. Facilities: 53 camp and picnic sites, 19 picnic only; 6 boating sites; Taft Mountain Winter Sports Area. Resorts, dude ranches, motels. Nearby towns: Canyonville, Cottage Grove, Roseburg.

**Wallowa-Whitman National Forests** (2,238,000 acres — two National Forests).
Baker, Oreg. Highways: US 26, 30; Oregon 7, 86, 82. Attractions: Snowcapped peaks; Wallowa and many other lakes; glaciers; alpine meadows and rare wild flowers; Minam River, famous fishing stream. Grand spectacle of Snake River and Imnaha Canyons from Grizzly Ridge Road and Hat Point. Blue and Wallowa Mountains, Anthony Lakes, Eagle Cap Wilderness. Stream and lake trout fishing; elk, deer, bear hunting. Saddle and pack trips, scenic drives. Facilities: 50 camp and picnic sites, 3 picnic only; Anthony Lake

Winter Sports Area. Resorts, dude ranches, motels. Nearby towns: Baker, Enterprise, Halfway, La Grande, and Union.

**Willamette National Forest** (1,667,000 acres).
Eugene, Oreg. Highways: US 126, 99, 20; Oregon 58, 22. Attractions: Most heavily timbered National Forest in the United States. Snowcapped peaks, lakes, waterfalls, and hot springs; McKenzie Pass Highway and lava beds. Historic Willamette Military Road. Three Sisters Wilderness Area including extensive volcanic formations; Mount Jefferson Primitive Area and the Mount Washington, and Diamond Peak Wildernesses. Sections of Oregon Skyline Trail from Mount Jefferson south to Maiden Peak. Stream and lake fishing, deer and bear hunting. Scenic drives, saddle and pack trips, winter sports. Facilities: 73 camp and picnic sites, 9 picnic only; 19 boating and 5 swimming sites, 2 winter sports areas. Motels, cabins, pack trip outfitters. Nearby towns: Albany, Eugene, Lebanon, and Salem.

**Winema National Forest** (909,000 acres).
Klamath Falls, Oreg. Highways: US 97, Oregon 66, 140. Attractions: Peaks and mountain lakes of southern Oregon Cascades, including Mt. McLoughlin, 9495 feet and Lake of the Woods and Fourmile Lake. Half the forest consists of former tribal lands of Klamath Indians; has great historical interest. Mountain Lakes Wilderness; teeming waterfowl areas in adjacent Upper Klamath Lake, Oregon's largest lake. Oregon Skyline Trail meanders along crest of the Cascades through the forest from Crater Lake to the forest boundary and on to the California line. Trout fishing, deer (both black-tailed and mule), and migratory bird hunting. Facilities: 26 camp and picnic sites, 9 picnic only; 6 boating and 2 swimming sites; Tomahawk Ski Bowl. Resorts, cabins, motels, pack trip outfitters. Nearby towns: Chemult, Chiloquin, and Klamath Falls.

## PENNSYLVANIA

**Allegheny National Forest** (495,000 acres).
Warren, Pa. Highways: US 6, 62, 219. Attractions: Allegheny Plateau country; Hearts Content and Tionesta virgin timber stands; Allegheny Reservoir; 260 miles of trout streams, 85 miles of bass fishing in Allegheny and Clarion Rivers, 32 acres of lake fishing in Twin Lakes and Beaver Meadows Pond; hunting for deer, turkey and bear; scenic drives. Facilities: 15 camp and picnic sites, 35 picnic only; 27 roadside tables; 4 swimming sites. Hotels nearby, cabins in Cook Forest and Allegheny State Parks. Nearby towns: Bradford, Kane, Ridgway, Sheffield, Tionésta, and Warren.

## SOUTH CAROLINA

**Francis Marion National Forest** (246,000 acres).
Columbia, S.C. Highways: US 17, 52; S.C. 41, 45. Attractions: Ruins and remnants of early colonial settlements and plantations. Many "Carolina bays" (small lakes, believed to be caused by meteors); picturesque moss-hung oaks, flowering yucca, dogwood, redbud, and holly. Bass and other fishing; alligator, deer, turkey, and quail hunting. Boating. Facilities: 1 camp and picnic site, 1 picnic only; 1 swimming site. Hotels and motels near the National Forest. Nearby towns: Charleston, Georgetown, McClellanville, and Moncks Corner.

**Sumter National Forest** (346,000 acres).
Columbia, S.C. Highways: US 25, 76, 123, 176, 221, 378; S.C. 28, 72, 107. Attractions: Piedmont and Blue Ridge Mountains, rank growth of rhododendron and other flowering shrubs; Walhalla Trout Hatchery. Trout and some bass fishing, quail hunting, scenic drives. Facilities: 11 camp and picnic sites, 23 picnic only; 4 swimming sites. Hotels and motels near the National Forest. Nearby towns: Abbeville, Clinton, Edgefield, Greenwood, Newberry, Union, and Walhalla.

## SOUTH DAKOTA

**Black Hills National Forest** (1,223,000 acres — partly in Wyoming.)
Custer, S. Dak. Highways: US 14, 16, 85, 385. Attractions: Spectacular canyons and waterfalls, crystal caves. Historic gold rush area where famous early-day characters lived and were buried, including Calamity Jane, Wild Bill Hickok, Deadwood Dick, and Preacher Smith; famous Homestake Mine. Harney Peak, highest east of Rocky Mountains. Mount Rushmore National Memorial. Lake and stream fishing; deer and elk hunting. Boating, saddle trips, and scenic drives. Facilities: 31 camp and picnic sites, 31 picnic only; 4 swimming sites, 1 winter sports area. Motels and dude ranches in and near the National Forest. Nearby towns: Belle Fourche, Custer, Deadwood, Edgemont, Hot Springs, and Rapid City, S. Dak.; Newcastle and Sundance, Wyo.

America's National Forests offer virtually every type of terrain, ranging from desert to mountain crags. One has only to choose the type of backpacking he desires, as is reflected in this scene in the Sawtooth Wilderness.

## TENNESSEE

**Cherokee National Forest** (615,000 acres).
Cleveland, Tenn. Highways: US 411, 421, 11, 19E, 19W, 25, 64; State 68, 67, 70. Attractions: Rugged mountain country, rhododendron and laurel blooming in season. Lake and stream fishing, rainbow and brook trout. Hunting for small and big game, including wild boar. Hiking, boating, swimming. Ducktown Cooper Basin, one of the Nation's worst examples of deforestation through air pollution, with consequent erosion. Facilities: 29 camp and picnic sites, 25 picnic only; 13 swimming sites. Hotels and tourist cabins in nearby towns. Nearby towns: Cleveland, Erwin, Etowah, Greeneville, Johnson City, Madisonville, Mountain City, Newport, Parksville, and Tellico Plains.

## TEXAS

**Angelina National Forest** (155,000 acres).
Lufkin, Texas. Highways: US 59, 69; Texas 147. Attractions: Flat to rolling sandy hills with longleaf pine-hardwood forest. Sam Rayburn Reservoir. Bass and catfish in rivers and lakes; quail and dove hunting. Facilities: 7 camp and picnic sites, 5 picnic only; 2 swimming sites. Nearby towns: Jasper, Lufkin, and San Augustine.

**Davy Crockett National Forest** (162,000 acres).
Lufkin, Tex. Highways: US 287; Texas 7, 94, 103. Attractions: Flat, shortleaf-loblolly pine woods; hardwoods in bottoms; timber management demonstration area at Ratcliff Lake. Bass and catfish in rivers and lakes; some deer hunting. Facilities: 2 camp and picnic sites, 4 picnic only; 1 swimming site. Nearby towns: Alto, Crockett, Groveton, and Lufkin.

**Sabine National Forest** (184,000 acres).
Lufkin, Tex. Highways: US 96; Texas 21, 87. Attractions: Southern pine and hardwood forest, Toledo Bend Reservoir, Boles Field Fox Hunt Area. Bass and catfish in river and lakes; fox hunting. Facilities: 4 camp and picnic sites, 4 picnic only; 1 swimming site. Nearby towns: Center, Hemphill, Jasper, and San Augustine.

**Sam Houston National Forest** (158,000 acres).
Lufkin, Tex. Highways: US 59, 75, 190; Texas 105, 150. Attractions: Flat shortleaf-loblolly pine woods, hardwoods in bottoms, numerous lakes and small streams; part of "Big Thicket" area. Bass and catfish in rivers and lakes. Facilities: 3 camp and picnic sites, 2 picnic only; 1 swimming site. Nearby towns: Cleveland, Conroe, and Huntsville.

## UTAH

**Ashley National Forest** (1,377,000 acres).
Vernal, Utah. Highways: US 30, 40; Utah 44. Attractions: East-half of Uinta Range; Kings Peak, at 13,498 feet, highest point in Utah; Red Gorge of the Green River, 1500 feet deep; exposed geological formations a billion years old; site of new Flaming Gorge dam; new High Uintas Primitive Area, mostly above 10,000 feet; numerous scenic gorges, natural erosion formations. Lake and stream fishing; big-game hunting, including deer, elk, and antelope. Riding trails, wilderness pack trips. Facilities: 50 camp and picnic sites, 12 picnic only; 1 winter sports site. Resorts, motels, dude ranches. Nearby towns: Green River and Rock Springs, Wyo.; Duchesne, Manila, Roosevelt, and Vernal, Utah.

**Cache National Forest** (679,000 acres — partly in Idaho).
Logan, Utah. Highways: US 30S, 89, 91; Utah 39. Attractions: Rugged mountains, Bear River and Wasatch Ranges, Minnetonka Cave, Logan and Ogden Canyons, Monte Cristo Mountain. Bear Lake nearby. Fishing; deer, and elk hunting. Scenic drives, riding and hiking trails. Facilities: 49 camp sites, 8 picnic only; Beaver Mountain and Snow Basin Winter Sports Areas. Nearby towns: Brigham, Logan, and Ogden, Utah; Montpelier, Preston, and Soda Springs, Idaho.

**Dixie National Forest** (1,885,000 acres).
Cedar City, Utah. Highways: US 91, 89; Utah 14, 18, 24. Attractions: Red Canyon, Panguitch and Navajo Lakes, Pine Valley Mountains, Boulder Top Plateau and its many lakes not accessible by road. Table Cliff Point with vista into 4 states (Colorado, Arizona, Nevada, and Utah). Spectacularly colored cliffs. Deer, elk, and cougar hunting; lake and stream fishing. Facilities: 27 camp sites, 4 picnic only; Cedar Canyon Winter Sports Area. Resorts, motels, dude ranches. Nearby towns: Cedar City, Enterprise, Escalante, Panguitch, Parowan, and St. George, Utah; Las Vegas, Nev.

**Fishlake National Forest** (1,427,000 acres).
Richfield, Utah. Highways: US 50-6, 89. 91; Utah 10, 13, 24. Attractions: Beaver Mountains, Thousand Lake Mountain Scenic Area. Fish Lake, Petrified Wood Scenic Area. Lake and stream fishing; big-game hunting, including deer and elk, Scenic drives: Beaver Canyon, Wayne Wonderland, Fish Lake-Salina, Marysvale-Balknap, and others. Facilities: 21 camping sites, 9 picnic only. Resorts, hotels, and motels. Nearby towns: Beaver, Delta, Fillmore, Kanosh, Loa, Monroe, Richfield, and Salina.

**Manti-La Sal National Forest** (1,263,000 acres — partly in Colorado).
Price, Utah. Highways: US 89, 50-6, 160; Utah 10, 29, 31, 46, 95. Attractions: Wasatch Plateau; Skyline Road penetrates high alpine meadows and sylvan glades; unique geology, Indian hieroglyphics and cliff dwellings. World's largest aspen trees. La Sal and Abajo Mountains. Fishing; deer and elk hunting. Scenic drives, riding and hiking trails, limited skiing. Facilities: 15 camp sites, 7 picnic only; Bluebell Flat Winter Sports Area. Nearby towns: Blanding, Ferron, Huntington, Manti, Moab, Monticello, Mount Pleasant, and Price.

**Uinta National Forest** (797,000 acres).
Provo, Utah. Highways: US 40, 50, 89, 91, 189. Attractions: Cool, high mountains rising out of the desert. Near Provo, deep canyons with spectacular waterfalls cutting through upthrust Wasatch limestone. Timpanogos Cave; Alpine Scenic Highway around Mount Timpanogos; Nebo Scenic Loop Road; maple, aspen, and oak make brilliant colored landscapes in fall. Fishing in mountain streams; deer and elk hunting; 6-mile hiking trail to top of 12,000-foot Mount Timpanogos. Facilities: 36 camp and picnic sites, 12 picnic only; 1 winter sports area; 4 valley view overlook points. Hotels, motels. Nearby towns: American Fork, Heber, Nephi, Provo, and Spanish Fork.

**Wasatch National Forest** (892,000 acres — partly in Wyoming).
Salt Lake City, Utah. Highways: US 30S, 40, 89, 91, 189; Utah 35, 150, 152, 210, 65, 36. Attractions: Big cool mountains on the city's doorstep; rugged back country; Wasatch, Uinta, Stansbury, Onaqui Mountain Ranges, High Uintas Primitive Area, with 12-13,000-foot peaks. Mirror Lake; Granddaddy Lakes; Bridger Lake; many others; picnic sites in Mill Creek and Big Cottonwood Canyons. Lake and stream fishing, deer and elk hunting. Boating, swimming; riding and hiking trails, wilderness trips, outstanding skiing, skating, and mountain climbing. Facilities: 45 camp and picnic sites, 29 picnic only; 4 winter sports areas including the famous developments at Alta and Brighton. Numerous resorts, motels, and dude ranches. Nearby towns: Heber, Kamas, Murray, Ogden, Provo, and Salt Lake City, Utah; Evanston, Wyo.

## VERMONT

**Green Mountain National Forest** (240,000 acres).
Rutland, Vt. Highways: US 4, 7. Attractions: Rugged mountains, scenery, picturesque valleys, quaint New England villages. Green Mountain Range traversed by the "Long Trail." Champlain Valley and points of historic interest such as famous battleground of Revolutionary and French and Indian Wars. Winter sports; scenic drives; hiking and bridle trails. Hunting for big and small game; principal game species are deer, ruffed grouse, rabbit, and black bear. Fishing in some 400 miles of streams and 30 lakes and ponds. Facilities: 29 camp and picnic sites (including 5 Adirondack shelters on Long Trail), 10 picnic only; 1 swimming site; Mount Snow and Sugarbush Winter Sports areas. Summer resorts and famous New England inns, hotels, and cabins. Nearby towns: Brandon, Burlington, Manchester, Middlebury, Rochester, and Rutland.

## VIRGINIA

**George Washington National Forest** (1,028,000 acres — partly in West Virginia).
Harrisonburg, Va. Highways: US 50, 11, 220, 211, 33, 60, 29; Virginia 42, 259. Attractions: Rugged mountainous terrain with elevations up to 4500 feet; Blue Ridge, Shenandoah, Allegheny, and Massanutten Ranges. Outstanding scenery: Crabtree Falls, limestone caverns, Lost River sinks, Devils Garden, Trout Run sinks, and otheer unusual geological sites. Duncan, Bald, High, Reddish, and Elliott Knobs. Shenandoah and Warm Springs Valleys. Civil War iron furnaces. Sherando Lake Recreation Area, with 20-acre swimming

USDA Forest Service Photo

*If you're the type who has a thing for snow and ice, the Portage Glacier of Alaska may be the type of terrain that will lure you as it did forest naturalist Jim Mitchell. However, such areas have their dangers outlined elsewhere.*

and fishing lake. Trout and bass fishing, 208 miles of cold-water fishing streams. Hunting, including black bear, deer, turkey, grouse, and squirrel. Panoramic views, scenic drives, Blue Ridge Parkway and 391 miles of foot trails. Facilities: 23 camp and picnic sites, 24 picnic only; 1 swimming site. Hotels, resorts, and numerous small cabins available nearby. Many secondary roads. Nearby towns: Fron Royal, Luray, Harrisonburg, Staunton, Lexington, Lynchburg, Waynesboro, Charlottesville, and Winchester, Va.; Franklin and Moorefield, W. Va.; Washington, D.C.

**Jefferson National Forest** (611,000 acres — partly in Kentucky).
Roanoke, Va. Highways: US 11, 220, 21, 52, 23, 58. Attractions: Blue Ridge Mountains; Mount Rogers, 5719 feet, highest in Virginia. Mt. Rogers National Recreation Area. Transitional zone between northern and southern flora; rhododendrons. Glenwood and Roaring Run Civil War iron furnaces; Appalachian Trail; Blue Ridge Parkway. More than 200 miles of fishing streams, 3 fishing lakes. Principal game species: White-tailed deer, grouse, squirrel, bear, raccoon, and elk. Facilities: 42 camp and picnic sites, 19 picnic only; 2 swimming sites. Resorts, hotels, and cabins. Network of good secondary roads. Nearby towns: Bristol, Bluefield, Lexington, Lynchburg, Marion, Radford, Roanoke, and Wytheville.


# WASHINGTON

**Colville National Forest** (944,000 acres).
Colville, Wash. Highways: US 395; Washington 22, 6, 4, 3P. Attractions: Roosevelt Lake, 151 miles long, 82,000 acres. Scenic drives. Old mission near Kettle Falls. Hunting in area noted for large mule deer, record weight of 440 pounds. Water transportation from Roosevelt Lake to Arrow Lakes in Canada. Huckleberries and mushrooms. Lake and stream fishing: Thomas, Swan, Sullivan Lakes, and others. Facilities: 25 camp and picnic sites, 7 picnic only; 6 swimming sites; Chewelah Peak Winter Sports Area. Resorts and cabins. Nearby towns: Chewelah, Colville, and Republic, Wash.; Grand Forks, British Columbia, Canada.

**Gifford Pinchot National Forest** (1,272,000 acres).
Vancouver, Wash. Highways: US 5, 12; Washington 14; Interstate 5. Attractions: Mount Adams, 12,300 feet, reached by scenic Evergreen Highway; Spirit Lake, many other lakes; snowcapped peaks; Mineral Springs. Wind River Forest Nursery. Goat Rocks and Mount Adams Wildernesses. Lake and stream trout fishing; deer and bear hunting; historic Indian huckleberry fields. Cascade Crest Trail extends through the National Forest. Specacular auto tours, saddle and pack trips, mountain climbing, winter sports. Facilities: 65 camp and picnic sites, 15 picnic only; 5 boating sites. Resorts, motels, cabins. Nearby towns: Castle Rock, Morton, Stevenson, Vancouver, and White Salmon.

**Mount Baker National Forest** (1,283,000 acres).
Bellingham, Wash. Highways: US 99, Washington 1, 17A. Attractions: Superb mountain scenery; snowcapped peaks, including Glacier Peak; numerous glaciers; alpine lakes; heavy stands of Douglas-fir up to 200 feet in height. Glacier Peak Wilderness. Pasayten Wilderness. Mount Baker Recreation Area featuring both summer and winter recreation. Segments of Cascade Crest Trail from Harts Pass to Glacier Peak. Steelhead and rainbow trout fishing, deer and bear hunting, skiing, saddle and pack trips, mountain climbing. Facilities: 87 camp and picnic sites, 6 picnic only; 3 boating sites; Mount Baker and Mount Pilchuck Winter Sports Areas. Hotels, resorts; experienced guides. Nearby towns: Bellingham, Darrington, Everett, and Granite Falls.

**Okanogan National Forest** (1,521,000 acres).
Okanogan, Wash. Highways: US 97; Washington 20. Attractions: Alpine meadows, snow peaks, and glaciers. Cascade Crest Trail, a segment of the Pacific Crest Trail system, originates at Canadian boundary and extends southward to Harts Pass. North Cascade Primitive Area. Pasayten Wilderness. Lake and stream fishing, boating, saddle and pack trips, mountain climbing, winter sports. Facilities: 61 camp and picnic sites, 2 picnic only; 9 boating and 2 swimming sites; Loup Loup Winter Sports Area. Dude ranches, motels. Nearby towns: Brewster, Okanogan, Tonasket, and Twisp.

**Olympic National Forest** (622,000 acres).
Olympia, Wash. Highways: US 99, 410, 101. Attractions: Dense rain forests, big trees, spectacular snow peaks, scores of lakes and streams. Fishing includes salmon and steelhead trout; hunting for deer, bear, cougar, and elk. Scenic drives; saddle and pack trips. Facilities: 20 camp and picnic sites; 2 boating sites; 1 swimming site. Resorts, motels, dude ranches. Nearby towns: Aberdeen, Olympia, Port Angeles, Quilcene, and Shelton.

**Snoqualmie National Forest** (1,211,901 acres).
Seattle, Wash. Highways: US 2, 90; Washington 410; Interstate 5. Attractions: Snoqualmie Falls, 250 feet high; scenic Chinook and White Pass Highways; giant Douglas-firs, snow peaks, lakes, fishing streams. Sections of Cascade Crest Trail from Cady Pass to Goat Rocks. Mather Memorial Parkway, Goat Rocks Wilderness. Stream and lake fishing, including salmon and steelhead trout; hunting black-tailed and mule deer, bear, and elk. Scenic drives, saddle and pack trips, skiing. Facilities: 103 camp and picnic sites; 9 boating sites; 5 winter sports areas. Motels and outfitters locally available. Nearby towns: Cle Elum, Everett, Seattle, Tacoma, and Yakima.

**Wenatchee National Forest** (1,602,000 acres).
Wenatchee, Wash. Highways: US 10, 2, 97. Attractions: Lake Chelan, 55 miles long, between precipitous mountain ranges; lake bottom 389 feet below sea level. Glacier Peak Wilderness. Snowcapped peaks, lakes, alpine meadows, rare wild flowers in Tumwater Botanical Area; fishing streams; Lake Wenatchee. Stream and trout fishing; deer and bear hunting. Cascade Crest Trail between Rainy Pass and Blowout Mountain. Scenic drives, Lake Chelan boat trip, saddle and pack trips, winter sports. Facilities: 120 camp and picnic sites, 5 picnic only; 4 winter sports areas. Motels and dude ranches. Nearby towns: Cashmere, Chelan, Cle Elum, Ellensburg, Leavenworth, and Wenatchee.


# WEST VIRGINIA

**Monongahela National Forest** (824,000 acres).
Elkins, W. Va. Highways: US 33, 60, 219, 220, and 250. Attractions: Appalachian and Allegheny Mountains; Spruce Knob, 4860 feet, highest in West Virginia; Blackwater Canyon and 60-foot falls; spectacular Seneca Rocks on historic Seneca Indian Trail. Botanically curious Cranberry Glades; rhododendrons in early July; unexplored limestone caves; bear colonies. Parsons Forest Nursery, Smoke Hole, rugged mountain scenery. Some 1900 miles of trout and bass fishing streams; hunting for deer, turkey, squirrel, bear, grouse, and other game. Swimming, horseback riding, scenic drives. Manmade lakes at Spruce Knob, Summit, and Sherwood offer trout and bass fishing with good camp sites nearby. Facilities: 43 camp and picnic sites, 17 picnic only; 5 swimming sites. Tourist homes and motels. Nearby towns: Charleston, Elkins, Lewisburg, Petersburg.

# WISCONSIN

**Chequamegon National Forest** (837,000 acres).
Park Falls, Wis. Highways: US 2, 8, 63; Wisconsin 13, 64, 70, 77, 182. Attractions: Hundreds of large and small lakes. Pine, spruce, and balsam forests; extensive jack pine plantations. Lake and stream fishing, particularly for muskellunge; hunting for deer and small game. Canoe travel on Flambeau and Chippewa Rivers; skiing. Facilities: 21 camp and picnic sites, 21 picnic only; 11 swimming sites; 1 winter sports area. Resorts and cabins. Nearby towns: Ashland, Eau Claire, Hayward, Medford, Park Falls, Superior, and Washburn.

**Nicolet National Forest** (650,000 acres).
Rhinelander, Wis. Highways: US 8, 45; Wisconsin 32, 52, 55, 70, 64, 139. Attractions: Northern Wisconsin lake region, trout streams and scenic rivers. Pine, spruce-balsam, hardwood, and cedar-spruce swamp forests. Lake and stream fishing for muskellunge, pike, bass, and trout. Deer, bear, grouse and duck hunting. Swimming; boating; canoe trips; snowshoeing and skiing. Facilities: 24 camp and picnic sites, 17 picnic only; 16 swimming sites. Sheltered Valley Ski Area. Numerous resorts and private cabins on private lands within and near the National Forest. Nearby towns: Eagle River, Green Bay, Marinette, and Rhinelander.

# WYOMING

**Bighorn National Forest** (1,114,000 acres).
Sheridan, Wyo. Highways: US 14, 16, 87. Attractions: Bighorn Mountains, snowcapped peaks, glaciers; more than 300 lakes. Curious prehistoric Indian Medicine Wheel on Medicine Mountain; Indian battlefields. Cloud Peak Primitive Area. Fishing; elk, deer, bear, and duck hunting. Saddle and pack trips; scenic drives. Facilities: 40 camp and picnic sites, 14 picnic only; 2 winter sports areas. Motels and dude ranches in and near the National Forest. Nearby towns: Buffalo, Greybull, Lovell, Sheridan, and Worland.

**Bridger National Forest** (1,712,000 acres).
Kemmerer, Wyo. Highways: US 26, 89, 189, 187, 30N. Attractions: Salt River, Wyoming, and Wind River Mountain Ranges, live glaciers, Bridger Wilderness; Gannett Peak, highest in Wyoming at 13,785 feet. Lots of remote country: lake and stream fishing; hunting for

252

*In the Pisgah National Forest of North Carolina, the Toxaway River features falls that rival those in the West.*

bear, moose, elk, mountain sheep, and deer. Scenic drives: Pinedale Skyline Drive, Greys River Road. Wilderness trips. Facilities: 23 camp sites, 2 picnic only; 1 swimming site; Divide and Surveyor Park Winter Sports Areas. Resorts, hotels, cabins, and dude ranches. Nearby towns: Afton and Pinedale.

**Medicine Bow National Forest** (1,092,000 acres).
Laramie, Wyo. Highways: US 30; Wyoming 130, 230. Attractions: Medicine Bow, Sierra Madre, Laramie, and Pole Mountains. Many lakes and fishing streams; numerous beaver colonies. Fishing and deer hunting. Saddle and pack trips; scenic drives. Facilities: 36 camp and picnic sites, 10 picnic only; 3 winter sports areas. Motels and dude ranches in and near the National Forest. Nearby towns: Cheyenne, Encampment, and Laramie.

**Shoshone National Forest** (2,431,000 acres).
Cody, Wyo. Highways: US 14, 20, 12, 287. Attractions: Rugged Absaroka Mountains and Beartooth Plateau, Wind River Range with perpetual snow; Gannett Peak, 13,785 feet, highest in Wyoming; largest glaciers in Rocky Mountains; hundreds of lakes. North and South Absaroka Wildernesses. Glacier, Stratified, and Popo Agie

Primitive Areas. Fishing; hunting for mountain sheep, elk, moose, deer, antelope, black and grizzly bear, and game birds. Saddle and pack trips. Scenic drives: Red Lodge-Cook City Highway, Sunlight Basin Road, Cody-Yellowstone Road, Togwotee Pass Road. Facilities: 30 camp and picnic sites, 9 picnic only; 2 winter sports areas. Motels and dude ranches in and near the National Forest. Nearby towns: Cody, Dubois, and Lander, Wyo.; Cooke City and Red Lodge, Mont.

**Teton National Forest** (1,701,000 acres).
Jackson, Wyo. Highways: US 89, 187, 26, 287; Wyoming 22, 1. Attractions: Unspoiled scenic back country famous for big-game herds. Gros Ventre Slide; Gros Ventre, Teton, and Wind River Ranges; Continental Divide. Teton Wilderness; famous Jackson Hole country. Outstanding skiing; stream, lake fishing; big-game hunting, moose, elk, deer, mountain sheep, grizzly bear. Scenic drives: Hoback Canyon, Snake River Canyon, Wind River Highway. Facilities: 10 camp sites, 2 picnic only; 2 swimming sites; 3 winter sports areas including Jackson and Teton Pass Ski Runs. Resorts, dude ranches, cabins. Nearby towns: Dubois and Jackson, Wyo.; Rexburg, Idaho.

# GLOSSARY OF TERMS

**ABS** — A compound plastic material used in the construction of canoe hulls: Acrylonitrile, Butadiene, Styrene.

**A-Frame** — Tent design which uses lightweight poles positioned to resemble the letter **A**.

**Artificial Respiration** — The first-aid technique of introducing air into a person's lungs until they are able to do so on their own.

**Azimuth** — Horizontal direction expressed as the angular distance between the direction of a fixed point and the direction of the object.

**Backpacking** — The act of carrying items necessary for survival strapped to your back, normally contained within a pack.

**Baffles** — Panels sewn between the inner and outer shell of sleeping bags and used to stabilize the fill.

**Bow Plate** — Reinforcements at either end of a watercraft, often containing the craft's identification numbers.

**Breathable** — A characteristic of material in which its pores are said to allow the passage of air, but too small to permit passage of liquids.

**Canoe** — A long, narrow, lightweight boat, normally paddled.

**Catenary Cut** — The built-in sway of a tent roofline, designed to add tension to the tent for stability.

**Cookhole** — An area within a tent floor which can be withdrawn to provide bare ground for cooking.

**Compass** — A magnetic needle set inside a dial which, when permitted to turn freely, will always face toward magnetic North.

**Compress** — A pressure bandage held in place until bleeding has been retarded.

**Condensation** — The formation of moisture on a tent wall, caused by a difference in internal and external air temperatures.

**Contour Lines** — Used to indicate terrain elevation and shape.

**CPR** — Cardiopulmonary resuscitation. The restoration of heart and lung activity by artificial contraction of the heart coupled with mouth-to-mouth resuscitation.

**Dayhike** — A hike limited to one day's duration.

**Dead Air** — Air trapped within layers of material, the best form of insulation available.

**Declination Scale** — A scale indicating the degree of difference between true North, magnetic North and grid North.

**Dehydrated Foods** — Food stuff that has had all moisture removed before packaging, retaining its nutritional benefits but lacking in bulk weight.

**Dehydration** — Insufficient levels of liquids within the body, causing the mouth to taste dry and foul, legs to weaken, lips to crack.

**Differential Cut** — A type of sleeping bag construction in which the outer shell is cut larger than the inner shell, creating a tube effect in which the fill is contained.

**Dingle Stick** — A green stick suspended over a campfire from which a cook pot can be hung.

**Down Fill** — Insulating material composed of duck or goose down.

**External Frame Pack** — A pack that is strapped to an outer frame, normally of lightweight aluminum, for carrying heavy loads.

**Fanny Pack** — A small specialized pack that rests around the hips. Normally used as an emergency or day pack.

**Feather** — The quill section of down; has little or no insulating capabilities.

**Field of View** — In optics, the width and depth of a view seen through binoculars or scopes.

**Flotation** — The buoyancy of a canoe.

**Freeboard** — The measure of sidewall left above the water.

**Free Standing** — A design of tents that allows them to be erected without the need to anchor them to the ground.

**Freeze-Dried** — Foods that have been flash frozen to a very low temperature, followed by the conversion of the ice to a gas which is removed, leaving the food dry.

**Frostbite** — The freezing or partial freezing of a part of the body.

**Goodyear Welt** — Welt sewn over inturned upper shoe, offering water repellency to the union between upper sole and sole.

**Grid Lines** — Equidistant lines running North and South, East to West, on a map.

**Grid North** — (GN) North as it is given on the map.

**Gunwale** — The lip running along the top of the canoe, whose function it is to deflect water spray from inside the boat.

**Guy Lines** — Cords attached to a tent and staked to the ground to stabilize.

**Heat Exhaustion** — Overheating of the body, causing profuse perspiration, nausea, weakness and dizziness.

**Heat Stroke** — A life-threatening condition caused by overheating of the body. A heat stroke victim is no longer capable of giving off heat through perspiration. Temperature may exceed 108.

**Heimlich Maneuver** — Preferred method of clearing a lodged object from the throat by forcing air up from the abdomen.

**Hollofil II** — A synthetic fill produced by DuPont, non-allergic, odorless and consistent in loft.

**Hypothermia** — A life-threatening drop in internal body temperature to a point where the body's mechanisms can no longer function.

**Index Contour** — Contour lines, spaced at specified distances, heavily inked to stand out, and providing a known elevation.

**Internal Frame Pack** — A pack whose frame is tucked inside the pack as an integral part of that pack.

**Inwale** — The width of the lip on the inside of the gunwale, held to a minimum for ease of bailing.

**Keel** — A strip of wood or metal lining the bottom of watercraft, offering guidance and stability.

**Kevlar** — A high-strength, high-modulus non-organic fiber used in canoe hulls.

**Lap-Felled** — A type of seam used to join two pieces of fabric in which the edges have been interlocked to prevent raveling.

**Layering** — The application of clothing in several layers, allowing for the adaptation of body temperature to environmental temperature.

**Lean-To** — A simplified shelter made of a tarp suspended between two trees, and anchored to the ground.

**Legend** — The margin around maps in which is located important information regarding how to read the map.

**Load Limit** — The weight capacity a canoe can safely hold without capsizing.

**Loft** — The thickness of insulation.

**Magnetic North** — (MN) The direction in which the compass points, toward the magnetic North Pole, actually located in Canada.

**Magnification** — The enlargement of an object when seen through binoculars or a scope. Referred to as the power (X) of that optic.

**Mountain Boot** — A thick, inflexible soled boot, usually ankle high, used for mountaineering.

**Mummy Bag** — A fitted cut bag, offering the greatest insulation capabilities but confining.

**Norwegian Welt** — Welt sewn to the outside of a boot, overlapping the turned-out upper shoe. Used in construction of heavy-duty backpacking boots.

**Outwale** — The width of the lip on the outside of the gunwale, providing deflection of spray away from the craft.

**PolarGuard** — A continuous-filament polyester fiberfill manufactured by Celanese Fortrel and used for insulating bags and clothing.

**Portaging** — The carrying of a canoe from one body of water to another.

**Quilting** — A type of construction in which insulation material is sewn in between an inner and outer shell.

**Radiation** — The loss of body heat emitted by the body in an effort to heat the environment.

**Rainfly** — A waterproof shield placed over a tent to keep it dry.

**Rectangular Bag** — A style of sleeping bag cut rectangularly. The most economical of bags, it is also the heaviest in weight and least heat efficient.

**Resection** — Determination of your position by comparing the position of landmarks as seen in reality to that seen on the map.

**Ripstop** — A nylon material with heavy thread lines designed to prevent tearing of the fabric.

**Rocker** — The amount of curve in the hull of a canoe from bow to stern.

**Royalex** — A canoe hull compound, layered with vinyl/ABS/foam/ABS/vinyl.

**Rucksack** — A frameless pack intended to carry light weights, for brief hikes.

**Scale** — A consistent comparison of the features as they appear on a map to those as they exist on the earth.

**Scree-Guard** — The padding at the top of hiking boots, used to protect the ankles.

**Shell** — The inner and outer material of sleeping bags, insulating fill being sandwiched in between.

**Side Wall Pull-Outs** — Sewn flaps at sides of tents that allow the tent walls to be expanded outward.

**Sternum Strap** — A strap connecting the front pack straps, which reduces lateral sway and eases shoulder pressure.

**Symbols** — The language of maps, the meanings of which can be found in the legend.

**Synthetic Fill** — Insulating material made from man-made fibers.

**Tacks** — Extra reinforcements at stress points of tents, bags, etc.

**Tapered Bag** — A compromise between the mummy and rectangular bag, it provides the light weight and heat retention abilities of the mummy with the roominess of the rectangular bag.

**Thwart** — Braces spanning the width of water craft, used to maintain shape and provide added strength.

**Topographic Map** — A map illustrating the contours of terrain.

**Tracking** — The tendency of water craft to travel in a straight line.

**Trail Boot** — A thick lug-soled boot with flexible uppers and laced front.

**True North** — (TN) The direction of the geographic North Pole.

**Tub Construction** — The extension of the floor of tents several inches above ground, for added water-repellency.

**USGS** — United States Geological Survey, a federal organization whose job it is to collect, analyze, and publish detailed information about the nation's mineral, land and water resources.

**Vestibule** — The protected entryway of a tent.

**Water-Line** — The measurement of how deep the canoe is riding in the water.

**Waterproof** — The characteristic of fabric, leather or other material which prevent moisture from penetrating.

**Water Purification** — The introduction of chemicals to kill germs and make water drinkable.

**Water-Repellent** — The tendency to retard the absorption of moisture for a period of time.

**Welt** — A narrow strip of leather attached to the seam between a boot's sole and upper shoe, to aid in water repellency.

**Wicking** — The absorption of moisture into a garment by seepage.

# Directory Of MANUFACTURERS

**A16 Wilderness Camping Outfitters**
4620 Alvarado Canyon Road, San Diego, California 92120
Backpacking equipment through mail order. Manufactures their own external frame pack, half dome tent, goose down sleeping bag and parka.

**Air Lift**
2217 Roosevelt Avenue, Berkeley, California 94703
Air Lift sleeping bag mattresses.

**Alaska Wilderness**
P.O. Box 450, Girdwood, Alaska 99587
Four season, multi-top sleeping bag.

**Alpine Aire**
P.O. Box 926, Nevada City, California 95959
Foods.

**Blue Hole Canoe Co.**
Sunbright, Tennessee 37872
Royalex/ABS canoes and accessories.

**Browning**
Route 1, Morgan, Utah 84050
Full line of outdoor products.

**Camp 7**
802 South Sherman Street, Longmont, Colorado 80501
Sleeping bags, tents, clothing.

**Campmor**
205 West Shore Avenue, Bogota, New Jersey 07603
Mail order, all backpacking needs.

**Camp Trails Co.**
4111 West Clarendon Avenue, Phoenix, Arizona 85019
Sleeping bags, packs.

**Cannondale**
35 Pulaski Street, Stamford, Connecticut 06902
Tents, packs, bags, clothing.

**Cedar River Mountaineering, Inc.**
P.O. Box 347, Enumclaw, Washington 98022
Sleeping bags.

**Coleman Company, Inc.**
250 North St. Francis, Wichita, Kansas 67201
Tents, packs, sleeping bags, camp needs.

**Danner Shoe Manufacturing Co.**
P.C. Box 22204, Portland, Oregon 97222
Boots.

**Early Winters, Ltd.**
110 Prefontaine Place South, Seattle, Washington 98104
Mail order, all backpacking needs.

**Eureka Tents**
P.O. Box 966, Birghamton, New York 13902
Tents.

**Force 10**
4304 West Jefferson Boulevard, Los Angeles, California 90016
Clothing.

**Gerry Down**
6260 Downing Street, Denver, Colorado 80216
Clothing.

**Don Gleason's Campers Supply, Inc.**
Pearl Street, Northampton, Massachusetts 01060
All backpacking needs.

**Himalayan Industries, Inc.**
P.O. Box 5668, Pine Bluff, Arkansas 71611
Packs, sleeping bags, tents.

**Hine Snowbridge**
P.O. Box 4059, Boulder, Colorado 80306
Packs.

**Westcor Inc.**
565 East 4500 South, Suite A-205, Salt Lake City, Utah 84107
Instadome tents.

**JanSport**
Paine Field Industrial Park, Everett, Washington 98204
Packs.

**Kelty Pack, Inc.**
9281 Borden Avenue, P.O. Box 639, Sun Valley, California 91352
Packs.

**Hans Klepper Corp.**
35 Union Square West, New York, New York 10003
Canoes.

**Lowe Alpine Systems, Inc.**
802 South Public Road, Lafayette, Colorado 80026
Packs, mountaineering hardware.

**Marmot Mountain Works**
331 South 13th, Grand Junction, Colorado 81501
Sleeping bags, bivy sacks, clothing.

**Moss Tent Works**
Camden, Maine 04843
Tents.

**North Face**
1234 Fifth Street, Berkeley, California 94710
Tents, sleeping bags, packs, clothing.

**Oregon Freeze Dry Foods, Inc.**
P.O. Box 1048, 770 West 29th Avenue, Albany, Oregon 97321
Freeze dried foods.

**Outdoor Products**
530 South Main Street, Los Angeles, California 90013
Packs, gaiters.

**Precise International**
3 Chestnut Street, Suffern, New York 10901
Knives, compasses, backpacking stoves.

**Quabaug Rubber Co.**
North Brookfield, Massachusetts 01535
Vibram soles.

**REI Co-op.**
P.O. Box C-88125, Seattle, Washington 98188
All backpacking needs.

**Sierra Designs**
247 Fourth Street, Oakland, California 94607
Clothing, bags, tents.

**SierraWest**
6 East Yanonali Street, Santa Barbara, California 93101
Clothing, bivy sacks, sleeping bags.

**Slumberjack, Inc.**
P.O. Box 31405, Los Angeles, California 90031
Sleeping bags.

**Stephenson**
RFD 4, Box 145, Gilford, New Hampshire 03246
Sleeping bags, tents.

**Therm-a-Rest**
568 1st Avenue South, Seattle, Washington 98104
Therm-a-Rest air mattress.

**Tough Traveler**
1328 State Street, Schenectady, New York 12304
Packs.

**Woolrich, Inc.**
Woolrich, Pennsylvania 17779
Clothing, socks.

**Yak Works Corp.**
2030 Westlake Avenue, Seattle, Washington 98121
Clothing, packs, tents, camp needs.

**White Stag Camping**
5203 S.E. Johnson Creek Boulevard, Portland, Oregon 97222
Tents, sleeping bags, packs.

**Wigwam Mills, Inc.**
Sheboygan, Wisconsin 53081
Socks.